Published by 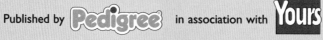 in association with

Pedigree Books Limited, Beech Hill House, Walnut Gardens, Exeter, Devon EX4 4DH

Yours is a monthly magazine for the young at heart. Look out for it in your local newsagent.
Yours, Bretton Court, Bretton, Peterborough PE3 8DZ. Tel: 01733 264666

Compiled by Marion Clarke, designed by David Reid. Sub edited by Christine Curtis.
Additional writing Caroline Chadderton and Sanchia Gorner. Heartfelt thanks to all the readers who
contributed so magnificently to this annual by sending in their letters, tips, stories and photos

£6.99

Hello!

Welcome to the fourth edition of A Year with **Yours** – our pot-pourri of titbits, advice, seasonal know-how and memories. We hope we've produced an indispensable guide to the year – with a handy calendar thrown in.

Just like the magazine, the Year Book is built on your contributions – whether it's photos that tell a story, precious first memories, things that have made you chuckle or a prayer that has got you through hard times. But that's by no means all – you'll find tasty recipes, ideas for volunteering, the best of British wildlife – I don't know how we pack it all in!

I'd like to say a big thanks to the **Yours** team members who have worked so hard on the Year Book. Features Writer Marion Clarke put the whole thing together, ably assisted by Chris Terrey. And Features Editor Caroline Chadderton was the organiser behind the whole enterprise.

So once again – I hope you have a wonderful year with **Yours**!

Our best wishes for 2005

Valery McConnell
Editor

January 2005

Saturday

1

New Year's Day

Sunday

2

Monday

3

Bank Holiday (Scotland, England and Wales)

Tuesday

4

Bank Holiday (Scotland)

Wednesday

5

Thursday

6

Epiphany, London International Boat Show starts

Friday

7

Saturday

8

Sunday

9

Monday

10

Tuesday

11

Wednesday

12

Thursday

13

Friday

14

Saturday

15

Sunday

16

Monday

17

Tuesday

18

Wednesday

19

Thursday

20

Friday

21

Saturday

22

Sunday
23

Monday
24

Tuesday
25

Burns' Night

Wednesday
26

Thursday
27

Holocaust Memorial Day

Friday
28

February **Yours** on sale

Saturday
29

Sunday
30

Monday
31

IT HAPPENED THIS MONTH

3 January, 1987
Aretha Franklin was inducted into the Rock & Roll Hall of Fame

9 January, 1959
Clint Eastwood appeared on TV in the first episode of Rawhide

10 January, 1955
Annette Mills, creator of Muffin the Mule, died aged 60

16 January, 1759
The British Museum opened

22 January, 1959
World Champion racing driver Mike Hawthorn was killed in a road accident at the age of 29

22 January, 1901
Queen Victoria died at Osborne House on the Isle of Wight, aged 82

26 January, 1885
General Gordon was killed at the siege of Khartoum

27 January, 1927
The Harlem Globetrotters played their first game

17 January, 1956
Sun Records released Elvis Presley's Heartbreak Hotel

IN MEMORIAM

Ring out, wild bells, to the wild sky,
The flying cloud, the frosty light:
The year is dying in the night;
Ring out, wild bells, and let him die.

Ring out the old, ring in the new,
Ring, happy bells, across the snow:
The year is going, let him go;
Ring out the false, ring in the true.

Ring out the grief that saps the mind,
For those that here we see no more;
Ring out the feud of rich and poor,
Ring in redress to all mankind.

Ring in the valiant and the free,
The larger heart, the kindlier hand;
Ring out the darkness of the land,
Ring in the Christ that is to be.
Alfred, Lord Tennyson

PIC: REXFEATURES

January 1-9

═ Here's health ═

Gout playing you up?
If you've overdone the alcohol over Christmas you may be paying the price with a gout attack. Typical symptoms include sudden and severe joint pain, most commonly in the big toe, heel, ankle or instep initially. To prevent further attacks try eating 250 grams of cherries (fresh or canned) every day or buy a cherry fruit extract tablet from a health food shop.

Great garden idea

It's a new year and a new beginning. Take a look at the bare bones of your garden and plan what changes you'd like to make in terms of structure, extra evergreens for winter interest, a small pond to encourage wildlife or even a screen to divide the garden and create mystery. Draw up a list of achievable ideas and jot them on the calendar to remind you of what you'd like to do if you have a spare day.

A nice little earner

Ron Heninghem of London was a pioneer in the 'recycling' business.

My brother, who was four years older than me, found old bikes on rubbish dumps. We used to paint them, fit new tyres, and sell them for £2. The trouble was, when the war started we had about a dozen bikes we hadn't sold so my dad took them down to the local dump where they had come from in the first place!

 Let's get cooking!

Beef, Mushroom and Red Wine with Thyme Suet Crust

(Serves 4)
- 1 lb (450 g) lean beef cubes (braising or stewing cubes; chuck and blade or shin and leg cuts)
- 1 tablespoon (15 ml) oil
- 1 onion, sliced
- 2 cloves garlic, crushed
- 5 oz (150 g) mushrooms, halved
- ¾pt (450ml) red wine
- 1 tablespoon (15 ml) gravy granules
- 1 tablespoon (15 ml) redcurrant jelly

For the Suet Crust:
- 10 oz (275 g) self-raising flour
- 5 oz (150 g) suet
- 2 tablespoons (30 ml) fresh thyme, chopped
- Salt

1 Heat the oil in a pan and cook the lean beef cubes for 3-4 minutes until browned. Add the onion, garlic, and mushrooms and cook for 2-3 minutes.
2 Pour over the red wine, and add the gravy granules and redcurrant jelly. Heat for 3-4 minutes until thickened, then transfer to an ovenproof pie dish.
3 To make the suet crust, place self-raising flour in a bowl with the suet. Add the fresh thyme and season with salt. Add enough water to bind, approx 6 fl oz (175 ml), and roll out on a floured surface to cover the pie dish.
4 Place on top of the meat, cover with foil and cook in a preheated oven, Gas Mark 3, 170°C, 325°F, for 2 hours. Remove the foil for the last 15 minutes of cooking time to brown the topping.
5 Serve with mashed potatoes and seasonal vegetables.

RECIPE COURTESY OF ENGLISH BEEF AND LAMB EXECUTIVE

OLD-FASHIONED CLEANING REMEDY

If your shoes are badly scuffed and will not take the polish, rub them with a banana skin first.
Ruby Ainsworth, Wakefield

Oh, happy day!

One particular birthday stands out for Susan Elston of the Wirral

On my 52nd birthday I had my name mentioned on the local radio. Nothing unusual about that, except that I was on Norfolk Island in the South Pacific. I was there in search of family history as my grandmother's name was Nobbs, the same as that of the Reverend George Hunn Nobbs, who was pastor to the mutineers on the Bounty.

We breakfasted in a three-bedroomed, A-framed house called Tania's Place, listening to the radio. Take me Back to Norfolk Island had been requested by my cousin Charles Nobbs and his wife,

Joan, who had accompanied us.

A horse-and-carriage ride followed to Steele's Point, a very good tour with a stop for photographs and tea or coffee. We took a look at the Banyan Tree and the Cable Centre before lunch at the Homestead restaurant. The menu was extensive. I chose Scotch beef with garlic butter and a salad. We spent a relaxing evening with newly acquired friends at their Hideaway, drinking the locally brewed liqueur, Convict's Curse, and eating freshly made dips and snacks. What hospitality we were shown. Thank you, Norfolk Islanders.

It makes me smile

We took my 97-year-old father on an outing to 11th century Knaresborough castle. He contemplated it for a while and then remarked 'I don't remember this, it must have been built since I was here last.'
Mrs D Kirby, Harrogate

My pet

Boom! Boom!
Miss C E Archer of Weymouth's dog, Honey, went to a dogs' fancy dress party dressed as Basil Brush.

Top tip

Having boiled the kettle, tip the remaining water down the sink plug-hole to keep it clear.
Jane Thomas, London

MY PRAYER

Dear God, when I am lonely and I feel despair
Let not my aching heart forget you; hear my every prayer.
Remind me that no matter what I do or fail to do
There still is hope for me as long as I have faith in you.
Let not my eyes be blinded by some folly I commit
But help me to regret my wrong and to make up for it.
Inspire me to put my fears upon a hidden shelf
And in future never to be sorry for myself.
Give me the restful sleep I need before another dawn
And bless me in the morning with the courage to go on.
Anne Greig, Doncaster

January 10-16

It makes me smile

As a young teacher I always found dinner money and savings confusing. One Monday the dinner money just would not add up. I counted the children yet again and suddenly remembered: "Oh, John, you're free aren't you?" John's reply: "I'm not free, I'm 5!"

Eleanor Reeves, Sidcup

My pet

Sarah Thomas of London says her cat, Chelsea, is a very keen solitaire player – but she has a few problems with chess!

MY PRAYER

I do not ask for an easy life
Or sunshine every day
I only ask for guidance
As I move along life's way.
And as I climb each hurdle
With You close by my side
In faith and trust I'll overcome
If You will be my guide.
So please stay close beside me
To share each heavy load
With love, I put my trust in You
However rough the road.
Cynthia Shum, Burton-on-Trent

OLD-FASHIONED CLEANING REMEDY

Use strong cold tea to clean varnished woodwork.

Make a difference - volunteer!

Watch the birdie!

At this chilly time of the year we all prefer to be indoors in the warm. Luckily, you don't have to leave the comfort of your armchair to volunteer for the RSPB's 26th Big Garden Birdwatch which takes place on the last weekend of January every year. Nor is it necessary to be a member of the RSPB to participate; in 2004 around 400,000 people made a record of all the feathered friends that visited their backyard in the course of two days.

As a result of their observations the RSPB was able to build up a picture of how well our common birds are doing and found, among other things, that the numbers of starlings, house sparrows and blackbirds continue to decline.

All you need to do is spend one hour during the specified two days watching the birds in your garden or local park and note the highest number of each species observed at any one time.

◆ **If you are not an RSPB member you can obtain a form (which has helpful pictures of the birds you are most likely to see) by phoning Richard Bashford (tel: 01767 680551) or from the website www.rspb.org.uk/birdwatch**

Remember the '60s?

Marjorie Edwards of Swanage was on her marks for TV's hippest show – Ready, Steady, Go!

As a London girl, I used to go and hang around outside the TV studio in The Strand on Friday night (when the show was broadcast). Sometimes there would not be enough people in the audience so the director would open the stage door and invite some more of us in to dance. We bopped to Freddie and the Dreamers, Johnny Kid and the Pirates and Brian Poole and the Tremeloes.

Gene Pitney was top of the bill one night and we met him in the corridor. He was already made up for his appearance and his face shone with orange make-up under the bright lights. It didn't go too well with his purple velvet jacket, though! Another time, we came upon Billy J Kramer and the Dakotas. Billy J was my idol. "Kiss me, Billy J," I cried, and he did! It was ages before I'd wash that cheek again.

 Let's get cooking!

Bramley and Raspberry Cinnamon Crunch Crumble

(Serves 4)

- ◆ I lb (450 g) Bramley apples, peeled, cored and sliced
- ◆ 6 oz (175 g) frozen raspberries, defrosted
- ◆ I oz (25 g) caster sugar
- ◆ 8 oz (225 g) plain flour
- ◆ 2 oz (50 g) demerara sugar
- ◆ I tsp ground cinnamon
- ◆ 4 oz (100 g) butter
- ◆ I oz (25 g) porridge oats
- ◆ I oz (25 g) flaked almonds

1 Preheat the oven to Gas Mark 5, 190°C/Fan 375°F
2 Place the Bramleys and raspberries in a large ovenproof dish, add the caster sugar and toss together until the fruit is coated.
3 Place the flour, demerara sugar and cinnamon in a food processor, add the butter and blend until the mixture resembles crumbs. Stir in the oats and almonds. Scatter over the fruit.
4 Bake for 25-30 mins or until golden brown. Serve hot with custard.

Cook's tip
If you haven't got a food processor, rub the butter into the flour and cinnamon with your fingertips. It's easier if the butter has been cut into cubes first.

RECIPE COURTESY OF BRAMLEY APPLES

Great garden idea

Buy a small container of snowdrops from your garden centre and place it on a cool windowsill where you can enjoy the intricate wonderful flowers. Then order a catalogue from John Morley at North Green Only, Stoven, Beccles, Suffolk NR34 8DG. This company lists many different varieties and sells them 'in the green' – the best way to plant them; you'll have more success than by planting them as bulbs during autumn. Why not plant them in a raised bed where you can more easily enjoy the flowers.

Here's health

Small changes make big results
If your New Year's diet is going off the rails already, think small. Concentrate on small changes you can actually stick to and build up from there. Give up sugar in tea and coffee and use sweetener instead. Switch to skimmed milk, have one slice of toast not two, and ditch jam for Marmite, etc. A pound of body fat contains 3,500 calories, so cutting back 50-100 calories a day over a year will shift between five to ten pounds!

January 17-23

Let's get cooking!

Spicy Fish Stew

(Serves 6)
- ½ oz (15 g) butter
- 8 oz (225 g) leeks, sliced
- 8 oz (225 g) onions, chopped
- 2 celery sticks, sliced
- ½ oz (15 g) flour
- 1 pt (575 ml) hot fish stock
- 1 teaspoon cayenne pepper
- 1 tablespoon medium curry powder
- 1 tomato, chopped
- 1 lb (450 g) skinless white fish fillets
- 14 oz (400 g) packet frozen mixed seafood, thawed

1 Melt the butter in a large saucepan and add the leeks, onions and celery. Cover and cook for 10 minutes, stirring occasionally.

2 Stir in the flour, then add the fish stock with the cayenne pepper and curry powder. Simmer for 10 minutes. Stir in the tomato.

3 Cut the fish into large chunks and add to the pan with the seafood. Season, and simmer for five minutes, until the fish starts to flake, and then serve.

RECIPE COURTESY SLIMMING MAGAZINE

My first...

In 1948, at the tender age of 15, I started my first job at John Dickinson & Company Ltd, papermakers and envelope manufacturers. Nervously, I approached the main entrance gates where I had to clock in on a time machine. Even if you were only a minute late, a quarter of an hour would be deducted from your salary (which was the great sum of £1 17s 6d a week).

I was directed to my office where an extremely well groomed silver-haired lady greeted me with a firm handshake. She was the export manager's secretary and I was to be her assistant. My work was to include typing, filing, taking messages to other departments, and making tea. My first effort at making tea was poor as, when I began to pour it out in front of the export manager, it looked as weak as gnat's water. I felt such an idiot until I was informed it was China tea.

I had to do a lot of copy typing and, in the days before photocopiers, to obtain 12 copies of a document, 11 sheets of carbon were fed between each sheet of paper. I enjoyed taking letters and reports down in shorthand and eventually became a fully-fledged secretary.

Mrs F Scott,
Hemel Hempstead

MY PRAYER

I pray that each and every day
I can help everybody I meet on life's way,
That I may be a vessel for good to come through,
To uplift and encourage friends both old and new.
A cheery word, a friendly smile to all we meet on the road
Can oft ease the burden of even the heaviest load.
Give these things freely, they don't cost a thing,
And just by giving, your heart will sing.
The warmth and love you radiate will quickly spread around,
In caring and in sharing, true happiness you'll have found.

Dee Miller, Leeds

Make a difference - volunteer!

Your career skills can help others

It's a shame to let the valuable experience gained over a lifetime at work go to waste because you have retired. There are many voluntary organisations that are desperately in need of professional or managerial skills but can't afford to employ a full-time person. REACH specialises in matching people's career skills with the mentoring needs of voluntary organisations, large and small.

Mentors of all ages are sought from a wide variety of managerial, technical and business backgrounds. The work is part-time and you decide the amount of time you are able to spare – just a few hours a month can make a real difference. All expenses are paid. Being a mentor gives you the stimulation of keeping your mind active as well as the chance to meet new people who will appreciate your maturity and practical assistance.

◆ **If you would like to start the new year with an exciting new challenge, learn more on REACH by contacting the mentoring co-ordinator on 020 7582 6543 or by e-mail on mail@reach-online.org.uk. Website: www.reach-online.org.uk**

Here's health

Cold finger cures

Raynaud's Disease, a painful numbing and/or tingling feeling in your fingers and toes, is caused by intermittent blood supply. Try putting hot (wrapped) baked potatoes in your pockets to keep your hands warm or buy battery-operated socks (yes really!). Send an SAE for a free copy of Percy's Hot tips for Keeping Warm' to the Raynaud's and Sclerodama Disease Society, 112 Crew Road, Alsager, Cheshire, ST7 2JA or download from www.raynauds.org.uk.

Top tip

Cover a cat litter tray with a plastic carrier bag before you put the litter in. It's much easier to dispose of hygienically.
Charlotte Joseph, Lelant

My pet

Who's a pretty girl, then?
Mrs M Street of Wellow, Notts took this photo of her King Charles spaniel, Robyn, admiring herself in the bedroom mirror.

Senior moment

I needed some cash so I put my card in the hole in the wall machine. It told me to go to the inquiry desk. Halfway there, I looked at my card – it was a Tesco bonus points card!
Mrs M Birch, Leeds

Great garden idea

Save money be growing some of your bedding plants from seed. Although many annuals can be sown successfully from March onwards, slow-maturing bedding plants, such as petunias, should be started off now in a heated propagator. They need plenty of time to mature so should be sown early and given plenty of bottom heat. Stroke your seedlings gently – they will develop stronger stems and thus become healthier plants with more flowers during the summer.

January 24-30

Every picture tells a story

In 1972 my brother, Bob, emigrated to Australia with his young family. When they returned to England for a holiday ten years later, Bob drove round to look at the cottage where he was born and spent his first eight years. To his dismay he found that the back-to-backs at Undercliffe in Bradford, were being demolished.

By a quirk of fate, demolition was just taking place on Number 29, the cottage where Bob was born, so he asked the builders if he could have one of the stones. As he had no way of transporting the large stone to Australia it sat in our parents' garden until their deaths, when it was transferred to my sister's garden. There it sits to this day, in the hope that we may one day be able to have it moved to Australia, so that Bob can pass this piece of his personal history on to his grandsons. The photo shows him sitting on the stone in our parents' garden in 1982.

Kay Spurr, Okehampton

Top tip

Before you use your oven, make up a paste with bicarbonate of soda and water and wipe this all over the inside, including the bars, with a damp cloth. After you have finished and your oven has cooled down, wipe over with a hot damp cloth. Any fat splashes will be removed.

Mrs J Lewer, London

Let's get cooking!

Orange Scented Crème Caramel
(Serves 4)
◆ ¾ pt (450 ml) skimmed milk
◆ 3 oz (75 g) Tate & Lyle granulated cane sugar
◆ Zest and juice of 1 large orange
◆ 1 teaspoon coriander seeds, lightly crushed
◆ 3 medium eggs

1 Heat the milk with 1 tablespoon of the granulated cane sugar, the orange zest and coriander seeds until almost boiling. Set aside for 20 mins for the flavours to develop.

2 Meanwhile, place the remaining sugar in a heavy-based small pan and cook over a gentle heat for 1-2 mins, shaking the pan occasionally until all the sugar has melted, then caramelised. Remove from the heat and pour in 2 tablespoons of the orange juice (take care, as the mixture will splatter) and stir until a smooth sauce forms. Divide the sauce between four ¼ pt (150 ml) ramekin dishes.

3 Preheat the oven to Gas Mark 3, 170°C, 325°F. Beat the eggs. Strain the hot milk, discarding the zest and seeds. Mix the eggs and milk well then pour into the ramekin dishes.

4 Place the ramekins in a large roasting tin and pour hot water from the kettle to come halfway up the outside of the dishes.

5 Bake for 25-30mins, or until the custards are set in the middle. Remove from the tin and leave to cool. Chill for at least 1 hour.

6 To serve, invert the crème caramels on to plates and top with spun sugar, if liked.

RECIPE COURTESY OF TATE & LYLE

My pet

'Is it supper time?' ask Charlie (left) and Daisy, inseparable companions who belong to Kay Probert of Shoebury.

Here's health

Get out in the midday sun
Did you know older Brits just don't get enough sunshine to make vitamin D for healthy bones and teeth? Experts say our long grey winters mean many over 70s may suffer, especially the housebound and those living in residential homes.

OLD-FASHIONED CLEANING REMEDY

Rinse crystal glassware in a weak solution of vinegar to give a sparkling finish.

Great garden idea

If you're sowing seeds on a windowsill, take a piece of cardboard the same length as the seed tray and cover it with a piece of aluminium foil. Place the cardboard behind the seed tray so it reflects light coming through the window back on to the seedlings – this will prevent them bending towards the window as their only light source. Fold the card, sit the tray on one piece and it will hold it in position.

MY PRAYER

After I have said The Lord's Prayer I say the following prayer:
'Hear my prayer, oh heavenly Father, ere I lay me down to sleep. May Thy angels pure and holy around my bed their vigils keep.'
Cordelia Holman, Moseley

Make a difference - volunteer!

Cat lovers step forward

If you are a 'cat person', promoting the welfare of your favourite pet will make you purr with satisfaction. Cats Protection has branches throughout the country and all of them are glad of help with everything from fundraising to fostering. Thanks to its volunteers, Cats Protection has rescued and rehomed more than 350,000 cats and reunited 20,000 lost pets with their owners.

Voluntary work can range from helping with office duties to visiting new homes to ensure the owners are suitable for a chosen cat. Answering the phone at your local branch could involve giving advice on all kinds of queries from 'my cat is stuck on the roof' to 'my mum is going into a nursing home, can you take her cat?' Car owners are needed to ferry cats to the vet.

PIC: CP PHOTOGRAPHIC LIBRARY

◆ **All you need is enthusiasm and a few spare hours a week. If you have these, then contact Cats Protection, 17 Kings Road, Horsham, West Sussex RH13 5PN. Tel: 01403 221900. Website: www.cats.org.uk**

A Walk in the Wild
Snowy hunter on silent wings

PIC:BOB SHEPPARD

The ghostly sight of a barn owl in the gloaming is now quite rare

Once common at dawn or dusk, the beautiful barn owl has become a rarity in many areas of the British countryside. The loss of rough grassland where it hunts voles, shrews and mice, is mainly to blame. The supply of traditional nesting sites is also dwindling as barns are converted to houses and hollow trees are felled.

Very keen hearing enables the barn owl to locate prey in the undergrowth, even in the dark. Its acute senses, combined with soundless flight, make it the perfect nocturnal hunter. Like many birds of prey, barn owl

pairs work together to rear their young, with the male bringing food to the nest and the female feeding it to the owlets.

The Hawk and Owl Trust has spearheaded barn owl conservation since 1988, working with farmers and landowners to reinstate rough grassland as wildlife corridors along river valleys, on farms and along woodland edges. Nest boxes in areas of suitable habitat compensate for the loss of natural nesting sites and it is thought that as many as 60 per cent of Britain's barn owls now breed in boxes. These measures

have helped to stabilise the population but it is estimated there are still only 4,000 breeding pairs in the UK compared with 12,000 in the 1930s. Putting up the nest boxes, which are almost as large as dog kennels, is specialist work and checking them requires a Government licence. Owl lovers can support this conservation work by adopting a nest box.

To learn more, contact Adopt a Box, The Hawk and Owl Trust, 11 St Mary's Close, Abbotskerswell, Newton Abbot TQ12 5QF. Tel: 01626 334864.

WARTIME WEDDINGS
Love letters straight from the heart

Muriel Golding of Rochdale and her fiancé did most of their courting by post

Jack and I met when I worked in the Salvation Army canteen at the barracks on the West Cliffs at Dover in 1941. I was 18 and he was 23, a regular soldier from Rochdale. We hadn't known each other long when he was transferred so we did our courting by letter like many other couples in those times. It should have been a December wedding in 1943 but the army cancelled Jack's leave so we had to put it off until 5 January 1944. I borrowed a dress and a veil from my cousin, Joyce, and had underwear made out of white parachute silk (not the softest of underwear).

We did not have flowers in the church or on the tables but I did have a lovely bouquet of bronze and yellow chrysanthemums – about the only flowers available as the allotments were taken up with growing essential food. Our reception was held at the girls' youth club I belonged to. We had gramophone records

for our music – Victor Sylvester played on. There wasn't any enemy activity that night so when it ended about 9pm we walked home in the blackout. The next day we travelled by train to Rochdale and got the bus to my new in-laws' house. Next morning we had a nice surprise; a knock on the bedroom door and in came my 13-year-old sister-in-law, Betty, with a mug of tea each and two rounds of toast and beef dripping for our honeymoon breakfast!

Puzzles

Crossword

Across
1 Religious cult (4)
3 Picturesque (6)
8 Pungent vegetable (5)
9 Diplomat (5)
10 Decorative metal (7, 4)
11 Dylan - - -, Welsh poet (6)
12 Dull pain (4)
15 Caribbean republic (5)
16 Cattle farm (5)
18 Location (4)
19 Urban bird (6)
21 At the required level (2, 2, 7)
23 Of the same value (5)
24 Light crown (5)
25 Dig up (6)
26 Search for (4)

Down
1 Device used for timing races (9)
2 Foot doctor (11)
4 Make (6)
5 At no time (5)
6 Very hot, ground red pepper (7)
7 Mysterious, hard to pin down (9)
13 Focus one's attention (11)
14 Mediate, settle a dispute (9)
17 The - - - of Notre Dame,
     Victor Hugo novel (9)
18 Compress (7)
20 Mental hospital (6)
22 Feel with the fingers (5)

Numbers

With this puzzle, each symbol represents a single-figure number. The given numbers show the totals when each row or column is added together. If we tell you that the telephone has the value 6, can you work out the rest?

Turn to Page 157 for puzzle answers

Janey is keen to make use of Granddad's store of memories but, for once, he's not keen to talk

All our yesterdays

PIC: ILLUSTRATION WORKS

"Granddad, I've been asked to take Betty Grant's reminiscence class while she's away on her ski-ing holiday," I gabble down the phone, wondering if he's still listening. "D'you fancy coming along? I really need your help with you knowing all about the war and everything."

Silence. Did I really think he'd say yes? Normally, Granddad loves talking – about the war, politics, the new baby down the road – anything, but since I moved out of his house and into my own flat, he's been what you might call 'off' with me. And it really hurts. I ring him most days, but he never phones me. "Got to go out, Janey," he mutters, when I suggest a visit. He didn't want me to leave even though he knew my living there was only temporary.

I hated leaving him in that big old house alone but I do need my own space. When I suggested he might join a club, he didn't want to know. His friend, Bob, has been trying to get him to go along to the Ramblers for ages but 'I do enough rambling round the garden' is his answer to that.

I try again. "We're meeting at two o'clock on Saturday in the Community Centre, just around the corner from you," I wheedle. "Please, Granddad! I do need you!" After I put down the phone, I panic. Why did I agree to do this? How can I reminisce with people who have lived longer and experienced a great deal more than I have? It's easier for Betty, who is in her fifties – I'm just twenty-two. They'll eat me alive!

At a quarter to two on Saturday, I sit at the end of a large table with a stack of library books covering past decades at the ready. My fingers are crossed, in the vain hope that Granddad's familiar, ruddy face will appear round the door.

An immaculately dressed elderly man – a retired bank manager, I decide – comes in, followed by a forbidding-looking woman who I recognise as a local councillor. Then three grey-haired ladies giggle and jostle their way to seats around the table. I smile and relax a little. Maybe we can have a laugh, if nothing else!

I glance at my watch; two

I hated leaving him in that big old house alone but I need my own space

I wonder if I dare look up accumulator in one of my books

World War with Betty," says 'bank manager' Tom, somewhat sharply. "Ah, right!" I smile, "How far had you got?"

"Accumulators," calls out Mary, one of the giggling ladies. "We was all runnin' about with them during the war. Nasty things, they were!"

"You wouldn't get kids today doin' it," says another of the trio.

"I had to go three miles to get ours filled," someone else chips in.

And they're off, all talking at once. I wonder if I dare look up 'accumulator' in one of my books. I glance around the table. Debbie is laughing with the others although her poor mother, Greta, sits silently, completely out of it. Well, you can't win them all, Janey…

The conversation moves on to food rationing. I am about to ask what dried egg tasted like – it sounds revolting – when someone mentions singing in air-raid shelters. I see a flicker of interest on Greta's face. Great! Suddenly, it's important to get Greta involved. I raise my voice. 'Why don't we do a list of songs from the war?' I suggest, knowing my contribution will be almost zero.

"As Time Goes By – that was my favourite," says Mary, looking wistful.

"The White Cliffs of Dover." Tom adds: "I worked with Vera Lynn once." I blink. My 'bank manager' was in show biz!

Then someone starts singing – very softly, but perfectly in tune: "There'll be bluebirds over the white cliffs of Dover,

Tomorrow – just you wait and see…" It's Greta! We all listen, spellbound, then she stops and smiles radiantly.

Someone claps and Debbie is wiping her eyes. My own are brimming, and I feel strangely elated. Maybe Granddad didn't turn up and I feel this is all way out of my league but I reckon we've all got something out of this session.

At the end of the class, Debbie comes up to me. "Thank you," she says. "Mum's really enjoyed it." Greta certainly looks better than when she arrived.

As I go through Reception, I spot a lone figure sitting with a carrier bag on his knees. My heart does a somersault. "Granddad! The class has finished!"

"Yeah. Can't be doin' with classes, Janey," he says, looking at the floor. "But I brought you a war video and a few books." He thrusts the carrier at me. "One of the books is Bob's. I joined the Ramblers," he mutters.

I want to hug him there and then, but daren't ruffle his pride. "D'you fancy going for a coffee?" I say, tucking my arm in his. "You can tell me about accumulators."

He stops in his tracks. "Accumulators? We used 'em in wirelesses. Things you got filled up with acid you didn't dare spill when you ran home with 'em." He is still talking when we are on our second coffee. I just listen. And the hot drink is not solely responsible for the warm glow inside me.

o'clock. No Granddad. I feel disappointed and sad. He would have been a real asset. More important, had he turned up it would have meant that this silly 'feud' was over.

I am about to start when a girl comes in with a pale middle-aged lady. The girl whispers to me. "Is it okay if we sit in? Mum's been ill and I think it might do her good."

"Of course!'" I say, heartily. My heart thumping like mad, I beam at the small group and take down their names. Then I begin brightly: "Shall we start with fashion? Has anyone any memories of past fashion disasters? What about the Sixties – remember flower power? Psychedelic colours, hippies…"

Seven faces stare at me blankly. I gulp. Desperate, I hone in on the councillor. "What did you wear in the Sixties, Doreen?"

"School uniform," she responds icily. Oh dear! I've never been good at guessing people's ages.

"We were on the Second

February 2005

Tuesday *1*	**Saturday** *12* Cheltenham Folk Festival
Wednesday *2*	**Sunday** *13* Cheltenham Folk Festival
Thursday *3*	**Monday** *14* St Valentine's Day
Friday *4*	**Tuesday** *15*
Saturday *5*	**Wednesday** *16*
Sunday *6*	**Thursday** *17*
Monday *7*	**Friday** *18*
Tuesday *8* Shrove Tuesday (Lent begins)	**Saturday** *19*
Wednesday *9* Chinese New Year	**Sunday** *20*
Thursday *10*	**Monday** *21*
Friday *11* Cheltenham Folk Festival	**Tuesday** *22*

Wednesday *23*	**Saturday** *26*
Thursday *24*	**Sunday** *27*
Friday *25* March **Yours** on sale	**Monday** *28*

UP IN THE MORNING

Cauld blaws the wind frae east to west,
The drift is driving sairly;
Sae loud and shrill's I hear the blast,
I'm sure it's winter fairly.

CHORUS: Up in the morning's no for me
Up in the morning airly;
When a' the hills are covered with snaw,
I know it's winter fairly.

The birds sit chittering on the thorn,
A' day they fare but sparely;
And lang's the night frae e'en to morn.
I'm sure it's winter fairly.

CHORUS: Up in the morning's no for me
Up in the morning airly;
When a' the hills are covered with snaw,
I know it's winter fairly.

Robert Burns

IT HAPPENED THIS MONTH

1 February, 1930
The Times printed its
first crossword,
compiled by Adrian Bell
(father of Martin Bell)

3 February, 1821
Elizabeth Blackwell, the
first English woman
doctor was born

5 February, 1953
Sweet rationing ended
in Britain

6 February, 1952
King George VI died at
Sandringham where he
had been born 56 years
earlier.

7 February 1958
Seven Manchester
United players and
three officials were
killed in a plane crashed
at Munich airport

8 February, 1586
Mary, Queen of Scots
was beheaded at
Fotheringhay Castle

9 February, 1540
The first recorded
horse race was run at
Chester

14 February, 1929
Al Capone killed seven
members of a rival gang
in the St Valentine's Day
Massacre in Chicago

16 February, 1923
The tomb of
Tutankhamun in the
Valley of the Kings was
entered for the first time

17 February, 1867
The first ship passed
through the Suez Canal

24 February, 1981
Prince Charles announced
his engagement to Lady
Diana Spencer

PIC: REXFEATURES

January 31-February 6

OLD-FASHIONED CLEANING REMEDY

To clean very neglected brass or copper, take equal quantities of salt and flour, mix to a paste with vinegar, coat the items and leave for 24 hours. Wash off in very hot soapy water. Dry, then coat with metal polish. Leave to dry, then polish with a soft cloth.

Mrs M Woodhouse, Halesowen

Top tip

Don't throw away old shower curtain rings. Use them in the garden shed to keep canes in neat bundles, or around electric cables of lawn mowers when wound up.

Mrs D J Tapscott, Dunfermline

It makes me smile

Many years ago my 11-year-old daughter was walking along with her 3-year-old brother when she realised he was having difficulty keeping up with her. "Am I going too fast?" she asked him. "No," he replied, "but I am."

Gwen Candy, Basingstoke

My pet

Sweet dreams!
Mrs J Porte of St Leonards on Sea says her Shih-tsu, Barnaby, didn't kick the dummy habit until he was two years old.

MY PRAYER

Lord, you are in control. You are sovereign. You know why everything happens and why everything comes to an end. I cannot grasp how You operate. I don't know why You do the things You do, but help me to trust You. Thank you, Father, that my life is in Your hands – every bit of it! You are the Lord. Amen.

Catherine Reid, Donaghadee, Co. Down

Oh, happy day!

Jane Price of Luton walked the Inca Trail to thank Great Ormond Street hospital for the care of her son Joe

My most memorable day has to be my first glimpse of the lost city of Machu Picchu after a gruelling four-day trek on the Inca Trail in Peru. We had begun day one by crossing River Urubamba. After six hours of a steady climb up a high rocky trail I felt exhausted and relieved to see camp.

Day two was a 5 am start to pack up tents and breakfast on porridge. The big climb was gruelling! As I reached Dead Woman's Pass, at 4,200m, my feeling of elation was intense.

After ten hours of trekking, our tents looked like a five-star hotel.

Day three involved walking through rain forest and cloud forest. Exotic flowers, cacti and humming birds rewarded us. After seven hours of trekking the sight of 2,000 steps down to the camp was almost enough to make me want to give up!

We rose early and as the clouds began to disperse the sightings of Machu Picchu were magical and mystical. As we arrived, I celebrated a real sense of achievement.

A nice little earner

As a horse-mad teenager, Joan Ramsden had a hobby that paid for itself!

In the 1950s I was living in West Ealing, London. By mucking out the stables and cleaning some tack at the local riding school I could make my half-hour ride up to an hour. To go on the two-hour ride to Norwood Green, I would bag up the manure from the midden and take it on a wheelbarrow round the local houses. I'd knock on the door to see if they would like to buy some for their roses. At 3d a bag it was snapped up.

I attended a convent school and we occasionally organised a raffle in the classroom during lunch break of chocs left over from Christmas (probably illegal!) and that went on rides at the local riding school.

Great garden idea

February is a dreary month so cheer yourself up with a bowl of hyacinths. They're excellent on a bathroom windowsill where they'll scent the air more delicately than an artificial air freshener. Keep the plants cool and they'll flower longer. Once the blooms have faded allow the leaves to die back, then plant the bulbs out in the garden where they'll flower again next spring.

Here's health

Lippy protects
Lipstick not only gives your makeup that finishing touch it also protects your lips from chapping and drying out. Wearing lipstick (but not the matte kind) or lip balm before going out in cold weather can prevent loss of moisture. Choose a lipstick that contains a sunscreen but don't buy a flavoured lip balm as you'll end up licking it off!

Let's get cooking!

Chilli Lamb Korma with Fragrant Pilau Rice
(Serves 2)
- 8oz (225 g) lean lamb leg steaks (cut into small cubes)
- 1 tablespoon (15 ml) oil
- 1 onion, sliced
- 1 clove garlic, crushed
- ¼ pt (150 ml) coconut milk
- 1 tablespoon (15 ml) korma curry paste
- 1 teaspoon (5 ml) sugar
- ½ fresh red chilli, sliced – flaked almonds (optional)

For the rice:
- 1 tablespoon (15ml) oil
- 1 red onion, sliced
- 1 cinnamon stick
- 1 teaspoon (5 ml) coriander seeds
- 1 teaspoon (5 ml) cardamon pods
- 8 oz (225 g) Basmati rice

1 For the rice, heat the oil in a pan and cook the red onion for 4-5 minutes until golden. Add the cinnamon stick, coriander seeds, cardamon pods and Basmati rice.
2 Pour over ½ pt (300ml) water and bring to the boil. Then cover with foil and a tight fitting lid and cook over a low heat for 10 minutes. Once cooked, remove from the heat and leave covered to stand for a further 5 minutes.
3 For the korma, heat the oil in a pan and cook the onion, garlic and lean lamb leg steaks for 4-5 minutes until browned. Add the coconut milk, the korma curry paste, sugar and red chilli, and cook for a further 3-4 minutes.
4 Sprinkle the curry with flaked almonds, if desired, and serve with the rice, naan bread and pickles.

RECIPE COURTESY OF BRITISH MEAT INFORMATION SERVICE

February 7-13

 Let's get cooking!

Chunky Fish Bolognese

(Serves 4)

- ◆ I tablespoon (15 ml) olive oil
- ◆ I small onion, finely chopped
- ◆ I stick celery, thinly sliced
- ◆ I carrot, peeled and finely diced
- ◆ Half a red pepper, deseeded and chopped
- ◆ I small courgette, chopped
- ◆ 4 oz (100 g)) mushrooms, sliced
- ◆ I x 14 oz (400 g) can chopped tomatoes
- ◆ 2 tablespoons (30 ml) tomato purée
- ◆ 2 teaspoons (10 ml) dried Italian herbs
- ◆ 8 oz (225 g) cod loin or thick cod fillet, skinned and cut into chunks
- ◆ 8 oz (225 g) dried pasta shells, cooked
- ◆ Fresh basil leaves, to garnish

1 Heat the oil in a large frying pan and fry the onion until soft. Add the celery and carrot, and fry gently for 5 minutes.
2 Add the pepper, courgette, mushrooms, tomatoes, purée and dried herbs. Simmer gently for 10-12 minutes until the vegetables are tender. Season to taste.
3 Add the fish and simmer for a further 4-5 minutes until the fish is cooked and starting to flake. Spoon over the cooked pasta and garnish with fresh basil leaves.

RECIPE COURTESY OF SEA FISH INDUSTRY AUTHORITY

Remember the '60s?

Thoughts of surfin' USA sent Alun Rees of Dyfed off around the world

Of all the bands around at that time, the Beach Boys had the biggest influence on me. Their songs about life on America's Pacific coast, beautiful girls, sports cars and surfing kindled a desire to travel. We all aspire to be like our heroes, but it wasn't easy. I got some very strange looks as I walked around my village in rural Wales wearing shorts and a Hawaiian shirt on a cold winter's day.

At the age of 16, I joined the Merchant Navy. I travelled widely during my time at sea but never did make it to California. I still get a kick whenever I hear one of those Beach Boys hits on the radio. As for Hawaiian shirts – my wife only lets me wear them to fancy dress parties.

 ## MY PRAYER

I live alone dear Lord, stay by my side
In all my daily needs, be Thou my guide.
Grant me good health for that I pray
To carry on my work from day to day.
Keep pure my mind, my thoughts, my every deed
Let me be kind, unselfish, in my neighbours' needs.
Spare me from fire, from flood, malicious tongues,
From thieves, from fear, from evil ones.
If sickness or an accident befall
Then humbly Lord, I pray, be Thou my call.
And when I'm feeling low or in despair
Lift up my head and help me in my prayer.
I live alone dear Lord yet have no fear
Because I feel Your presence ever near. Amen

Grace Grogan, Canvey Island
and Midge Fieldhouse, Lee-on-Solent

Make a difference - volunteer!

So much more than meals on wheels

Think of the WRVS and the Meal on Wheels service comes first to mind, but there is much more to this charity than its valuable role of serving hot dinners to the housebound. As a volunteer, you could find yourself involved in any one of a number of schemes, all aimed at supporting your local community.

The Good Neighbours scheme helps with shopping or collecting prescriptions or just by paying a regular visit to people who are living alone. The Home from Hospital scheme offers assistance with cooking and household chores for those who are still convalescent after an illness.

Drivers with their own cars are needed to transport people to a medical appointment or to the shops. Customers pay a small mileage charge directly to the volunteer driver.

◆ **Other WRVS activities that would welcome your help include a home library service and providing trolley rounds in hospitals for patients who can't walk to the hospital shop. To find out more call 0845 601 4670.**

Here's health

Brain boosters

Age-related memory decline is not as serious as Alzheimer's but distressing nonetheless. In 'Optimum Nutrition For the Mind' (Piatkus £12.99), nutritionist Patrick Holford recommends eating oily fish (mackerel, tuna, pilchards) rich in omega 3 oils, three times a week. He also advocates eating antioxidant-rich foods such as fruit and vegetables to boost blood supply to the brain, plus gingko biloba, the herb that improves circulation. Keeping fit, learning new things and reducing stress can also prevent memory decline.

Top tip

A corner cut from a used envelope makes a handy book marker.
K Croft, Hayling Island

My pet

Hard to believe that Pru was once a feral cat! Her owner, Mrs F B Hancock of Hitchin, says she is proof that it is possible to make a house pet of a feral cat – but it does take time and patience.

Senior moment

In the supermarket, I reached into my pocket for my reading glasses, only to discover I already had some on the top of my head, and another pair round my neck.
Jacqueline Wilkins, Frome

Great garden idea

Buy a scrapbook and fill it with new ideas for your garden. Stick in pictures of planting combinations you like, inspirational articles from magazines or even the image of a plant you'd like to try. Keep a throw-away camera handy in the shed to take photos of your borders through the year so you can compare the results.

February 14-20

Here's health

Benefits of sex
Good news for Valentine's Day romantics – experts say sexually active older people live longer and stay healthier. Sadly, as many as one in three men aged over 60 suffers from impotence, and many are too embarrassed to get it treated, despite the availability of new drugs such as Viagra.

For more information call the Sexual Dysfunction Association helpline on 0870 774 3571 or log on to: www. sda.uk.net.

Great garden idea

Warm the soil by covering it with a cloche; this will raise the temperature by a few degrees and help to dry it out ready for sowing your first hardy crops such as broad beans, cabbages, peas, spinach and turnips. Alternatively, start them off in unheated greenhouse.

My first...

I well remember the first trip I made in my car after I had passed my driving test. I took my two daughters aged 13 and three years to the supermarket. Very proud of the fact that I had done the journey, packed my shopping into the boot, filled up with petrol, I was virtually home when I came to a busy crossroads. As the lights changed to green, I pulled away in the wrong gear and stalled the car right in the middle – nothing could move in any direction.

Two bus drivers were tooting me and I was in a lather. Instead of getting into first gear, I had the windscreen wipers going, the lights on and I pressed the horn by mistake.

When I eventually got going all the drivers honked their horns with glee. What a boost this must have been to their male egos!

Sheila Ford, Telford

Let's get cooking!

Love Heart Fruits
(Makes 12)
- 4 oz (100 g) raspberry jelly
- ½ pt (275 ml) boiling water
- 4 tablespoons (60 ml) vodka
- 12 raspberries, strawberries, or blueberries

1 Cut the jelly into cubes. Add the hot water and stir to dissolve.
2 Stir in the vodka and leave the jelly to cool slightly
3 Pour into an ice cube tray – heart-shaped, if possible – and pop a fruit into each segment.
4 Chill for three hours or until the jellies are set.
5 Turn out and enjoy your Valentine's treat!

RECIPE COURTESY OF SLIMMING MAGAZINE

Top tip

When arranging flowers, slip any broken stems into drinking straws and cut to the length required for display.
Mrs V Watson, Colchester

Make a difference - volunteer

Practical advice for all

If you are looking for voluntary work that is challenging, rewarding and varied, why not become an adviser with the Citizens Advice Bureau? The CAB says volunteers don't need any particular qualifications or experience to train as an adviser provided they have the following qualities:

- *Are good listeners*
- *Are able to work in a team*
- *Can read and write English and basic maths*
- *Are open-minded*
- *Enjoy helping people.*

The work is very varied and includes interviewing clients at drop-in sessions or over the phone, giving practical help by writing letters or completing forms. The problems that come up most frequently concern employment, debt, housing or benefits. Advisers keep

records of all clients' cases and can refer them to other agencies if they are better placed to help.

In addition to putting the experience they already have to good use, volunteers go through a comprehensive training programme that gives them the skills needed.

◆ **If you would like the chance to make a real difference, contact the CAB volunteer recruitment line 08451 264 264. Internet: www. citizensadvice.org.uk/join-us**

Wit and wisdom

All you need to know about luck for certain is that it's bound to change. Bret Harte (1836-1902)

It makes me smile

After reading about organ transplants, I said to my daughter: "I think I'd like to leave my body to help someone." Looking me up and down, she kindly said: "And which part do you actually think they may be interested in, Mother?"

Wendy Broughton, Loughton

MY PRAYER

Dear Lord I'm frequently unkind
Help me humility to find
In others goodness help me see
And let Your mercy shine on me.

In thoughtless haste, just passing by
Help me to recognise a cry
Of pain of sadness to be free
And let Your mercy shine on me.

In talk of someone else's sin
Do I too joyfully join in?
Help me of malice to be free
And let Your mercy shine on me.

You've given me hearing, sight and voice
So many blessings I rejoice
To use them wisely is my plea
So let Your mercy shine on me.
Enid Gill, Tavistock

My pet

This is our Dalmatian, Diana, thinking 'This is my basket' with my granddaughter Barbara. If she ever saw Barbara in the garden, Diana quickly jumped in first, before she could climb in!
Betty Howard-Cofield, Weedon, Northants

OLD-FASHIONED CLEANING REMEDY

To clean fragile china, sprinkle with Fuller's earth, leave overnight, then brush off.

February 21-27

Great garden idea

When you're next at a car boot sale, look out for old cutlery to make yourself a windchime. Heat the prongs of a fork and bend them out in different directions to create the arms of the chime then hang spoons and forks from these on clear fishing line. You can bend the prongs of the other forks around in a circle so to hold coloured glass beads. Hang the chime where you can hear it tinkle in the breeze.

My pet

A garden, a fireside, and walks in the wood,
I've learned to behave, and do as I should.
A wagging tail and a wet doggie kiss,
This is the life, and what I call BLISS!
Jan Clegg of Tadworth's rescue dog Jess is pictured with her late husband, Tom.

MY PRAYER

Oh Lord, please help me to drive safely and well today. Help me not to put anyone into any sort of danger and if I find myself in difficulty, please show me what to do and give me the courage to do it without hesitation. Amen
Sheila Wood, Herne Bay

Senior moment

My husband looked inside his birthday card from me and smiled. I had signed it from us both.
Mrs S Turner, Wisbech

Make a difference - volunteer

An understanding voice at the end of the line

This is the time of year when a great number of people feel at their lowest emotional ebb, often verging on the brink of suicide. Since the Samaritans was founded in 1953, an understanding voice on the other end of the phone has saved many from that last desperate act. Volunteers need to be sympathetic listeners who are prepared to do one overnight shift a month in addition to a shift of three or four hours a week.

New volunteers attend a series of seven preparation sessions with a group to learn about active listening and the different types of calls they are likely to receive. They will also take part in skills' practice exercises and group discussions.

When answering the phones, there is always an experienced volunteer on hand to give support and no one is left to deal with a harrowing call on their own.
◆ **For more information call the volunteer hotline 08705 627282. Internet: www.samaritans.org.**

Every picture tells a story

We went away on a special holiday to Austria to celebrate our 40th wedding anniversary. Imagine our surprise when, on the actual day, we walked into our hotel room to find the most beautiful arrangement of flowers, sent by our children. It brought tears to our eyes. We certainly didn't expect to receive them, being such a long way from home, but it is something we will never forget. In the photo we are standing on the balcony of our hotel, with the flowers. And when we returned home, the house was filled with more flowers and balloons from family and friends.

Jim and Christine Jay, Southampton

Here's health

Check your cold remedy

If you're suffering from a runny, blocked-up nose you may be using a decongestant cold remedy to clear your airways. Some brands of over-the-counter medicine contain a stimulant called phenylpropanolamine, which has been linked to strokes in young people in the US. Although those sold in the UK have a lower phenylpropanolamine content, they are best avoided if you have high blood pressure, heart disease or an overactive thyroid disease, so check the ingredients with your pharmacist before you buy.

Top tip

To keep bananas separate from other fruit, hang them on big cup-hooks attached to kitchen or pantry shelves.

Mrs D F Haslam, Warrington

Let's get cooking!

Hotpot
(Serves 4)
- 1 lb (450 g) lean minced lamb
- 4 oz (100 g) mushrooms, sliced
- ¾ pt (450 ml) stock
- 2 tablespoons (30 ml) gravy granules
- 1 tablespoon (15 ml) fresh thyme, chopped
- Salt and pepper
- 2 leeks, finely sliced
- 2 oz (50g) Lancashire cheese, grated
- 1½ lb (700 g) potatoes, sliced
- Butter

1 In a non-stick pan, dry fry the lean minced lamb with the mushrooms for 4-5 minutes until browned.
2 Add the stock, gravy granules and fresh thyme, and cook for further 2-3 minutes until thickened. Season with salt and pepper and transfer to an ovenproof casserole dish.
3 Cover the mince with the leeks and Lancashire cheese. Layer over the potatoes, peeled and sliced, and brush with a little melted butter.
4 Cover with foil and cook in preheated oven, Gas Mark 4-5, 190°C, 375°F for 1½ hours. Uncover for the last 30 minutes to allow the potatoes to brown.
5 Serve with pickled red cabbage or seasonal vegetables.

RECIPE COURTESY OF ENGLISH BEEF & LAMB EXECUTIVE

A Walk in the Wild
At home in town or country

Now is the time to see the first fox cubs of the year

PIC: THE FOX PROJECT

The red fox's mating season lasts from Christmas until around February. Vixens are in season for only three days. Successful pregnancies last 53 days, resulting in average-sized litters of four or five cubs. Although they are social animals, foxes are not pack animals and cubs may disperse as young as five months of age. The UK's red fox population peaks at 600,000 after the annual breeding season with over half that number being lost before the next. A fox's natural lifespan is around 11 years, although few of them survive beyond four years and cub mortality brings the urban average life expectancy down to 15 months. Traffic, disease and domestic pets account for most of these deaths. Foxes are very adaptable and 13 per cent of today's population have urban or suburban territories. Basic food resources include mice, rats, birds, voles, worms, insects and, for a short season, fruit.

A fox has upwards of 28 different calls, varying from the vixen's shrill communication call to the dog fox's 'triple bark'. Lower grunts are used to control cubs and 'hacking' noises and 'whoops' warn off rivals. Jousting cubs will sort out their pecking order with a protracted, high pitched cough – often heard in the early hours!

Foxes are not classified as vermin and the population is generally healthy. They are not aggressive, despite 'silly season' stories in the media about foxes attacking babies and cats. The Fox Project is an information bureau that offers advice on fox deterrence as well as running a wildlife hospital for sick animals.

To learn more, contact The Fox Project, The Old Chapel, Bradford Street, Tonbridge, Kent TN9 1AW. Tel: 01732 367397. Website: www.thefoxproject.fsnet.co.uk

WARTIME WEDDINGS
They weren't too young at all

Dolly Harmer of Leighton Buzzard had to persuade her parents she was ready for marriage

Sometimes I still feel guilty I was able to enjoy 56 years of married bliss by courtesy of Hitler. Had the war not fast-forwarded our romance, our parents would have said I was too young at 20 and Peter (at 25) too old for me.

We got engaged in September 1939 and the wording of his proposal was: "If the war is still on in July, will you marry me then?" Peter was in the Royal Navy and suddenly in January he heard he was due for leave so our wedding was fixed for Sunday 4 February, 1940 at St Albans, Golders Green.

Our vicar was very accommodating. He called the banns straight away, instead of waiting seven days. On that last Sunday the banns were called at matins and we were married the same afternoon. My godfather used his precious petrol to pick me up by car even though the church was only at the end of the road. Daddy insisted I should not arrive late, as was traditional, as everyone would want to get away as soon as possible because of the blackout.

There had been snow all week but on the Sunday it was beginning to thaw, making everywhere grey and damp. I had developed

laryngitis and went to Boots and whispered that I wanted to be heard saying 'I will'. The dispenser suggested that I gargle with port. What a waste – but it worked. I wore an edge-to-edge coney fur coat with a little pill box hat to match made in that very short time by a furrier friend.

Who's a pretty boy then?

Doreen Mayers knew you should never pick up a bird that had fallen out of the nest but with cats about, she had no choice. And that was only the beginning…

He was a tiny, scrawny little chick, with just the beginning of the odd feather, when we found him on the front path. He lay there on his side, cold and shaking.

Not quite sure what to do, I took him indoors and wrapped him in a warm scarf, while my husband made him an 'incubator', a cardboard box and a low wattage light bulb. We lined it with twigs, leaves and moss, in which to lay him.

I kept a vigil, and when he started to move I helped him sit up, and he stayed upright. Then wondering if he was thirsty, I put some warm water in a pipette and rested it on the edge of his beak. To my surprise, he opened and shut his beak and swallowed.

Trying to be 'Mummy bird', I chewed up some bread, then put tiny bits into his now ever-open beak. I continued this feeding method for a few days, then gradually changed to baby cereal. He seemed to like it and eventually progressed to eating it from a spoon.

My husband and I were thrilled when we heard his first chirrup – a bit like hearing baby's first words.

To our great relief, he seemed to be getting brighter and stronger each day. One morning I found him walking round his cardboard home, so I borrowed a bird cage to give him more scope, and a better view of the world.

By now he was quite happy to hop on my finger, and I'd put him on the swing in the cage and rock him gently but he'd no idea how to get down. No matter how long I left him he'd wait for my finger to lower him to the floor of the cage.

One morning I noticed he'd started to spread his wings. Time to teach him to fly, I thought. I lifted him out and sat him on the rocky piece of cactus but he never budged. I decided it wasn't high enough, so putting cushions on the floor in case of mishap, I stood on a chair with him perched on my finger, then dropped my arm suddenly. What a fluttering and spluttering that first attempt was! He finished up in a heap on the table with a rather startled expression. By the third try he could fly!

It was not long after this we had serious misgivings about keeping him indoors. We must let him go.

I walked down the garden with him, kissed him goodbye and said, 'off you go, Tweet', and off he flew.

When I opened the back door the next morning, in he flew, tweeting away. I left the door open for him and he came and went as he pleased.

One day when I popped to the shops, Tweet spotted me and flew round me. He waited patiently on a low wall until I reappeared, then flew to my outstreched hand.

I would have loved this state of affairs to have gone on, but one day he never returned. We like to think he found a mate, but we will never know. We really loved that little bird and will never forget him.

March 2005

Tuesday

1

St David's Day

Wednesday

2

Thursday

3

Friday

4

Saturday

5

Sunday

6

Mothering Sunday

Monday

7

Tuesday

8

Wednesday

9

Thursday

10

Crufts Dog Show, NEC, Birmingham

Friday

11

Crufts Dog Show, NEC, Birmingham

Saturday

12

Crufts Dog Show, NEC, Birmingham

Sunday

13

Crufts Dog Show, NEC, Birmingham

Monday

14

Tuesday

15

Wednesday

16

Thursday

17

St Patrick's Day (Bank Holiday N Ireland)

Friday

18

Saturday

19

Sunday

20

Monday

21

Tuesday

22

Wednesday
23

Thursday
24

Friday
25
Good Friday (Bank Holiday)

Saturday
26

Sunday
27
British Summer Time begins, clocks go forward

Monday
28
Easter Monday (Bank Holiday, except Scotland)

Tuesday
29
April **Yours** on sale

Wednesday
30

Thursday
31

CARGOES

Quinquireme of Nineveh from distant Ophir
Rowing home to haven in sunny Palestine,
With a cargo of ivory,
And apes and peacocks,
Sandalwood, cedarwood, and sweet white wine.

Stately Spanish galleon coming from the Isthmus,
Dipping through the Tropics by the palm-green shores,
With a cargo of diamonds,
Emeralds, amethysts,
Topazes, and cinnamon, and gold moidores.

Dirty British coaster with salt-caked smoke stack
Butting through the Channel in the mad March days,
With a cargo of Tyne coal,
Road-rail, pig-lead,
Firewood, iron-ware, and cheap tin trays.

John Masefield

IT HAPPENED THIS MONTH

4 March, 1675
John Flamsteed was
appointed the first
Astronomer Royal

5 March, 1953
Joseph Stalin died in the
Kremlin, aged 73, after
28 years as the ruler of
Russia

8 March, 1887
Everett Horton patented
the telescopic
fishing rod

12 March, 1969
A coup in the Caribbean
island of Grenada
toppled prime minister
Sir Eric Gairy

16 March, 1976
Harold Wilson resigned
after nearly eight years
as Prime Minister

18 March, 1891
The first telephone link
between London and
Paris was made

24 March, 1603
Queen Elizabeth I
died at Richmond Palace
in Surrey

29 March, 1981
Thousands of people
ran in the first
London marathon

21 March, 1961
The Beatles appeared at the
Cavern Club in Liverpool
for the first time

PIC: REXFEATURES

February 28-March 6

Great garden idea

Dig over a new border and mark out several different areas using sand poured from a bottle. Using a hoe, make shallow drills in each section about 6 in (15 cm) apart and sow hardy annuals seeds. Cover them with a little soil and water thoroughly. By sowing in rows you can easily spot which seedlings are flowers and which are weeds and be able to remove the latter.

Let's get cooking!

Citrus Pork Patties
(Serves: 2-4)

- 1 lb (450 g) lean pork mince
- Zest of 1 lemon
- Zest and juice of 1 lime
- 1 tablespoon fresh parsley or coriander, chopped

1. In a bowl place the lean pork mince, the lemon zest, the lime zest and juice, and fresh parsley or coriander. Season well and mix together thoroughly.
2. Divide into 8 and shape into patties. Cook under a preheated grill for 4-6 minutes per side until cooked through.
3. Serve in toasted pitta breads with salad and hummus. Alternatively, serve with oven chips or potato wedges and sweetcorn.

RECIPE COURTESY OF BRITISH MEAT INFORMATION SERVICE

A nice little earner

Mr J E Fletcher of Scarborough made a few pennies from being the fisherman's friend

We lived not far from a large drainage canal that was full of fish. The railways ran special fishermen's trains from Sheffield to Boston. I used to buy lemonade in glass bottles from the nearby pub to sell to the thirsty fishermen at a small profit. When the trains had departed for Sheffield I went round and collected the empty bottles and took them back to the pub and got the 2d back, making myself a handsome profit.

I also had a side-line in maggot farming and selling little red worms for bait. I had several old oil drums with the tops cut off with coloured sawdust in the bottom. Above the sawdust were pieces of mesh from sieves through which the decaying offal etc fell. The smell was awful. For the worms, I had large pieces of wet hessian laid out at the bottom of the garden – the worms stuck to the underside. I collected moss from the dyke banks and put the worms in it. The fishermen said the moss made the worms more attractive to the fish, and who was I to argue?

Oh - happy day!

Ann (seated) with Engelbert on a special day

Pam Lawrance of Leicestershire shares a heartwarming memory tinged with sadness

A surprise outing was arranged for my cousin Ann who was terminally ill with cancer. The surprise was to meet Engelbert Humperdink who she had known in his early days as Gerry Dorsey at the Palais de Dance in Leicester. He used to call her Pixie as she was under five feet tall. She had no idea what was going to happen as we had just told her to put her glad-rags on.

Engelbert was playing in a celebrity match at Oadby golf course in aid of cystic fibrosis and, with the kind help of the club's secretary and captain, had agreed to meet Ann. As you can see by her face, Engelbert was fantastic with her and made her feel so special. We all went to see him tee off and, on returning to the club house, who should come out and have a chat but Jasper Carrot, who also made her feel very special.

After putting up a very brave fight, Ann died three months later and we all miss her but feel so pleased she had this special day.

It makes me smile

I have an aunt of 93 years who is still driving a car. When I rang her one weekend, I was told: "Joan is out – she has taken an old lady shopping." I wondered how old the 'old lady' was!

Beryl Collins, Uckfield

MY PRAYER

Show me the way oh, Lord my God,
For here I am lost and alone.
Out of my depth, old, fighting to survive,
I need Thee at my side.
Now in my need, please believe
You are my all, on You I call,
Be there lest I fall.

Mrs F Arkinson, Hatfield

My pet

Knock, knock, who's there? Tootsie the tabby and her big pal Holly think it's time their owner, Susanne Stevenson of Buckland St Mary, let them back indoors in the warm.

Here's health

Leeks are good for you

It's St David's Day this week, so why not celebrate the Welsh patron saint by eating some delicious leeks? The French call them the 'asparagus of the poor' and the Welsh have relished them since 640AD, when they wore them on their hats to distinguish themselves from invading Saxons. Leeks are a member of the onion family but have a much milder taste than onion or garlic and they're also extremely healthy: low calorie (100 g contains just 22 calories), cheap, and packed full of fibre, vitamin C and iron.

March 7-13

 Let's get cooking!

Mixed Seafood Braise

(Serves 6)

- 1 tablespoon (15 ml) sunflower oil
- 1 clove garlic, crushed
- 1 medium onion, peeled and sliced
- 12 oz (350g) tomatoes, skinned and chopped
- 1 tablespoon (15 ml) tomato purée
- 5 fl oz (150 ml) red wine
- 12 oz (350 g) coley fillets, skinned and cubed
- 6 oz (175 g) peeled prawns, fresh or defrosted
- 8 oz (225g) fresh mussels, debearded and scrubbed
- 3 king scallops, fresh or defrosted, sliced
- Salt and black pepper
- 1 tablespoon (15 ml) fresh chopped parsley, to garnish

1 Heat the oil in a large shallow pan. Cook the garlic and onion until slightly soft.

2 Stir in the tomatoes, tomato purée and wine and simmer for about 10 minutes to make a rich sauce.

3 Add the coley fillets, cover and cook for 5 minutes.

4 Add the prawns and mussels. Cover and cook for a further 5 minutes, stirring occasionally.

5 Stir in the scallops, cook for 2-3 minutes. Remove and discard any mussels that have not opened. Season to taste.

6 Sprinkle with parsley and serve hot with pasta, rice or crusty bread.

RECIPE COURTESY OF SEA FISH INDUSTRY AUTHORITY

Remember the '60s?

Richard Sirot will never forget the night he was a mere three feet away from Jimi Hendrix

My friends and I saw many great names at the blues club that used to be at the rear of the Bromley Court Hotel. The club had no real stage so if you could fight your way to the front you were practically on top of the performers. One Saturday we turned up to see the Animals but their manager came out to say they would not be playing as three of the group had flu. Big moans! He then told us he was going to let us see a new black guitarist /singer from the States – his name was Jimi Hendrix. No one had ever heard of him but within minutes of him starting to play I was in rock and roll heaven. He poured lighter fluid on his guitar, ignited it and began playing the fret with his teeth. I was so close I could feel the heat. It was a fantastic and unforgettable evening. Little did I know that I had just witnessed a rock legend and that within months his concert tickets would be like gold dust.

MY PRAYER

The void you've left cannot be filled:
So sad my aching heart,
But grateful thanks there'll always be
As memories play their part.
A perfect wife, a loving Mum
Throughout so many years,
We'll always see your smiling face
Come shining through our tears.
And as we travel on through life
We know that Heaven's gate
Has let another angel in
To smile on us and wait
Until the day we pass like you
Through Heaven's open door,
Where everlasting joy and love
Will blossom as before.

Roy Hobbs, Christchurch

Make a difference - volunteer!

Help the needy of the world

Voluntary Service Overseas (VSO) is not just for the younger generation. The average age of volunteers is late thirties but the age range goes right through from the early twenties to early 70s. People who retire early but are fit and healthy and have professional as well as life skills are welcomed.

Since 1958 VSO has sent over 30,000 volunteers to work in Africa, Asia, the Caribbean and Pacific regions, as well as Eastern Europe. The volunteers are skilled professionals who live and work in some of the poorest communities in the world, sharing their expertise and knowledge with local colleagues. Jobs vary, but placements exist for small business advisers, management advisers, midwives, primary teachers and foresters.

Comments from older people who have applied to VSO include: 'I wanted to live in a different culture rather than just visiting' and 'I wanted to do something while I was still keen and fit'.

◆ **If you feel the same, contact VSO, 317 Putney Bridge Road, London SW15 2PN. Tel: 020 8780 7500. Internet: www.vso.org.uk**

Here's health

Get that duster out

Microscopic dust mites colonise our homes and four million people in the UK suffer from house dust mite allergies. You can protect yourself by opening windows, washing bedding at temperatures over 60 degrees centigrade, spraying curtains and blinds with a fine water mist to prevent dust collection, vacuuming carpets and soft furnishings and investing in anti-dust mite covers for mattresses.

Top tip

When carving meat, put a few sheets of damp kitchen towel under the plate to stop it from sliding around on the counter-top. This helps to prevent accidents with the carving knife!
Sheila Ford, Telford

It makes me smile

When my boyfriend unloaded some clean clothes from the washing machine he found 74p in shiny new change – now he is worried he might be a money launderer!
Patsy Collins, Lee-on-Solent

My pet

Sonny makes his owner, Anneliese Holden of Bexleyheath, laugh at his antics. One of his favourite games is batting table tennis balls around the room for her to retrieve!

Great garden idea

Plant summer-flowering bulbs, corms and rhizomes such as camassia, triteleia, lilies, gladioli and schizostylis now because they will add extra colour in borders that can look a little tired after July. Gladioli don't mix well with other herbaceous plants so grow them separately and cut them to bring indoors.

March 14-20

Here's health

Is it all Blarney?

St Patrick's Day, March 17, is the traditional day to enjoy a pint of Ireland's national tipple Guinness. The company was forced to drop its 'Guinness is Good For You' advertising slogan years ago, but now a US university has compared the health-giving properties of stout versus lager by giving it to dogs who had narrowed arteries. The dogs given Guinness (but not lager) had reduced clotting, making them less prone to heart attacks. Researchers said it's possible antioxidants found in Guinness may slow down deposits of cholesterol in the artery walls – making it good for you after all!

Great garden idea

Create a wigwam of canes and sow one sweet pea seed at the base of each. These hardy annuals will not be killed by frost but it's worth sowing a few extra seeds under glass so that if any fail you can replace them at a later date. Once the seedlings are a few inches high, pinch out the growing points to encourage sideshoots for bushy plants with more flowers.

Let's get cooking!

Mango Chicken with White Wine

(Serves 6)
- ◆ 2 fl oz(50 ml) sunflower oil
- ◆ 2 lb 4 oz (1 kg) chicken pieces
- ◆ 2 fl oz (50 ml) soy sauce
- ◆ 4 fl oz (100ml) white wine
- ◆ 2 cloves garlic, crushed
- ◆ 1 green pepper, diced
- ◆ 2 mangoes, sliced

1. Heat oil in a heavy based pan and brown the chicken in batches.
2. Add the soy sauce, wine and garlic, and toss in the green pepper.
3. Transfer to an oven-proof dish.
4. Cover and bake at 350°F, 180°C, gas mark 4 for 30 minutes.
5. Add mangoes and bake for a further 10 minutes

RECIPE COURTESY OF THE MANGO ASSOCIATION

My first...

Drina Brokenbrow of High Wycombe had hopes and dreams for her first baby

'William' we called him
As he kicked around the womb,
While we prepared his room
With non-committal colours
(For we couldn't be sure –
And we had no reason to assume.)
But 'William' he became
And I could see the football game
Where his father would stand by
And say with a proud sigh,
'That's my boy, that's William'.

A bonny child he'd be,
A lot like him, a bit like me,
His father's face when asleep,
With crumpled hair beneath the sheet.
A young man with a mind of his own,
Impetuous, impatient, but never alone.
All his friends will fill the kitchen
Begging for coffee and someone to listen.
But it's 'Come on mother, one more push,
Very soon you can have a look'.
And, as they hand me a cup of tea,
They show me a girl, who's a lot like me!

Make a difference - volunteer

Insider healing

No special qualification is needed to become a prison visitor but it is essential to be a good listener and to have enough free time to make regular visits. It is an asset if a volunteer can speak an ethnic minority language.

Regular visits and chats enable the prisoner to establish a no-strings-attached relationship with someone unconnected with authority. The role is that of a friend to whom the prisoner can unburden their fears and share the ups and downs of life inside.

Visitors are appointed by the prison governor who should be the initial contact (have a look in your phone book to find the address of a prison near you). In addition to completing an application form, volunteers have to supply two

references before being invited for an interview. If you are accepted, the rules and regulations of prison visiting will be explained.

The majority of prison visitors are middle-aged but anyone from the age of 21 to 70 can apply.

◆ **For more information, contact The National Association of Prison Visitors, tel: 01234 359763.**

My pet

Prince and Pussy lived in London during the Second World War. Lily Gardner of Longfield in Kent says that when the bombs fell, Prince dived under the kitchen table with the rest of the family.

OLD-FASHIONED CLEANING REMEDY

Make beeswax polish by melting 3 oz (75 g) pure beeswax in a bowl placed over a pan of warm water. When wax has melted, stir in ¼ pint (150 ml) turpentine. Pour into a tin with a lid and add ten drops of lavender oil.

March 21-27

It makes me smile

I was showing my grandson Jack (aged six) a photo album of when his mother was a little girl. Next day he asked his mum: "Did Nannie always dress you in black and white?"
Mrs C Corbett, Birmingham

Here's health

Spring forward, fall back

Losing an hour's sleep when the clocks go forward can play havoc with your body clock for several days. Studies have shown that it can cause extra day-time sleepiness and this is enough to generate a significant rise in traffic accidents. Fatal accidents peak on the day after BST begins. Minimise the effects of the disruption by investing in some blackout blinds to make sure your bedroom is as dark as possible (they're good for people who suffer from early waking, too), and lie in bed an hour later than usual, to adjust.

My pet

Mrs J M Chambers of London had the bright idea of turning a wooden clothes airer into a budgie playground – and Joey thought it was great fun!

Make a difference - volunteer

Holidays for handicapped

With the Easter weekend coming up, many of us are planning a short holiday, but spare a thought for those who do not find it so easy to take an independent holiday. The Winged Fellowship Trust depends on the help of 5,600 volunteers to provide 7,000 breaks every year for visually impaired and disabled people.

There are opportunities all year round at the Trust's five UK centres where volunteers spend one or two weeks helping disabled guests with personal care. Although the hours are long, much of the time is spent accompanying guests on outings, entertainments and other leisure activities. These include trips to the theatre and cinema, bowling and shopping. Socialising with guests and other volunteers is a key part of the experience.

All volunteers receive free food and accommodation, travel costs within the UK and full insurance cover. No experience is needed as training is given. There are also day volunteering opportunities.
◆ **To find out more, write to Winged Fellowship Trust, Angel House, 20-32 Pentonville Road, London N1 9XD. Tel: 020 7833 2594.**

Every picture tells a story

When my husband retired we moved to our present address and soon afterwards some friends came to visit us. We had a very happy time and I told them all about my little granddaughter, Isabella Hope Collins, and how she loved fairies. When they left they insisted upon giving me a cheque 'to buy a little fairy for the bottom of the garden, for Isabella'. This we did. On Isabella's next visit, she wandered down the garden, to the spot

where she liked to play hide-and-seek, and this photo shows her delighted reaction upon finding Fairy Candytuft. (I was ready with my camera!)

Norma D Bona,
South Molton, Devon

Great garden idea

Place several dahlia tubers in a container of moist compost, with the crown just showing above the surface, and put them somewhere warm and light. The tubers will produce fresh new shoots which you can use as cuttings to create more plants. Dahlias with simple flower shapes look much more natural than complex blooms in herbaceous borders.

MY PRAYER

Keep your faith in the daffodil flower.
Keep your faith in the tranquillity of the hour.
Whatever torments come your way,
Do not be dismayed.
Remember the tranquillity of a flower.
Peace in abundance.
Pray through each hour for the peace
And purposeful faith of a tranquil flower.
Anne Hadley, Slough

Let's get cooking!

Chocolate and Bramley Apple Nests

(Makes 12)
- 4 oz (100 g) butter
- 4 oz (100 g) light soft brown sugar
- 4 tablespoons (60 ml) golden syrup
- 4 tablespoons (60 ml) cocoa powder
- 8 oz (225 g) Bramley apples, peeled, cored and grated
- 3 oz (75 g) porridge oats
- 4 oz (100 g) All-bran
- 1 oz (25 g) milk chocolate
- Mini Easter eggs for decoration

1 Preheat the oven to Gas Mark 4, 180°C, 350°F. Line a 12-hole patty tin with paper cake cases.
2 Place the butter, sugar and golden syrup together in a pan, stir until the sugar dissolves. Remove from the heat, then stir in the cocoa powder until smooth.
3 Stir in the apples, oats and All-bran, mixing well. Place heaped spoonfuls into the cake cases, making a hollow in the middle of each, then bake for 15-20mins. Cool in the tin.
4 To decorate, melt the chocolate and spoon a little into each of the nests. Place a few mini eggs in each and leave until the chocolate sets.

RECIPE COURTESY OF BRAMLEY APPLE INFORMATION SERVICE

March 28-April 3

Great garden idea

Companion planting helps to reduce pest damage. Try setting rows of beans between your brassicas – you will have fewer problems with cabbage root fly and mealy aphid on your cabbages and fewer blackfly on your beans. Thyme planted near brassicas is reputed to keep flea beetles away. Tagetes, rue, mint, lavender, rosemary and artemisia are commonly grown as companion plants – all have a strong scent that can mask the smell of susceptible plants close by.

OLD-FASHIONED CLEANING REMEDY

Clean tortoiseshell with a paste made by adding a few drops of olive oil to jeweller's rouge. Rub on gently with a soft cloth, leave for a few minutes then polish with a clean duster.

Dear diary

In the 1950s, Jim Ashby of Ashford in Kent, was serving in the navy and jotted down his first impressions of Portugal

10 March 1958
We arrived at Ponta Delgarda at 0600 this morning and came straight alongside the jetty to fuel. From the berth we could see right across the town to the hills behind – and what a welcome sight it was. It seemed like home to see fields on the mountain slopes – a mosaic of greens and browns – so different from the heavy growth of the West Indies. The town looked so different, too, all white in the early morning sun, with red and brown roofs.

Suddenly, it all seemed very European. We were soon surrounded by trading boats loaded with basket-work of every kind, and huge boxes of pineapples. The basketwork was absolutely superb.

We sailed at 1215 and have since been putting the miles behind us... homeward bound. It's dull, rainy, the sea calm...

Let's get cooking!

Lamb Moussaka
(Serves 4-6)
◆ 1½ lb (700 g) lean lamb mince
◆ 1 onion, chopped
◆ 1 clove garlic, crushed
◆ 3 tablespoons (45 ml) tomato purée
◆ 2 tablespoons (30 ml) mint jelly
◆ Salt and pepper
◆ 2 aubergines, thinly sliced
◆ 3 oz (75 g) feta cheese
◆ 500g carton Greek yoghurt
◆ 2 eggs

1 In a non-stick pan, dry fry the lean lamb mince for 4-5 minutes with the onion and garlic. Add tomato purée and mint jelly. Season with salt and pepper and cook for 2-3 minutes.
2 Lightly brown the aubergines slices on both sides in a hot frying pan.
3 Place half the mince mixture into an ovenproof dish and top with some of the aubergine slices. Crumble over the feta cheese and cover with the rest of the mince and the remaining aubergine.
4 Mix together the Greek yoghurt with 2 eggs and pour over the aubergines.
5 Bake in a preheated oven, Gas Mark 4, 180°C, 350°F, for 30-35 minutes until golden brown.
6 Serve with a baked Greek salad – roast tomatoes, slices of red onion and olives topped with crumbled feta cheese.

RECIPE COURTESY OF BRITISH MEAT INFORMATION SERVICE

Make a difference - volunteer

Guide to gracious living

Working in beautiful surroundings is a pleasure. If you live near one of the National Trust's 300 properties, enjoy history and like meeting people, why not become a room steward? Room stewards welcome the visitors and bring rooms to life by explaining stories connected with the property. They also keep a watchful eye on security and deal with visitor safety in emergencies.

Most properties are open from April through to November and room stewards are expected to commit at least one day a fortnight for those months (allowance is made those taking their annual holiday).

The hours are 10am to around 5.30pm. Although volunteers are unpaid, they do receive travel expenses.
◆ **To find out more about voluntary work for the Trust, contact its Volunteering and Community Involvement office, tel: 0870 609 5383. Internet: www.national-trust.org.uk/volunteering**

MY PRAYER

A simple cross of simple wood
Upon a hilltop silent stood
And on the cross a simple man
Was crucified – it was God's plan.
He gave His son to cleanse our sin
But what a mess the world is in.
Oh God you must be in despair
To see such mayhem everywhere.
Yet standing here on Easter morn
While watching such a perfect dawn,
That simple cross just seems to me
A symbol of eternity.
So on this special day of days,
Man rues the error of his ways,
Prays that forgiveness, peace and love
Come to the world from God above.
Mrs Paddy Jupp, Helston

Top tip

When labelling packets and containers for cupboard, fridge or freezer, use masking tape to write on. It comes off easily when no longer needed.
Mrs M Hotston-Moore, Milborne Port

My pet

He looks very comfy wrapped in his blanket but Jack once had a near-death experience when he got his head stuck in a large glass jar that had been used as a bottle garden. His owner, Jean Smith of Castle Barnard in Co. Durham, rushed him to the vet who managed to release him, with only a small nick on his neck to remind him of his misadventure.

Here's health

Guilt-free choc

Too much chocolate may make you fat, but it's hard to resist a seasonal Easter egg. Don't feel guilty, because chocolate can have some health benefits – it contains phytochemicals called flavonoids which can stop damage to the artery walls and inhibit blood clotting, preventing heart attacks or stroke. Dark chocolate with higher concentrations of cocoa is best.

It makes me smile

My wife had just had her hair done and when our friend saw it she exclaimed: "Oh, Judy, you have had skylights in your hair!"
Mr D Oldham, Milton Keynes

A Walk in the Wild
The gardener's prickly friend

Hedgehogs like to feast on garden pests

The hedgehog comes from an ancient family and fossils indicate that hedgehog-like creatures have been on Earth for around 15 million years – long before sabre-toothed tigers! The hedgehog is covered in one-inch (25mm) spines that are really modified hairs. There are between five and seven thousand spines on an adult hedgehog. They are not present on the chest, belly, throat and legs, which are covered with coarse grey-brown fur.

The hedgehog's natural food includes slugs, snails, woodlice and beetles. If you wish to supplement the diet of the hedgehogs in your garden, you should put out non-fish flavoured pet food and fresh water.

Provided a hedgehog survives its early life in the nest and its first hibernation, its life expectancy is around four years, although some have been known to live as long as ten years. Breeding starts in April and litters of two to six hoglets are born from May through to October.

When a hoglet goes out into the world it faces many dangers, not only from traffic and predators but also from gardeners. Injuries from strimmers and lawn mowers are usually fatal but hedgehogs also suffer from poisoning by garden chemicals, stabbing by garden forks and becoming entangled in netting. Although hedgehogs are good swimmers, they can drown if the sides of the ponds are too steep for them clamber out.

For more information send an A5 sized sae to The British Hedgehog Preservation Society, Hedgehog House, Dhustone, Ludlow, Shropshire SY8 3PL.

WARTIME WEDDINGS
Wot, no vicar?

Win Kenway of Colchester was almost wed without benefit of clergy

We were married in 1943. My husband Henry (nicknamed Bud) and I were both in the army and it was touch-and-go whether or not we would get leave at the same time. Having lost all my possessions in the bombing of my home town, Southsea.

I was married from my school friend's house, where I luxuriated in a tin bath (none of the pampering preparations of today). The wedding dress was given to me by an ATS colleague who had to cancel her wedding because her husband-to-be in the RAF had been shot down.

On arrival at the church, there was no vicar – he had been called away and the curate was gardening and had forgotten! He eventually arrived and we were consequently late at the photographer's (in those days we went to the studio) and also for the reception which was just a small affair in a tea room at the local cake shop. We managed to get one bottle of sacramental wine and the ingredients for the cake were scrounged from the officers' mess. No icing, just a dusting of icing sugar.

We went on honeymoon to Branksome Chine. We couldn't get on the beach because of all the barbed wire but we had a happy week before returning to our respective units. Afterwards I returned to Leicester where I was stationed and Bud went through the D-Day landings with the Royal Welch Fusiliers.

Puzzles

I See No Ships

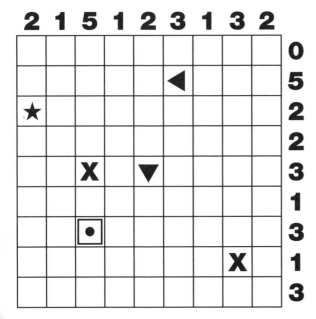

A fleet of ships is hidden in the grid. They may be lying horizontally or vertically, but they are not touching each other, even diagonally. The numbers along the side and top of the grid show you how many parts of ships can be found in each row or column. We've started you off with four hits and two misses. Can you fill in the rest?

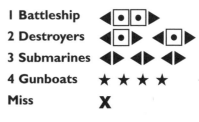

1 Battleship	◀ • • ▶
2 Destroyers	◀ • ▶ ◀ • ▶
3 Submarines	◀ ▶ ◀ ▶ ◀ ▶
4 Gunboats	★ ★ ★ ★
Miss	X

Vowel Play

The letters A, E, I, O and U have been removed from the words listed below — can you insert the full words into the grid?

Across
1 HRSM (7)
5 TTH (5)
8 NTL (5)
9 GNN (7)
10 T (3)
11 CHPLT (9)
12 DNTY (6)
14 VNSH (6)
18 BJCTN (9)
20 CG (3)
21 SRS (7)
22 SPR (5)
23 SDL (5)
24 VSV (7)

Down
1 HNTD (7)
2 RT (5)
3 LLCT (7)
4 MGP (6)
5 TNG (5)
6 RGM (7)
7 HYN (5)
13 NJRD (7)
15 MNS (7)
16 HYGN (7)
17 TSS (6)
18 SS (5)
19 CHK (5)
20 CRG (5)

Turn to Page 157 for puzzle answers

Short story

After going on a pilgrimage, Albert finds that he is nearer to God than ever before

To be a pilgrim

My brother-in-law Albert – now he's a strange one. Suddenly, in the middle of the night, he says to my sister Millie: "Millie, I've decided to become a wandering pilgrim for a while – one of those holy hermit chaps."

"You do get some funny ideas, Albert," she says, "Go back to sleep, there's a dear – I'm on earlies tomorrow."

After his breakfast, on a fine spring morning in April, Albert leaves. He is dressed in some old sandals from a jumble sale and a green flowing gown borrowed from the hospital laundry. His hair is shaved off and he carries a plant pot holder for a begging bowl. Millie doesn't know he's gone until she gets back from her early shift at the factory and finds the note in Albert's handwriting, 'Millie dear – just off on my pilgrimage'.

Albert takes a tube to Trafalgar Square where he joins a band of holy pilgrims setting off for Canterbury. All he has in his plastic carrier bag is his toothbrush, a Kit Kat, a banana and Millie's little radio for the Test Match commentary. In the pocket of his allotment trousers with the knee patches are five pound coins – Millie's launderette money. He falls in alongside this holy man, Archie, who's not happy. "Throw away that radio, my son. It ain't possible to walk in holiness with all that talking going on."

"It's from Lord's," explains Albert.

"It'll have to go even if it is the Lord's," replies Archie.

So Albert hands Millie's radio to a small boy sitting on a wall. "What's this for, Granddad?"

"To listen to the cricket. You can have it."

The kid looks at it: "Where d'ye get this – out of a bin? You keep it, Granddad – you ain't got nothin'."

Albert takes it back and removes the batteries.

"What happened to your hair, my son?" asks Archie, "Are you sure you're in the right march – we ain't goin' to Canterbury for a rumble!"

"Just thought it best, " says Albert. He's feeling rather low, not being able to listen to the cricket. "You know – pilgrim and that."

His friend raises his eyebrows and they stay silent all the way to Orpington.

Albert offers his new friend a finger of his Kit Kat – but this is an experienced pilgrim. "Keep it for later, my son, till after the chippy."

Albert has never liked fish so he gets double chips. Also, he only has five pounds as he has not yet tried his luck with the begging bowl.

Archie wipes his mouth with the paper serviette from the chippy, folds it and places it neatly in the top pocket of his sports jacket. "What's happened to your clothes, Albert?" he inquires, "that green gown – it's Health Service."

"I'm walking in the manner of Diogenes. You know – that Greek bloke in the picture."

"Yeah? I don't go to the pictures much," says Archie. He rubs his mouth with his hand: "You'd better say you're a green, if anyone comments."

"A green what?"

"You know – Friends of the Earth."

"Yes, I like that," says Albert, who has two allotments.

"What happened to your hair, my son?" asks Archie

By Richard Cutler

Eventually, on the fifth day, they arrive at Canterbury Cathedral. A figure in a long white gown with a large, heavy cross around his neck comes towards them.

"I'll have a word with that chap," says Albert.

"It's the Archbishop!" Archie backs off but Albert falls on his knees in front of the man in the white gown. The Archbishop's thoughts are far away, dwelling on the sung matins, and he almost trips over Albert.

"Hello? Had a tumble, my son?" He lifts Albert up and they sit down on a bench together. "Has something

"Millie dear –just off on my pilgrimage"

Albert falls on his knees in front of the man in the white gown

happened to your hair, my son?" asks the prelate.

Albert rubs his bristles: "My cousin Herbert suffered from alopecia but I just had mine cut for my pilgrimage."

"Got it," says the Archbishop. He touches Albert's arm: " What's this robe? Do I recognise it?"

"Green, your Grace," says Albert quickly.

"Ah, yes. Now which green order would that be?"

"Can't say exactly. Allotments… you know. Sort of thing."

"Would that be why you are carrying a plant pot holder, my son?"

"It's a begging bowl, your Holiness. I'm walking in the footsteps of Diogenes."

"Really? Remarkable! But I must tell you something, my son."

"I am listening, Father."

"Those who express too much humility are guilty of the sin of pride,"

Albert is a bit shocked at that.

"And remember, Albert, a man can do more in a day's work for his fellow men than in a year of contemplation and sacrifice."

Impressed by this saintly wisdom, Albert says: "Well, I'm looking for work. Know what I mean. I'm a cleaner. You name it, I clean it. No problem."

"Then you can clean my cathedral, Albert, especially the stained-glass windows." So Albert gets a really big cleaning job – just like that.

He leaves his pilgrim band and hitches a lift back to London.

"Hello, Albert," says Millie, "had a good pilgrimage?"

"I got a job, Millie. Something high up."

They value Albert at the cathedral. His cleaning skills, I mean. He's as spry as a goat. No fear of heights. Last time I'm down there he's sixty foot up on some scaffolding with his bucket and shammy leather.

I calls up: "Albert, if you get much higher, you'll be doing the Lord's windows." He shakes his head and gives me a strange look. Like I said, my brother-in-law Albert – he's a funny chap. I can almost see him as a monk. He's different. Not quite in the real world. Know what I mean?

April 2005

Friday *1* All Fools' Day	**Tuesday** *12*
Saturday *2*	**Wednesday** *13*
Sunday *3*	**Thursday** *14*
Monday *4*	**Friday** *15*
Tuesday *5*	**Saturday** *16*
Wednesday *6*	**Sunday** *17*
Thursday *7*	**Monday** *18*
Friday *8*	**Tuesday** *19*
Saturday *9*	**Wednesday** *20*
Sunday *10*	**Thursday** *21* The Queen's birthday
Monday *11*	**Friday** *22*

Saturday
23
St George's Day

Sunday
24

Monday
25

Tuesday
26

Wednesday
27

Thursday
28

Friday
29
May **Yours** on sale

Saturday
30

LOVELIEST OF TREES

Loveliest of trees, the cherry now
Is hung with blooms along the bough,
And stands about the woodland ride
Wearing white for Eastertide.

Now, of my threescore years and ten,
Twenty will not come again,
And take from seventy springs a score,
It only leaves me fifty more.

And since to look at things in bloom
Fifty springs are little room,
About the woodland I will
To see the cherry hung with snow.

A E Housman

IT HAPPENED THIS MONTH

1 April, 1957
The BBC made April
Fools of viewers when
Panorama showed
spaghetti being grown
on trees

4 April, 1968
Martin Luther King Jr
was assassinated on the
balcony of the Lorraine
Motel in Memphis

11 April, 1689
William and Mary were
crowned as joint rulers
of Britain

14 April, 1865
Abraham Lincoln was
shot while at the
theatre by actor
John Wilkes Booth

18 April, 1906
Two earthquakes killed
700 people in San
Francisco and left
400,000 homeless

20 April, 1902
Pierre and Marie Curie
isolated the radioactive
element radium

27 April, 1746
The British army
defeated Jacobite rebels
at the Battle of
Culloden

28 April, 1986
A nuclear leak
at Chernobyl
contaminated
thousands of miles
of the Ukraine

19 April, 1956
MGM had the exclusive film rights when
actress Grace Kelly (26) married Prince
Rainier III of Monaco (32) in a civil ceremony

April 4-10

Great garden idea

If your garden is shorter than you'd like then make it feel longer by planting white-flowered plants at the far end. Pale colours recede, while vibrant colours jump out at you and feel nearer than they really are.

Oh, happy day!

Anne L Harvey of Bolsover was thrilled to see her name in print

Among my most memorable days was the one when I saw my first published short story in A Year with Yours 2004. After three novels gathering dust in the loft and a dozen or so unpublished short stories, there was the proof that I was a published fiction writer at last! I had written non-fiction for some years with moderate success, yet I never seemed to get it right for the fiction market.

My hands were shaking and my knees turned to jelly as I flicked through the pages to find my story. There it was in the July section – The Breakaway by Anne L Harvey. And who better to share that exceptional day with but a dear friend from Australia, Judith, who had arrived that afternoon to stay with me. She had always encouraged my writing. You can see in the picture how excited we were (I'm on the right) – mind you, the bottle of Shiraz she'd brought with her might have boosted our silly smiles!

Let's get cooking!

Posh Beef Steak Sandwich and Chips
◆ 8 oz (225 g) lean beef rump steak
◆ I teaspoon (5 ml) oil
◆ I small onion, sliced
◆ 2 tablespoons (30 ml) mayonnaise
◆ I teaspoon (5 ml) black peppercorns, crushed
◆ Fresh bread

For the chips:
◆ I lb (450 g) potatoes
◆ I tablespoon (15 ml) oil
◆ I teaspoon (5 ml) chilli powder

1 Peel potatoes and cut into chunky chips.
2 Place into a roasting tin with the oil and chilli powder and cook in a preheated oven, Gas Mark 6, 200°C, 400°F, for 20-25 minutes until golden.
3 Heat oil in a pan and cook the beef rump steak for about 4 minutes each side (for a medium steak) with the onion slices.
4 When onion slices are golden brown, remove from the pan and mix with the mayonnaise and black peppercorns.
5 Cut the steak into thick slices and serve on a slice of fresh bread.

RECIPE COURTESY OF BRITISH MEAT INFORMATION SERVICE

Here's health

Put a spring in your step
Spring is a great time to start exercising more but if you don't fancy aerobics or jogging, go for something gentler that fits in with your everyday routine. A couple of brisk walks round the park could do you more good than an hour in the gym. 'Little and often' is the key and a moderate level of activity introduced into daily life can be more effective than high-impact activity.

A nice little earner

Norma Reeves (*below right*) earned sixpence a week helping in her father's business

My father was a shoemaker and in 1940 I was tall and strong enough to ride the tradesman's bicycle to deliver the shoes. They were packed into the basket at the front; laced shoes were hung on the saddle and the crossbar. I had a satchel on my back to put the money in. The bike was very heavy at first and quite difficult to keep upright.

I must have cycled between six and ten miles. Luckily, during the war there were few cars on the roads. There were vast numbers of planes in the sky; very often I would stop to watch dog-fights.

I would leave home at 8.30am and arrive back in time for dinner at 1pm. Everyone was very trusting and the doors were left unlocked. If there was no one at home, the shoes would be left in the kitchen and I made a note in my book to collect the money next week.

OLD-FASHIONED CLEANING REMEDY

Paraffin can be used to remove the tide mark from a bath.
Mr A Barker, Northallerton

MY PRAYER

Maybe one day we shall all realise
Of the wasted years of our lives
Jesus was crucified upon a cross
He gave his life, have you forgot?
Let us pray, that for us it's not too late
To lift up our hearts with renewed faith
To show our faith and belief in the Lord
And pledge your soul by giving your word.
As the church bell beckons come this way,
You enter the church and kneel to pray,
Asking the Lord for forgiveness in your prayers
As you look ahead to the future years.
Your way along the righteous path is well trod
As you whisper the words 'Thanks be to God'.
William Reilly, Liverpool

Senior moment

My clock chimed the hour while my son was chatting to me on the phone. He said: "Mum, your clock is ten minutes fast." I said: "That doesn't matter as the clock in the hall is ten minutes slow."
Mrs K P Gillgrass,
Chorley

My pet

Maureen Davies of Swansea was inspired to write a poem about Barbie, her cockatiel.
Barbie sat upon her eggs,
Soon the babies grew quite big,
Crowding out the nest,
So we gave them to the pet shop –
I think we did what's best.
Waiting patiently.
Three weeks went by, then cheep, cheep, cheep,
The chicks had hatched – all three.

Top tip

If you are going out in the rain, take a spare carrier bag to put your umbrella in; it stops everything getting wet.
Joyce Wright,
Hurstpierpoint

April 11-17

Great garden idea

If you have a frost-free greenhouse, plant up summer hanging baskets now and grow them on inside. As a liner, use a thick layer of moss removed from the lawn (as long as it hasn't been treated with chemicals within the last few weeks). Choose wire baskets so you can position trailing plants through gaps in the sides. Include a controlled release fertiliser that will give nutrients throughout the growing season.

My pet

Len Pearce of Frome snapped his German Shepherd Poppy enjoying a nap with her pal the ginger tom.

MY PRAYER

Life is precious.
Each day upon waking
I am amazed
You, God, have given me
More time for the journey
With many crossroads,
Many sorrows
Many joys.
I pray the journey will
Not be in vain,
That what little contribution I make
Is sustaining to someone,
Whether human or animal
Who comes my way.

When I trip over I know
You, God, will pick me up and
Dust me down and restore me to new paths.
The world seen with new eyes
Which are no longer blurred,
Colours dazzling.
An entrancing vision of life,
Which all can acquire.

Joyce Gale, Bristol

OLD-FASHIONED CLEANING REMEDY

To remove white rings caused by water or heat on polished furniture, rub gently with a paste of salt and cooking oil on a soft cloth. Polish with a dry cloth.

Wit and wisdom

I've never hated a man enough to give him his diamonds back.
Zsa Zsa Gabor (1919-)

Make a difference - volunteer!

Once upon a time, I learned how to read

Curling up with a good book is one of the enduring joys of childhood so teaching children to read has to be one of the greatest gifts we have to bestow. If you can give time regularly each week, are patient and understanding as well as liking children and books, then Volunteer Reading Help (VRH) would love to hear from you. The charity recruits volunteers to offer one-to-one support to primary school children who find reading a struggle. Helping the same child for two half-hour sessions a week, and supporting up to three children, volunteers are placed in a local school. They receive training plus the on-going support of a VRH fieldworker.

VRH provides a box of books for each reading helper, with termly book exchanges and social events. In the sessions with the children, the emphasis is on fun, encouragement and boosting confidence.
◆ **To find out if VRH has a branch in your area, call 020 7729 4087.**

Remember the '60s?

Pat Martin of Bristol was at the London Palladium

My husband and I got married in 1960 and decided on London for our honeymoon. We had tickets for Sunday Night at the London Palladium and jokingly said that if the contestants for Beat the Clock were picked from the audience, we would be ready.

Just before the interval, Bruce Forsyth began picking the contestants. He went to the left and asked if there was a nurse in the audience, then he went to the right and asked for a honeymoon couple. We were up like a shot. We had to sign an insurance form – my hands were shaking so much no one could have read my signature. We played a few games and then it was my turn for the word game. I had to unscramble 'everything comes to those who wait'. We won a television with sliding doors. People still remember us being on TV.

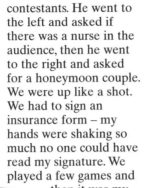

Left and above: Pat's wedding day and a reminder of her time on the TV with Brucie

Let's get cooking!

Thai Mango and Tuna Salad
(Serves 4)

For the salad:
- ◆ 4 oz (100 g) egg noodles
- ◆ 1 tablespoon (15 ml) sunflower oil
- ◆ 1 medium mango, peeled and cut into strips
- ◆ 1 small red onion, peeled and finely sliced
- ◆ 1 packet fresh mint, leaves stripped
- ◆ 1 packet fresh coriander, chopped
- ◆ 1 lb 2 oz (500 g) fresh tuna steak, cut into cubes

For the dressing:
- ◆ 1 garlic clove, peeled and finely chopped
- ◆ 1 fresh red chilli, seeded and finely chopped
- ◆ 4 tablespoons (60 ml) light soy sauce
- ◆ 2 tablespoons (30 ml) Thai fish sauce
- ◆ Juice of 4 limes
- ◆ 2 tablespoons dark sugar

1 Place noodles in a bowl, pour over boiling water and leave for 5 minutes. Drain.
2 Whisk all the dressing ingredients together.
3 Pour half the dressing over the noodles and toss to coat evenly. Arrange the noodles on four plates.
4 Heat the oil in a non-stick frying pan until very hot. Add the tuna and cook until cooked through.
5 Combine tuna with the rest of the salad ingredients and the remaining dressing and toss until well coated. Spoon on top of the noodles and serve.

RECIPE COURTESY OF THE MANGO ASSOCIATION

Top tip

Pour a can of coke down a blocked up sink plughole. It works; try it!
Mrs F Easton, Dagenham

Senior moment

I hurriedly got into my car and put my hands on the steering wheel – it wasn't there! I realised I was sitting in the back seat!
Ken Smith, Coventry

Here's health

Oriental wisdom

Living in harmony with the seasons of the year is one of the tenets of Chinese medicine. Spring and summer are 'yang' months; a time of warmth, growth and activity. Spring, traditionally associated with the liver and gall bladder, is a good time of the year for cleansing, mental exercise and making new plans. Now is the time to drink plenty of water and juices and eat green vegetables and seeds to give your body a fresh start.

April 18-24

 Let's get cooking!

Pistachio Praline and Chocolate Mousse

(Serves 4)

- ◆ 1 oz (25 g) Tate & Lyle granulated cane sugar
- ◆ 1 tablespoon unsalted, shelled pistachios, chopped
- ◆ 3 oz (75 g) white chocolate
- ◆ ¼ pt (150 ml) reduced fat double cream alternative
- ◆ 2 medium egg whites

1 Place the granulated cane sugar in a heavy-based small pan and cook over a gentle heat for 1-2 minutes, shaking the pan occasionally until all the sugar has melted, then caramelised.
2 Stir in the pistachios and remove from the heat. Carefully pour the caramel mixture on to an oiled baking sheet and leave until cold. Smash the praline with a rolling pin, reserving a few pieces for decoration. Finely crush the remainder.
3 Melt the chocolate in a bowl placed over a pan of hot water. Whisk the egg whites and light double cream in separate bowls, until they form soft peaks, then fold into the chocolate with the crushed praline.
4 Divide between four dessert glasses and top with the reserved praline shards.

RECIPE COURTESY TATE & LYLE CANE SUGARS

My first...

Jean Ferrier of Saltash was four when she first saw her father

My father went to India to fight for King and country when I was six months old. I was happy living with my mother, who allowed me to stay up late in evenings, sometimes listening to the radio. On the day my father came home I was completely unaware of the changes this would bring to my life. The train had already arrived at the station and I saw swarms of men running four abreast down the steps to the platform. A tinge of fear crept over me; my childhood had been spent mostly with women and I was not used to seeing vast numbers of men.

"There he is," exclaimed my mother, "wave your flag!"

Suddenly, a man ran towards us and threw his arms around my mother. While I stood watching, I felt they were a pair but I was on my own. Eventually, my father looked down at me and said: "Is this our little girl?" I did not feel instinctively that he was my own flesh and blood. Nevertheless, it was the beginning of a happy relationship that was to last 55 years.

 ## MY PRAYER

Welcome the spring blossom for me.
Listen when our blackbird chants in the cherry tree,
When the cuckoo calls, remember how we used to be.
In summer nose the wild roses for me,
When leaves drip from the trees
And martins leave clay-potted eaves,
Watch the arrow-flighting geese for me.
My heart will not hang on the Christmas tree
Nor these eyes be there to see.
Hug our children for me, my love,
Live life to the full for me.

Beryl Johnson, Nottingham

Make a difference - volunteer!

Lightening the darkness

There are around two million people with sight problems in the UK and every day another 100 people go blind. The RNIB depends on the work of volunteers to rebuild the lives of people devastated by sight loss. One way in which you could help is by providing support for the charity's talking book service. This involves visiting people in their own homes, demonstrating how to use the talking book player and giving advice on any aspect needed to ensure the user gains maximum enjoyment from the facility.

◆ **To find out more, call the Volunteer Development Unit on 0845 604 2341 or send an e-mail to tcsvolunit@rnib.org.uk.**

Great garden idea

Plant up plain terracotta containers with small evergreen shrubs such as Choisya ternata 'Sundance' and use these as a backdrop for your summer bedding plants. The shrubs (one per pot) will last several seasons and provide a colourful background for spring bulbs as well as summer and autumn displays.

Here's health

Bending over backwards

If you are planning to tackle the garden this week, take care of your back. Bending for too long can cause the muscles that support your spine to go into spasm. Work with long-handled garden tools and change from one job to another frequently to use different sets of muscles. **A helpful booklet called Back in the Garden (£3.50) is available from Back Care, 16 Elm Tree Road, Teddington, Middx TW11 8ST.**

OLD-FASHIONED CLEANING REMEDY

Brighten up aluminium saucepans by adding one teaspoon of cream of tartar to one pint of water, then bring to the boil and simmer for a few minutes.

My pet

Heidi is remembered in a poem by Elizabeth Scarre of Hull
*A nicer natured dog
There could never be.
An irreplaceable friend
That's what you were to me.
You would sit by my side
With your head on my knee,
Then shuffle up close
As close as can be.
When the day came
To say our goodbyes
I walked away with tears in my eyes.
You were loyal and faithful
Until the end.
I will miss you so much,
My dog, my friend.*

Senior moment

As I was leaving my neighbour's house she gave me her bag of rubbish to put into her bin. When I arrived home, I still had it in my hand!
Mrs M Fardy, Leeds

Top tip

Fold clothes before you put them in the washing machine. They won't tangle and it's easier to unload them.
Charlotte Joseph, Leland, Cornwall

April 25-May 1

Great garden idea

Add style to your garden with a penny-saving piece of topiary. Instead of waiting years for box or yew to grow, plant several ivy plants at the base of a frame of green, plastic-coated wire formed into a simple shape such as a cone, sphere or pyramid. Encourage them to grow through it by tying in the twining stems and trimming any that grow in the wrong direction. Keep it well watered and give it a feed every spring and you'll be surprised by the results.

My pet

Tandy won the heart of Marian Brislee of Maidstone when she saw her in Battersea Dogs' Home. 'I asked: "Can you shake hands?" and she gave me her paw. That was it; she had me hooked'.

MY PRAYER

Give us some friends in retirement
With similar hobbies and views.
Let us have int'resting chats and debates
Discussing the latest news.
Show us the beauty of nature
Now that we have time to browse,
And lead us to wonderful places
As far as our pittance allows.
Grant us the health to enjoy it,
This holiday we have all earned,
And the will to share with others
The notions and skills we have learned.
Allot us an adequate pension,
But here's where this pleading all points:
Please give us all back a bit of our youth
And keep the pain out of our joints.
       Gina Spreckley. Hemel Hempstead

Wit and wisdom

I don't deserve this, but then, I have arthritis and I don't deserve that either.
       Jack Benny (1894-1974)

OLD-FASHIONED CLEANING REMEDY

It is easier to remove candle wax spilt on fabric if you freeze the article for an hour so that the pieces will crack off. Treat any colour left from the wax with white spirit, then rinse.

Make a difference - volunteer!

Get out into the great outdoors

Whether you live in the town or country, you can play a useful part in preserving your local area by working for a Wildlife Trust near to you. The Wildlife Trusts are a partnership of 47 local environmental charities and the whole movement has been built on its army of 23,000 volunteers. Volunteers of all ages and from all sectors of society are kept busy on a wide range of activities from managing nature reserves to community gardening. As well as providing opportunities for people to enjoy the outdoors, get involved and find out about wildlife close to home. The Trusts aim to make a positive contribution to quality of life, health and social networks. Typical tasks might include creating nature trails, clearing invasive

plant species or maintaining ponds. You could become a warden at a nearby nature reserve or, if you prefer a less active role, be part of a team running a visitor centre or a Wildlife Trust shop.
◆ **To find out more, call 0870 036 7711 or e-mail volunteer@wildlife-trusts.cix.co.uk**

Every picture tells a story

My father was an agricultural engineer, so I visited many farms with him from the 1930s to the 1950s. This photo was taken at Eric Kays' farm at Marston Moor near York where we went to see the newborn lambs. (I am the smallest one – in white – with my two sisters). The countryside was so lovely in those days with lots of meadows, bluebell woods and blackberry copses. We saw rabbits, foxes and badgers because the farmers knew where they were.

Ruth Wright, York

Top tip

If you want to cut back on alcohol but still like the taste, add just a few drops of gin to a glass of tonic water. You'll find the taste is just as good.

Mrs O Sherrington, Chelmsford

It makes me smile

I had taken my two daughters to visit a stately home. It was rather chilly inside and Amy (aged nine) said: "I'm not surprised it's cold; there's a frieze on the wall!"

Angela Higinbotham, Congleton

Here's health

An avocado a day...

Add slices of avocado to your salads and sandwiches. Avocados are a rich source of vitamin E which is believed to slow the ageing process. They also contain potassium which has been shown to reduce blood pressure and the risk of stroke. Although avocados are high in fat, it is the monounsaturated type of fat that lowers cholesterol.

Let's get cooking!

Seared Tuna with Asparagus, Mushrooms and Cherry Tomatoes

(Serves 4)

- 1 lb (450 g) British asparagus
- 8 oz (225 g) button mushrooms
- 12 cherry tomatoes
- 1 clove garlic, crushed
- 1 tablespoon olive oil
- Black pepper
- 4 x 6 oz (175 g) tuna steaks
- Handful of fresh basil leaves
- 1 lime cut into four wedges

1 Clean and trim asparagus, snapping off any woody ends.
2 Preheat oven to 190°C/375°F/Gas Mark 5.
3 Toss the asparagus and mushrooms in 2 teaspoons of olive oil and garlic, plus black pepper and transfer to a large baking sheet.
4 Roast in the oven for 5 minutes, then add the tomatoes. Roast for a further 10 minutes or until tender.
5 Season the tuna steaks with black pepper and sear them for 1 minute each side in a very hot non-stick griddle pan lightly rubbed with oil.
6 Toss the vegetables and basil together and pile on to plates. Top with the tuna steaks and serve immediately with the lime wedges.

RECIPE COURTESY OF BRITISH ASPARAGUS

A Walk in the Wild
A brilliant blue flutter by

The Holly Blue butterfly makes its home in ivy as well

The small, lively Holly Blue is one of the few butterflies that seems as much at home in urban parks and suburban gardens as in the countryside. This is thanks to the happy coincidence that some of our favourite garden plants are also very much to the taste of Holly Blue caterpillars; holly and ivy, to name but two.

You may be lucky enough to see this pretty butterfly anytime from late March through to October but, in fact, there are two separate generations in most areas each year. Females of the spring generation lay their eggs mainly on the developing flower buds of holly trees. Their caterpillars are tiny and difficult to spot, even if you search for them. Unfortunately, for the Holly Blue, its natural enemies, particularly small wasps, don't have the same problem in finding the caterpillars. The surviving caterpillars develop (via the pupal stage) and a new generation of Holly Blue emerges in the latter part of the summer. This generation's females choose ivy buds on which to lay their eggs. Thus, the holly and the ivy take turns to nurture successive generations.

Although it is a familiar sight to garden butterfly watchers in southern England and Wales, the Holly Blue is scarcer in the north and is not normally seen in Scotland at all. Here, the Common Blue is the only blue butterfly likely to be seen in gardens.

While the Holly Blue has fared well in modern Britain, most of our butterflies are in decline. Butterfly Conservation is trying to make a difference.

To find out how you can help please contact Butterfly Conservation on 0870 7744309.

WARTIME WEDDINGS
Just get me to the church on time

Jackie Dilley of Reading was confined to barracks but still made it to her wedding

Bert and I were both in the army and the week before we wed I was on company orders for accidentally burning the CO and the adjutant's clothes and Sam Browne when they were being aired in front of the fire, ready for a big parade. When Exhibit 3, a tie nine-tenths burned, was shown, I laughed – and got an extra week confined to barracks, making it three weeks in all, starting that day. When I informed them I was getting married the following Saturday, they allowed me to go, but with my punishment to start on my return to barracks.

I borrowed my wedding dress from our corporal and a pair of shoes that pinched like the devil. My hubby-to-be had been in hospital for fourteen months after being badly wounded so had to have a makeshift suit.

We had Spam sandwiches and a little

home-made cake. The bombs were dropping and there was a real pea-souper – you couldn't see your hand in front of you. When we went to meet my sister-in-law from Reading she told us my brother couldn't come because he had to fly over Germany on an air raid. We learned later that his Lancaster bomber was blown up over France on our wedding day. We didn't have a honeymoon – we only had 4s 6d left – but God gave me a wonderful husband. We had sixty years together and were sweethearts to the end.

Puzzles

Cryptogram

This quotation from politician Aneurin Bevan has been put into code by substituting one letter of the alphabet for another. We've started you off, so it's now up to you to decipher the rest.

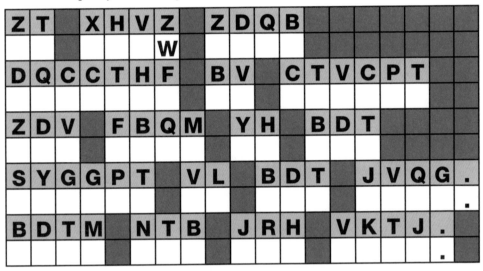

| Z | T | | X | H | V | Z | | Z | D | Q | B | | | | | | |
| | | | | | | **W** | | | | | | | | | | | |

| D | Q | C | C | T | H | F | | B | V | | C | T | V | C | P | T | |
| | | | | | | | | | | | | | | | | | |

| Z | D | V | | F | B | Q | M | | Y | H | | B | D | T | | | |
| | | | | | | | | | | | | | | | | | |

| S | Y | G | G | P | T | | V | L | | B | D | T | | J | V | Q | G | . |
| | | | | | | | | | | | | | | | | | . |

| B | D | T | M | | N | T | B | | J | R | H | | V | K | T | J | . |
| | | | | | | | | | | | | | | | | . |

Takeaway

By shading out one letter in each square, words can be formed reading across and down the rows and columns of the grid. It's best to use a pencil for this one in case you slip up. We've formed the first word to show you how the puzzle works, so now you can take it away!

Turn to Page 157 for puzzle answers

Dandelion

A poignant tale of young love during a time of conflict

The camp seemed to appear almost over night. When I cycled home on Friday afternoon the fields were empty except for the dandelions. On Monday morning there were men and machines everywhere, tanks covered with camouflage netting, lorries, jeeps, rows of khaki tents and lots of noisy young American soldiers. Young men terrified me.

There was another way to school, but it was along the main road and three times as far, so I had to put up with the wolf whistles and invitations. I was in my last school year and what was euphemistically termed 'beginning to blossom'. And now there was this young man in uniform sitting on the gate I wanted to go through. I could feel a blush rising up from my neck and covering my face. He grinned at me. "Can I pass through the gate, please?"

"Sure," he replied, with a Yankee drawl. Still smiling he jumped down and opened the gate for me.

"Thank you," I said, primly. I caught his 'You're welcome, Ma'am' as I shot off along the track as fast as I could pedal.

A few days later he was there again. "Hi," he greeted me as he opened the gate to let me through. A brief 'Hello' and 'Thank you' and I was off again at top speed. But this time I couldn't resist looking back. He was watching me; he grinned and waved.

The next day he was standing in front of the gate. There was a determined look about him. My heart lurched, and I had a feeling there would be no quick getaway today. "Hi!" He always seemed to be smiling.

"Why are you forever in such an all-fired hurry?" He wasn't going to let me pass without an answer. I grinned foolishly. "My name's Danny. What's yours?" he asked.

"Ruth," I replied.

"Well, Ruthie, how about playing hooky and spending some time with me?"

"I can't," I gasped, horrified. "I have to go to school. I shall be in trouble if I'm late. Please let me pass."

"Okay, okay. But only if you'll say you'll meet me after school. Please." He was suddenly serious. I looked at him properly for the first time. He was very young, not much older than me, I guessed. He seemed nice and I wavered, losing some of my shyness. "All right," I said, "but I won't be able to stay long."

He opened the gate for me and I pedalled off wondering what my father would say if he knew. I had already been given a stern warning of the perils of talking to American servicemen as, I'm sure, had every other girl of my age in the town.

But Danny was nice. He was only 17; like a lot of young men he had lied about his age to join up, but he missed his family and friends. He came from Fond Du Lac, a small town in Wisconsin, and he needed a friend.

As we got to know each other we began to spend as much time together as we could. I had my studies, and he had his duties, and sometimes the whole camp would disappear on manoeuvres, but when they returned he would always be waiting at the gate for me. We had fun. The real reason for the soldiers being there seemed a long way away, if I ever thought of it at all.

Danny liked to make me

"Ruthie, how about playing hooky?"

By Ruth Ann Aldridge

dreams

laugh. One day he picked a dandelion and started pulling off the petals. "She loves me, she loves me not," he said to the flower, then looked at me. "That's not dandelions, that's daisies," I laughed, "Dandelions make you wet the bed."

"What? You're kidding."

"No, I'm not. In England we say if you pick dandelions you'll wet the bed."

So every time we met he would pick a dandelion and wave it at me. "Hasn't happened yet," he'd say. "You English and your crazy country customs." And he would wrap his arms around me tightly, so that I couldn't move, laugh, and kiss me on the nose.

There came a time when he held me tightly and, instead of kissing me on the nose, he kissed me on the lips. We both laughed self-consciously, but he kept hold of my hands and suddenly he wasn't laughing.

"I think we're pulling out soon." He put his hands on my shoulders. "There's a mighty strong buzz going round the camp. You will write to me, won't you? Promise me, Ruthie, please."

"I will, of course I will," I reassured him. "Try and stop me."

"Don't worry if you don't hear from me for a while," he told me. "I may not be able to write to begin with." I had never seen him so serious.

I wrote often, but no letters came from Danny

"But you keep writing, you hear. You're special to me."

"I will, I will."

This was scary stuff. Although the camp had only been there for a few months, to me it seemed like a lifetime. I hadn't really thought about Danny leaving. I suppose I thought he would be there forever. But he had to go to war – that was why he was in England. I couldn't imagine not seeing him. What was I going to do without him? We hugged each other again.

By the weekend they had all gone. There was nothing left but the churned-up grass and dandelions.

I wrote often, but no letters came from Danny. And then, one by one, my letters were returned to me, marked 'Missing – believed killed in action'. And that was that. I was heartbroken. I missed him desperately. He was my love, but I was only sixteen and life has to go on.

For a long time, as I cycled along the track to school, it was hard not to imagine him sitting on the gate, waiting for me. I actually thought I saw him once but, of course, it was just a trick of the light.

There's a housing estate now where the fields used to be and the gate has gone, but I think of Danny sometimes – still smiling, with a dandelion in his hands, still seventeen.

May 2005

Sunday *1*	**Thursday** *12*
Monday *2* May Day Bank Holiday	**Friday** *13*
Tuesday *3*	**Saturday** *14*
Wednesday *4*	**Sunday** *15*
Thursday *5*	**Monday** *16*
Friday *6*	**Tuesday** *17*
Saturday *7*	**Wednesday** *18*
Sunday *8*	**Thursday** *19*
Monday *9*	**Friday** *20*
Tuesday *10*	**Saturday** *21*
Wednesday *11*	**Sunday** *22*

Monday

23

Yours Summer Special on sale

Tuesday

24

Chelsea Flower Show
(RHS members only, provisional)

Wednesday

25

Chelsea Flower Show

Thursday

26

Chelsea Flower Show

Friday

27

Chelsea Flower Show

Saturday

28

Sunday

29

Monday

30

Spring Bank Holiday

Tuesday

31

June **Yours** on sale

CATS

Cats sleep
Anywhere,
Any table,
Any chair,
Top of piano,
Window-ledge,
In the middle,
On the edge,
Open drawer,
Empty shoe,
Anybody's
Lap will do,
Fitted in a
Cardboard box,
In the cupboard
With your frocks –
Anywhere!
They don't care!
Cats sleep
Anywhere.
Eleanor Farjeon

IT HAPPENED THIS MONTH

1 May, 1961
Britain's first betting
shops opened

3 May, 1926
The first day of the
General Strike which
lasted nine days

8 May, 1956
John Osborne's Look
Back in Anger opened
at London's Royal
Court theatre

10 May, 1940
Neville Chamberlain
resigned as Prime
Minister

13 May, 1912
The Royal Flying
Corps was created

14 May, 1926
Comedian
Eric Morecambe
was born

20 May, 1940
The helicopter
was unveiled by
its inventor Igor
Sikorsky

28 May, 1588
The Spanish Armada
set sail from Lisbon

29 May, 1871
The first Bank
Holiday in the UK

4 May, 1979
Margaret Thatcher became Britain's
first woman Prime Minister

PIC: REXFEATURES

May 2-8

Great garden idea

Now is a good time to feed your plants with fertiliser. Organic fertilisers such as pelleted chicken manure are much better for the environment than man-made ones. Weigh out enough to cover one square metre (according to the instruction on the container) and place it in an old cup. Mark the level with an indelible pen so you know how much to use next time.

Oh, happy day!

Mrs Bobby Hitchin tells of a sunflower-decked wedding

When our youngest daughter, Helen, married her partner David at Rye Town Hall it was a landmark in our family. We have three daughters and six grandchildren but as they all live in different places, we had never all been together for 15 years. What a celebration!

The day itself was blessed with beautiful sunshine. The medieval town hall was decked out in huge sunflowers. My daughter loves sunflowers and she looked beautiful when she came in with her four-year-old son, Matthew, and her proud dad. After the ceremony, the town cryer, in full regalia, announced the happy couple to the world in ringing tones.

We then went to the reception – more sunflowers – where we enjoyed wonderful food and the children in the party played together with toys thoughtfully provided by the happy couple. The day flowed so smoothly from beginning to end and, for us, having all our girls together made it a really memorable day.

Helen and Matthew on a sunshine-filled day

 Let's get cooking!

Watercress and Salmon Soup
(Serves 4)
- 1 tablespoon (15 ml) sunflower oil
- 1 large onion, finely chopped
- 13 oz ((350 g) potatoes, peeled and cut into rough cubes
- 2½ pints (1.5 litres) vegetable stock or water
- 8 oz (225 g) watercress, roughly chopped
- 3 tablespoons (45 ml) single cream or reduced fat crème fraîche
- 6 oz (175 g) salmon, skinned and cut into cubes
- Salt and ground black pepper

1 Heat the oil in a large saucepan and add the onion and potatoes. Cook gently for 10 minutes until softened.
2 Add the stock or water and bring to the boil. Turn the heat down and simmer for 20 minutes. Stir in the watercress and cook for 5 minutes.
3 Let the soup cool a little before liquidising it in batches.
4 Return the soup to the pan and stir in the cream or crème fraîche. Taste, and season with salt and black pepper.
5 When you are ready to serve the soup, heat it to a low simmer. Add the salmon cubes and gently simmer for 5 minutes.

RECIPE COURTESY OF WATERCRESS ALLIANCE

Here's health

Hay fever is no fun
One in four of us is affected by hay fever. Here are four tips to minimise the symptoms:
- Keep your windows shut at home and in the car.
- Smear petroleum jelly around your nostrils to trap pollen and stop you breathing it in.
- Wear sunglasses.
- Shower as soon as you come indoors and put your clothes straight in the wash.

A nice little earner

Barbara Edmondson of Warrington's Jewish neighbours relied on her help

Mrs Greene and her two grown up sons owned the shop on the corner of my street. They were strict in upholding the Sabbath, their day of rest. This meant no work of any description could be undertaken. The shop would be closed and family set out early to walk to the Synagogue.

I would be waiting for them on their return. It was my job to light the fire, which had been set the previous evening, and to boil a kettle of water and make a pot of tea. Sometimes I would be asked to slice and plate the cake that had been left out in readiness. My reward for this was usually a chocolate biscuit or two from the shop, selected (with great deliberation, of course) by myself.

Top tip

When buying watercress, to prevent damage when taking it home, blow into the transparent plastic bag the shop probably popped it in, then tie the top into a twisted knot, making sure it's sealed. This keeps it safe and fresh.

*Rosie Jones,
Cardiff*

My pet

Howard Robinson of Ebbw Vale says: "Our dog Gemma, a beautiful Labrador, has her own armchair to relax in. We covered it with a blanket and asked her to take her hat off indoors, but she never would!"

MY PRAYER

*Be with me Lord when I am glad
And all my skies are blue,
Never let me fail to give my gratitude
To You.*

*Be with me when the night is dark,
And shadows cross my heart,
That I may always keep the faith
And never grow apart.*

*Be with me Lord when I'm at home,
Or when I travel far,
And help me to appreciate
The beauty of a star.*

*Let not my heart be lonely
Or my footsteps go astray,
Help me to live my life
According to Your way.*

*Be with me, Father – everywhere,
In happiness and tears,
Be with me now and grant me grace
Through my remaining years.*

Hilda Watkins, Bream

Senior moment

My husband was amused when I said to him: "Don't have the hymn Abide With Me at my service when I die – it always reminds me of funerals!"

*Sylvia Haywood,
Headington*

OLD-FASHIONED CLEANING REMEDY

To remove limescale stains on an enamel bath, make a mixture of bicarbonate of soda and vinegar and paint this around the stain. After a few minutes use the reverse side of the tail of an EPNS spoon and lightly scrape the limescale off.

Doreen Flynn, London

May 9-15

Great garden idea

It's time to put out your tender summer bedding plants but it's worth buying a length of plant protection fleece to cover them just in case temperatures drop below freezing during the night. You can buy fleece by the metre from garden centres, but if money is tight, there's nothing wrong in using an old cardigan or sheet – although you may get odd looks from the neighbours!

Wit and wisdom

If music be the food of love,
let's have a Beethoven butty.
John Lennon (1940-1980)

My pet

Madeleine Forsdick of Ipswich will never forget how Shep, a Red Merle border collie, came to the rescue when her husband Robert was left in charge of cooking the dinner. Having lit the gas ring and put the chops in the frying pan, he fell asleep in the front room. With smoke rising through the house, Shep pawed him awake just in time to prevent a major disaster.

MY PRAYER

Another day draws to its end,
To the Lord my prayers I send.
I thank him for giving me today,
For guiding me along life's way.

I pray the night be quiet and calm,
For him to keep me free from harm,
That the day to come will bring peace,
For all worldly ills to cease.

When day breaks fresh and new,
I thank Him for the morning dew.
Welcome its newness like a bird,
I thank the Lord, my prayers He heard.
Josie Rawson, Selston

Top tip

If you are partially sighted but still like to make your own cuppa, place a clean ping-pong ball in the bottom of the cup before pouring the tea; when the liquid is at the top the ball will rise, and you'll know you can stop pouring.
K M Hoath,
Claygate

Make a difference - volunteer!

Brave it in your bra

Marathon walker Nina Barough set up the health charity Walk the Walk in 1998 following her fight against breast cancer. The charity organises the Playtex Moonwalk that takes place in London every May and mobilises women (and men) all over the world to power-walk marathons in their bras. The funds raised go to Breakthrough Breast Cancer for research and the Bristol Cancer Help Centre for cancer care.

Called the Moonwalk because it starts at midnight, it is a full marathon (26.2 miles) but less experienced walkers can opt for the half moon (13.1 miles). If walking is not your thing or you are not the extrovert type who is happy to parade the streets in a fancy bra, then you can help in many other ways. Volunteers are needed for all sorts of jobs including handing out goody bags and bottles of water.
◆ **For more information call 0207 924 7214. email: kate@ktb.uk.com**

Remember the '60s?

Beryl Lomas of Stockport reckons the Beatles rescued us from a sartorial mess

I was 13 in 1962 and a trip to the youth club meant a dash to C & A after school to find an outfit for the same night. I (*below left*) usually ended up buying a tight skirt and it was irrelevant whether it fitted or not as long as it was something you hadn't been seen in at school.

We spent most of our time standing up or dancing, restricted by the ever-present suspender belt, a hideous contraption of white nylon. If you tried to bend down, it cut through your stomach like a chainsaw. When tights came out they were hailed as a revolution. My first pair were black fishnet, which I tastefully combined with a pair of white slingbacks. Winklepickers, wide belts and Evening in Paris were all jumbled together.

All that changed when we first saw the Beatles. At last, a new style! Any colour we wanted as long as it was black. Bri-nylon polo necks, suede or leather coats – even the girls tried to look like John Lennon.

OLD-FASHIONED CLEANING REMEDY

Use a cut lemon to remove tea stains from kitchen sinks.

 Let's get cooking!

Penne with Asparagus and Parma Ham

(serves 4)
- 16 spears British asparagus
- 14 oz (400 g) penne
- A knob of butter
- 8 slices Parma ham roughly cut into strips
- 3 tablespoons crème fraîche
- Black pepper
- Grated Parmesan cheese

1 Cook the penne according to the instructions on the packet.
2 Meanwhile, steam the asparagus, cut each spear into three and toss in a little butter.
3 When the pasta is cooked, drain it and return to the pan.
4 Add the asparagus, Parma ham, crème fraîche and black pepper to the pan and toss well.
5 Serve in warm bowls with a sprinkling of Parmesan on top of each serving.

RECIPE COURTESY OF THE ASPARAGUS ALLIANCE

Here's health

Beware bee stings
If you are unlucky enough to be stung by a bee or other insect, use sterile tweezers to take out the sting and then apply a cold compress (a bag of frozen peas wrapped in a cloth is a quick way to make one). If you have any severe reactions such as swelling of the face and neck, breathing difficulties, blotchy skin or a rapid pulse, you may have anaphylactic shock and should immediately seek emergency treatment.

It makes me smile

Watching me put on moisturising cream, my granddaughter remarked that I had a lot in common with her other Nanna: "You've both got laughter lines. You must have heard a lot of good jokes!"

Judith Clephan, Liverpool

May 16-22

My first...

The thrills and spills of her first holiday seem like yesterday for Edna Lydiate of Preston

In July 1957, aged 15, I left school, and before starting my first job I went with my mother on my first holiday to Butlins holiday camp at Filey. I made friends with a girl who was also on holiday with her mum and we went around the camp together, having a go at everything. We went swimming in the outdoor pool at 6am, before breakfast, and at 8am every morning we would put our fingers in our ears when the 'Good morning campers' tune was bellowed out to wake everyone up. We went roller skating, watched films and played in the amusement arcades. We even went horse riding, which I found scary because, although I had never ridden before, I was put with the experienced riders. My horse was bad tempered and it took off, with me clinging on for dear life. We passed all the other riders and arrived back first. My friend laughed and said: "Boy, did you ride 'em, cowboy!"

In the evenings we used to go to the Viennese Ballroom where all the teenagers congregated, dancing quicksteps and waltzes. I met a Geordie boy called Bill. I'll never forget him, or my first holiday, even though it's so long ago.

Edna's 1957 Butlins holiday

Let's get cooking!

Curried Pasties
(Serves 6)
- 8 oz (225 g) lean minced beef
- 1 onion, chopped
- 4 oz (100 g) potato, peeled and cubed
- 2 tablespoons (30 ml) curry paste
- 2 tablespoons (30 ml) mango chutney
- 2 oz (50 g) frozen peas
- 1 lb 2 oz (500g) packet puff pastry
- 1 egg, beaten

1 In a non-stick pan, dry fry the minced beef with the onion and potato for 4-5 minutes until browned.
2 Add the curry paste, mango chutney and frozen peas and cook for a further 2-3 minutes. Allow to cool slightly.
3 Roll out the puff pastry on a floured surface to approx 15 x 15 in (38 x 38 cm). Cut into six equal sized squares.
4 Divide the mince between the six pieces of pastry, brush the edges with a little beaten egg and fold the corners over to seal.
5 Place on a non-stick baking tray and brush with the remaining egg. Bake for 20 minutes at Gas Mark 4, 180°C, 350°F until risen and golden brown.
6 Serve with chutney or yoghurt dip, mixed salad or potato wedges.

RECIPE COURTESY OF ENGLISH BEEF AND LAMB EXECUTIVE

Here's health

Show a leg!
Don't let varicose veins stop you going without tights in warm weather. Try making up a compress of essential oils to tone the veins and leg muscles. Add up to ten drops of cypress, juniper, rosemary and lavender to a bowl of warm water and use it to soak a large, clean piece of cloth. Put the cloth on your legs and leave for ten minutes. Remove, and splash with cold water.

Make a difference - volunteer

Helping teacher

No professional qualifications are needed to become a classroom assistant but patience and a fondness of children are essential. In addition (a sad reflection on our times) all applicants must fill in a form and submit to a police check – an essential precaution to protect children from crimes against them.

Classroom assistants have a vital role to play in primary education; not only do they ease the pressure on the teacher, they can give one-to-one attention to children who need it. Reading is an area where the assistant can be especially useful, working either with an individual child who has learning difficulties or with small groups of able

pupils. If a volunteer shows a particular aptitude for working with handicapped children, for example, they might receive training 'in-house' before being offered a paid position.

◆ **If you are looking for rewarding part-time work and can offer a couple of hours of your time on the same day each week, contact the head of your local primary school – the chances are that they will welcome you with open arms.**

Senior moment

I'd been gardening and was looking forward to a hot bath. I turned on the taps, put in a big dollop of bath bubbles, and went away while it filled. It really would have been better if I'd put the plug in!
Babs Painter, Bridgwater

MY PRAYER

God give me sympathy and sense,
And help me keep my courage high.
God give me calm and confidence,
And – please – a twinkle in my eye.
Joyce Halsall, Williton

My pet

Time for forty winks for Valerie Evans of Anglesey's grandson, Jonathan, and Rosie the Labrador.

Great garden idea

At what time of day do you usually sit in the garden? Create a seating area which gets the sun when you're most likely to use it, then fill containers with scented plants such as nicotianas, lavender, freesias, heliotrope, brugmansias and sweet alyssum. If you're a chocaholic, why not choose Cosmos atrosanguineus which has velvety maroon flowers with a mouth-watering smell of chocolate.

OLD-FASHIONED CLEANING REMEDY

To conceal scratches on polished furniture, rub them with the kernel of a Brazil nut.

May 23-29

 **Let's get cooking!**

Coley Fajitas

(Serves 4)
- 1 tablespoon (15 ml) vegetable oil
- 1 small red onion, finely chopped
- 4 oz (100 g) button mushrooms, sliced
- 1 green pepper, deseeded and cut into thin strips
- 1 red pepper, deseeded and cut into thin strips
- 1 lb (450 g) coley or cod fillets, skinned and cut into strips
- 2 tablespoons (30 ml) water
- 9 oz (240 g) jar Tijuana sauce
- 12 soft flour tortillas, warmed
- 7 oz Greek yoghurt

1 heat the oil in a large frying pan or wok and cook the onion and mushrooms for 2-3 minutes or until softened.
2 Add the peppers and stir-fry for a further 2-3 minutes.
3 Gently stir in the fish, add the water and sauce. Bring to the boil and simmer for 2-3 minutes.
4 Serve with warm tortillas and yoghurt.

RECIPE COURTESY OF SEA FISH INDUSTRY AUTHORITY

Every picture tells a story

In 1938 I was orphaned and placed in a Dr Barnardo's home. Barnardo's put the children in touch with adopted aunts who would write to them and visit, if possible, and send them presents for Christmas and birthdays. My aunt was Hilary, a young Welsh lady who had just joined the ATS. I remember Hilary visiting me – she looked so smart in her uniform. She would take me to the cinema whenever it was possible for us to meet.

At the end of war Hilary became a ballet teacher in London. I left Barnardo's and did my National Service in Egypt before starting work in London. We would often meet for a meal. Eventually, Hilary retired and returned to Wales. We kept in touch but we rarely saw each other until I was on a short visit to Swansea and visited her beautiful little cottage, where this photo was taken.

John Speirs, Wembley

senior moment

My husband Reg usually makes our morning coffee. One morning, he said: "Coffee ready!" It tasted horrible. When I went into the kitchen I found he had put gravy granules into the cups instead of instant coffee. His face was a picture.

Mrs E Smith, Bognor Regis

Make a difference - volunteer!

Speak up and become a newsreader

If you have a nice, clear speaking voice and like reading aloud, you are an ideal candidate for the Talking Newspaper Association, which is the membership organisation for most of the 540 local Talking Newspaper groups that exist around the country.

Each Talking Newspaper supplies, mainly on audio tape, local newspapers and magazines for blind, partially sighted and print disabled people in their area. The groups are all staffed by volunteers who not only read but also edit, copy and distribute the tapes to their members. The Association is also responsible for running the National Service for which volunteers read 250 publications as well as supporting the staff members with other duties such as editing, recording, copying and dispatching throughout the UK and overseas.

◆ **For information on volunteering within your area contact TNAUK, National Recording Centre, 10 Browning Road, Heathfield, East Sussex TN21 8DB or e-mail info@tnauk.org.uk. Tel: 01435 866102**

Here's health

Travel sickness cure

If you are planning a trip away over the bank holiday, there's no need to fret about travel sickness. Pressure on the pericardium 6 (an acupressure point situated three fingers' breadth down from the wrist crease) has been shown to prevent nausea. Try pressing on it for ten minutes, four times a day, or wear an acupressure wristband, available from chemist shops.

Top tip

When using plastic tubes of cream, when they appear to be empty just cut an inch off the bottom of the tube (keep it to use as a lid) and you will find there is still a quantity of cream inside. As you use it, just cut some more off the tube until it is completely empty.
Mrs R Daw, Birmingham

My pet

'Our collie Meg likes to be mum to the baby rabbits when they play out on the grass in our back garden', says Mrs Rae Bysouth of Ipswich.

MY PRAYER

A dog's favourite prayer
A master who is firm and kind,
And understands a doggie mind;
A walkie and a meal each day,
That's all I ask for when I pray.
Susan Carr, Thornton-Cleveleys

Great garden idea

Buy a strawberry pot from your local garden centre and fill each hole with a different herb. Place it by the backdoor so that you can go out and pick a few leaves when you need them in the kitchen. When planting the container insert a length of hose in the centre and make holes along its length. If you water through the hosepipe, water will be available to all the plants no matter what their position in the container. The plants will last a season in the container and most of them can be taken out and divided during the autumn.

A Walk in the Wild
The peregrine comes to town

PIC: NICK DIXON

Once on the decline, our largest falcon is adapting to modern life

Falcons that breed in Britain are the kestrel (a familiar sight hovering over motorway verges), the hobby (which resembles a large swift in outline) and the smallest and rarest, the merlin. Britain's largest falcon is the peregrine, noted for its breathtaking aerial pursuits as it hunts its prey on the wing. It will often soar high before zooming spectacularly down on to its quarry – usually other birds such as pigeons, gulls or ducks. This powerful falcon is one of our best survivors. Numbers declined dramatically to just 360 pairs in the 1960s, largely because of pesticide poisoning.

The Hawk and Owl Trust, which works to conserve wild birds of prey and their habitats, was founded in 1969 because of concern about the plight of the peregrine. With the banning of DDT, increased protection and intensive conservation, the population has slowly recovered to over 1,500 pairs. Peregrines, which usually pair for life, lay eggs on sheltered ledges or in disused nests of other large birds, such as ravens. Traditionally birds of mountain, moorland or coast, they began to breed in quarries during the 1980s.

Some now even nest in towns and cities. There are increased sightings of peregrines on buildings and other man-made structures that offer secure nest sites and vantage points from which to spot prey. These range from power stations, pylons and bridges to blocks of flats, churches and cathedrals.

The peregrine is the emblem of the Trust, which is completing a three-year study of this bird of prey's shift towards urban living. The aim is to discover how many birds are adapting to the modern world in this way and to understand their behaviour in their new man-made setting.

To learn more, contact Adopt a Box, The Hawk and Owl Trust, 11 St Mary's Close, Abbotskerswell, Newton Abbot TQ12 5QF. Tel: 01626 334864.

WARTIME WEDDINGS
Navy larks at Roedean

Her fellow Wrens formed a guard of honour for Vi Parsons of Hailsham

We met at Roedean School which the Navy had taken over for the war. I was a Wren and Jack was doing a naval course there. We were married at St Andrew's Church in Brighton on 5 June 1943. The night before the wedding there was an air raid. Jack and his parents were staying in digs and the landlady woke them up to ask if they wanted to come under the stairs but they preferred their beds!

I had no coupons for clothes so wore an evening dress I had in blue shot gold. I managed to get some gold netting for the headdress and flowers. I had six Wrens forming a guard of honour at the church and I am still in touch with two of them. I was lucky with our cake. The baker said if I could give him a pound of sugar, he would provide the icing sugar – which he did.

We had only a weekend break for our honeymoon and spent it at the Anchor Hotel just outside Brighton. We went by train but had to

walk across the fields to get to the hotel which was right in the middle of the country. As I had been given a week's leave I went back with Jack to Chatham as he was standing by there for his submarine – a new one – to be finished.

Puzzle

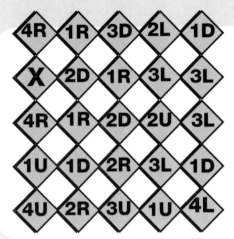

Making Tracks

Movement through this grid is determined by the instructions printed on each diamond. 3D, for example, is an instruction to move three places downwards. Can you work out where to start so that you finish on the spot marked X, and stop on each diamond only once?

Turn to Page 157 for puzzle answers

Quizword

ACROSS

7 In which TV series does David Jason play a veteran detective? (1, 5, 2, 5)
8 In the hit series Hi-De-Hi!, what kind of maid was Peggy, played by Su Pollard? (6)
9 What surname is shared by reclusive millionaire Howard and the poet Ted? (6)
11 What kind of Aboriginal weapon comes back when you throw it? (9)
14 Which Yorkshire city provided the setting for The Full Monty? (9)
18 Which Pacific island, capital Taipei, is claimed by China as part of its territory? (6)
20 What completes the title of the Arnold Schwarzenegger movie Total - - -? (6)
22 Which New Romantic group gave us True and Gold? (7, 6)

DOWN

1 Of which US state is Salt Lake City the capital? (4)
2 What name is given to the followers of Islam? (7)
3 In the Procul Harum hit, which word described the shade of pale? (6)
4 Which hound is noted for its grace and long hair? (6)
5 What is the surname of TV presenter and novelist, Melvyn - - -? (5)
6 What geographical term connects Dogs and Man? (4)
8 What team of ministers forms the main part of the Government? (7)
10 Which film deals with the Profumo affair? (7)
12 What term is used to describe a top card or a top pilot? (3)
13 What is the surname of the US president who emancipated the slaves in 1863? (7)
15 What is the first name of actress Ms Gordon, star of Upstairs, Downstairs? (6)
16 What stage name did ukulele-playing comedian George Booth adopt? (6)
17 American band leader Benny Goodman was known as the King of what? (5)
19 Mont Blanc is the highest peak of which mountain range? (4)
21 Which vegetable shares a name with a town in Staffordshire? (4)

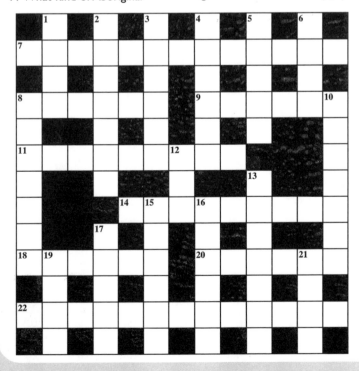

Reader article

The plane now

Heather Grange found that being an air stewardess in the 1960s was not quite as glamorous as she thought...

'I have pleasure in confirming your appointment with this company as Air Stewardess. Please arrange to commence duty on March 4, 1968. Rate of Pay: £9.00 per week. Standard Allowances'. My letter of acceptance lies yellowing with age in my drawer.

"One of the first things I notice about a woman is her nails," the Channel Airways Training Captain said. Luckily, mine were well cared for. After that, training began – lectures, visits to Catering, (overseen by a handsome Catering Officer) emergency drills and Customs formalities – so much to remember. We practised speaking over a public address system and throwing ourselves down a shute.

What a change from commuting from Rainham to Fenchurch Street as a short-hand typist, poring over a manual typewriter in a shipping office where the highlights were the coffee break and the outing to an Italian sandwich bar.

So now the glamorous life awaited…

Needing to live near the airport, I boarded at Mrs C's with other fledgling stewardesses – tall redheaded Ula, a German girl whose home was near the Czech border and much relieved that she didn't get teased about her red hair in England. Kim, half-Chinese and half-Portugese who came from Hong Kong and whose prime objective was to find an English husband (which she did). Christine, South American sexy and ambitious, and laid-back Anna who came from Rotterdam.

Anna was romantic and lived in a world of fantasy. We shared a bedroom and I lay enthralled at night listening to tales of her parents' resistance activities during the Second World War. She digressed from time to time to tell me how she'd fought off the sexual advances of a handsome First Officer. A wild exaggerator was how her friend described her.

We used to meet up in Mrs C's kitchen.

A bird in its cage swung solitarily on its perch spreading bird seed everywhere; Anna in her dressing gown would be cutting off bits of Dutch cheese with a sharp knife and Ula washing through the underarm of her uniform blouse.

I'd be ironing mine, then the phone would ring. It was usually one of Kim's boyfriends. Or 'Operations, anyone want to do a Rotterdam nightstop?' We all looked at Anna, who would change into her rumpled uniform and race out of the door, her makeup bag half open. A few months later she left the airline. The reason was shrouded in mystery but it had something to do with the cabin smelling strongly of whisky fumes. She went back to Rotterdam and married Hans.

My first nightstop was Rotterdam and I was warned not to open my bedroom door. When the knock came at about 2.30am I was prepared. "Got any aspirins?" asked a glum voice which I recognised as the First Officer's. "No," I said firmly. He wasn't going to use a headache as a pretext for any hanky panky!

Cologne became a regular daytime stopover. Going to Cologne meant driving to Stansted and leaving very early in the morning, the Captain and crew arranging to meet me at 4.30am. I always arranged to wait in a cinema doorway near where I lived which, in more romantic circumstances, might have made me think of myself as a spy, except that I was too tired to think of anything but getting out

boarding...

of the cold wind as it whipped around me. Some glamour!

The drive to Stansted was long. Our passengers were businessmen working for the Ford Motor Company due in Cologne and scheduled for meetings at 9am. Arriving at our hotel exhausted, we would sleep until midday, have lunch and then walk round the city and include a visit to the cathedral. It was disorienting and tiring but was all part of the job. We looked forward to days off which were spent recuperating.

My passport soon became full of stamps from Italian and Spanish resorts. There were occasions to bring back presents: Pearls from Palma, banana liqueurs from Brindisi and white wines from Venice. The trips were mostly charter flights, taking off in the evening and arriving before 6am so that airport landing fees would be low.

While the aircraft was cleaned and fresh water brought on board, we catnapped on a verandah, the crickets the only sounds in the heat of the early morning. They were quick turn-arounds. In Ostend, we browsed round the harbour and had meals in restaurants of mussels and white wine. When we flew to Guernsey the greenhouses were so near we almost touched them and then we took back their tomatoes to the mainland.

The job had its dangerous moments and they were never far from our minds, although I was seldom frightened. One of the fleet, Papa Charlie, aquaplaned in bad weather and came to rest at the end of the runway. Nobody was hurt but we were shaken. The other flights, mine included, were transferred to another airport. It meant transporting already tired passengers by coach and driving through the pouring rain back to base a few hours away.

Passengers could be irate or confrontational. One whom I refused to serve with more alcohol, said he would report me. It was not an idle threat.

Working in pressurised cabins had its drawbacks too, ankles could swell, and it was not adviseable to fly with a head cold. Seats for the cabin staff were near the doors where the sounds of the engines were loudest which might mean hearing loss later in life.

Working long and odd hours could mean losing contact with old friends. Some marriages were made, others un-made. Some cabin crew requested not to fly together, others had their favourites. Women were out to get husbands. Men were romantic or seemed to be, and liaisons were formed. I put it all down to the uniform.

Airline life was transitional. Many used the company as a stepping stone to international companies. Especially some of the younger pilots who had clocked up hours crop-spraying and were ready to move on. They wanted promotion. Like many of the others when the season came to an end I, too, moved on.

It was my grandfather who said incredulously: "You, an air hostess, don't you know your station in life?" If only he'd known…

June 2005

Wednesday *1*	**Sunday** *12*
Thursday *2*	**Monday** *13*
Friday *3*	**Tuesday** *14*
Saturday *4*	**Wednesday** *15*
Sunday *5*	**Thursday** *16*
Monday *6*	**Friday** *17*
Tuesday *7*	**Saturday** *18*
Wednesday *8*	**Sunday** *19* Fathers' Day
Thursday *9*	**Monday** *20* Wimbledon Championships start
Friday *10*	**Tuesday** *21* Summer solstice
Saturday *11*	**Wednesday** *22*

Thursday
23

Friday
24

July **Yours** on sale

Saturday
25

ADLESTROP

Yes. I remember Adlestrop –
The name, because one afternoon
Of heat the express-train drew up there
Unwontedly. It was late June.

The steam hissed. Someone cleared his throat.
No one left and no one came
On the bare platform. What I saw
Was Adlestrop – only the name

And willows, willow-herb, and grass,
And meadowsweet, and haycocks dry,
No whit less still and lonely fair
Than the high cloudlets in the sky.

And for that minute a blackbird sang
Close by, and round him, mistier,
Farther and farther, all the birds
Of Oxfordshire and Gloucestershire.

Edward Thomas

Sunday
26

Monday
27

Tuesday
28

Wednesday
29

Thursday
30

IT HAPPENED THIS MONTH

1 June, 1946
The first TV licences were issued in Britain

3 June, 1989
Soldiers of the Chinese People's Liberation Army used tanks to suppress a demonstration by pro-democracy students

6 June, 1868
Explorer Robert Falcon Scott was born

12 June, 1849
Lewis Haslett patented the gas mask

17 June, 1970
Decimal postage stamps were issued for sale in the UK

23 June, 1989
The film Batman was released

24 June, 1955
Walt Disney's cartoon Lady and the Tramp, based on the book by Ward Greene, had its premiere in New York

28 June, 1914
The assassination of Archduke Ferdinand by a Serb nationalist in Sarajevo led to the outbreak of the First World War

29 June, 1613
Shakespeare's Globe Theatre was destroyed by fire

18 June, 1815
Napoleon was defeated at the Battle of Waterloo by an Anglo-Dutch army lead by the Duke of Wellington

May 30-June 5

My pet

Scary Spike was rescued by friends of Mrs A Harriman of Harrogate who rehouse hedgehogs that have been in garden accidents. Unlike her prickly friends, Scary Spike chose not to hibernate – perhaps she was scared she would miss a meal!

Great garden idea

Azaleas and rhododendrons are in their glory right now but they are not suitable for every garden because they are acid-loving plants that require soils with a pH of around 6 or lower and dislike chalky alkaline conditions. In these soils some of the elements become unavailable to the plants and this causes a deficiency. So never try to grow acid-lovers in alkaline soils – plant them in a container using ericaceous (acidic) compost.

Top tip

To make quick work of scraping new potatoes, rub them with a nylon pan scourer.
Mrs L Childs,
Newton Abbot

Oh, happy day!

Doreen Clements of Bristol's husband Clem was on cloud nine in every sense

My husband Clem enjoyed an unforgettable day when his family gave him a surprise 80th birthday present – a flight in a Tiger Moth. As many of the family as were able to (we now number 26 including great grandchildren) gathered for a picnic at Staverton Airfield near Gloucester to watch Granddad take to the skies – something he hadn't done since 1942 when he was training with the Royal New Zealand Air Force in Canada.

He was in the capable hands of a very experienced lady pilot called Tizzie who handed over the controls after take-off for the 30 minute flight, only taking over again for the landing. His original log book, now a little dog-eared and yellow, was duly signed and he was presented with a certificate that said 'Absolutely brilliant and has forgotten nothing in 61 years'. The family clapped and shouted: "Well done, Biggles!".

His photo, standing by the Tiger Moth, adorns the reception area of the retirement complex we now call home.

A nice little earner

Celia Machin of Manchester recalls an unusual way of earning some extra money in the 1940s.

My husband, Stanley, had the nightly job of taking the newsreel after it was shown in one cinema as quickly as possible on his bike to a second cinema to be shown to the first house. He then waited to take it back in time for the second house at the first cinema where he waited again to return it in time for the second house of the other cinema. This earned him ten shillings a week.

Let's get cooking!

Creamy Mustard Pork
(Serves 2)
- ◆ 1 tablespoon (15 ml) oil
- ◆ 8 oz (225 g) lean pork fillet, sliced into thin medallions
- ◆ 1 onion, sliced
- ◆ 1 clove garlic, crushed
- ◆ 3 oz (75 g) mushrooms, sliced
- ◆ 5 tablespoons (75 ml) crème fraîche
- ◆ 1 tablespoon (15 ml) wholegrain mustard
- ◆ 1 tablespoon (15 ml) basil leaves, torn

1 In a large pan, heat the oil and cook the pork medallions for 1-2 minutes. Add the onion, garlic and mushrooms. Cook for a further 4-5 minutes.
2 Add the crème fraîche, mustard and basil to the pan. Heat gently for 1-2 minutes.
3 Serve on a bed of pasta ribbons with seasonal vegetables.

RECIPE COURTESY OF BRITISH MEAT INFORMATION SERVICE

OLD-FASHIONED CLEANING REMEDY

If your iron becomes sticky through using it too hot on synthetic fabrics, unplug it, and while it's still warm (not hot), apply toilet soap to the affected area then gently scrape it off with the blunt side of an old knife.

Doreen Flynn, London

Wit and wisdom

Talk to a man about himself and he will listen for hours.
Benjamin Disraeli (1804-1881)

Here's health

Veggie might
Now that summer vegetables are in season, add some to salads to give yourself a boost. Beetroot contains vitamin C, calcium, iron, magnesium, folic acid and potassium and is great for cleansing your digestive system. It can help to detoxify your liver and prevent gallstones. For healthy skin and eyes, add watercress which has anti-cancer properties and contains 15 essential vitamins including vitamin A and betacarotene.

It makes me smile

The doctor asked my dad if he was on any tablets, whereupon his prompt reply was: "Only Steradent, sir!"
Doreen King, Tunbridge Wells

June 6-12

Remember the '60s?

The Sunday School outing was a great day out for Linda Hill

My enduring memory of the 1960s was the annual Sunday School outing when we travelled by coach from Northamptonshire to Mablethorpe, Skegness or Hunstanton. The greatest excitement was receiving a real brown wage packet handed out by the vicar with my name on the front containing two shillings and sixpence pocket money.

The day itself was characterised by a swim in the grey sea, no matter how far out the tide was or how cold the weather, and a ride on a donkey. A sand-encrusted picnic would be supplemented by fish and chips eaten straight from the newspaper, using wooden forks that always failed to secure a chip from paper to mouth. We would just have time to spend our last pennies in the slot machine before getting the coach home. One year, my older sister and I (*below*) had our photographs taken with sweater-clad monkeys.

 ## Let's get cooking!

Warm Fennel and Squash Salad
(Serves 4)
- 1 lb (450 g) butternut squash, deseeded but not peeled
- 1 bulb fennel, trimmed, quartered and sliced
- 2 medium red onions, sliced
- 4 cloves garlic, unpeeled
- 1 tablespoon (15 ml) olive oil
- 1 tablespoon (15 ml) pine kernels
- 1 (85 g) bag of watercress

For the dressing
- 1 tablespoon (15 ml) olive oil
- 1 tablespoon (15 ml) clear honey
- 2 tablespoons (30 ml) red wine vinegar
- 1 teaspoon (5 ml) wholegrain mustard

1 Cut the squash into chunky wedges then place with the fennel, onions and garlic in a large roasting tray. Add the oil and toss well to mix. Season with salt and pepper then roast in the oven at 200°C, 400°F, Gas mark 6 for 15 minutes. Add the pine kernels and roast for another 5-10 minutes.
2 Remove the garlic and squeeze the flesh from the papery skins onto a chopping board. Mix to a paste with the blade of a knife then place in a screw-top jar. Add the remaining dressing ingredients and shake to mix. Season to taste.
3 Place the watercress leaves in a salad bowl, add the roasted vegetables and dressing and toss well to mix. Serve with crusty bread.

RECIPE COURTESY OF WATERCRESS ALLIANCE

Here's health

Barbecue common sense
When planning a barbecue, don't neglect basic food hygiene. Wash your hands, chopping board and utensils when you switch between preparing different types of food such as meat and vegetables. Chicken is a common cause of food poisoning so make sure it is cooked all the way through to kill off salmonella bacteria.

Make a difference - volunteer

Nosey parkers play their part

When it comes to preventing the spread of petty crime, we can all make a difference without leaving our own front rooms. The Neighbourhood Watch scheme has been shown to lower crime statistics (as well as the cost of home insurance) thanks to the vigilance of folk who keep an eye on what is going on in their own patch.

With most people out at work during the day, unattended properties are a tempting target for thieves and vandals. Retired people have time to take note of any suspicious behaviour and alert the authorities, if necessary.

◆ **If you are observant by nature, think about joining your local Neighbourhood Watch scheme. It's a good way of promoting a community spirit as well as giving protection to the vulnerable, especially the very young and very old. Speak to the Crime Reduction Office at your local police station or visit website www.homeoffice.govuk.**

Senior moment

My fishmonger looked puzzled when I asked for two cud cotlets.
*Doris Sheppard,
Isle of Man*

My pet

Another volunteer for Neighbourhood Watch? Evi Korsus of Coggeshall caught Simba peeping through the net curtains.

MY PRAYER

*Lord, my way seems hard today
But I thank You for being there.
Lord, sometimes I cannot go on
But I thank You for showing you care.
Lord, forgive me for doubting You,
But I thank You for the times You carry me.
Lord, I walk in light with You
But I thank You for giving me strength to see.
Lord, your plans are better than mine
But I thank You for I know You are truly kind.
Lord, with You all my needs are met
But I thank You for all my journeys set.
Lord, take my hand
And I will thank You
For taking me to Your better land.*
  Rosemary Medland, Letchworth Garden City

Great garden idea

Save those polystyrene trays of bedding plants from the garden centre to break up for use as crocking in the base of your containers. This material can't be recycled because, although it's plastic, most of it is made up of air. As a result it isn't cost effective for companies to collect it. What better way to keep it out of landfill than by using it for drainage to prevent your plants from becoming waterlogged.

OLD-FASHIONED CLEANING REMEDY

To remove grease marks from wallpaper, cover the stain spot with blotting paper and apply a warm iron to absorb the grease.

June 13-19

OLD-FASHIONED CLEANING REMEDY

To make your own air freshener, fill a spray bottle with 4 fl oz (115 ml) water and add ten drops of an essential oil such as lemon or cedarwood.

Let's get cooking!

Banana and Grape Layers
(Serves 4)

- 3 x 5 oz (150 g) pots of no-fat Greek yoghurt
- 2 teaspoons (10 ml) clear honey
- Few drops vanilla essence
- 2 bananas, peeled and sliced
- 4 oz (100 g) seedless red grapes
- 2 oz (50 g) Tate & Lyle dark brown soft cane sugar
- 1 teaspoon (5 ml) lemon juice

1 Place the yoghurt in a bowl and fold in the honey and vanilla essence. Reserve 8 slices of banana, 4 halved grapes and 1 teaspoon of the sugar for decoration.
2 Arrange half the remaining bananas and grapes in the base of four dessert glasses. Sprinkle with the sugar. Repeat the layers with the rest of the fruit and sugar.
3 Spoon over the yoghurt mixture. Toss the reserved bananas in the lemon juice then place on top of the yoghurt with the grapes.
4 Chill for one hour or until the sugar has dissolved to form a dark caramel sauce. Sprinkle over with a little more sugar and serve.

RECIPE COURTESY OF TATE & LYLE CANE SUGARS

My first...

Kay Spurr of Okehampton was led astray very early on

The first time my boyfriend joined my family on our summer holiday, I was just 13 years old and Paul was 18. There wasn't room for Paul and his mate, Keith, to travel with us in Dad's car so they hitchhiked down to Paignton from Bradford.

Funds being tight, they carried a tent with them and

pitched it in a field close to the hotel we were staying in. One morning a horse and rider entered the field. On seeing the tent, the horse reared up, almost throwing its rider. She approached us, telling us we had no right to be there and threatening to prosecute. She asked for our names and addresses and I followed Paul and Keith's example and gave false ones. He'd already started getting me into bad ways! What on earth possessed me to marry him, I don't know, but we're still together over 40 years later!

Top tip

Disguise chipped white paintwork by painting with correcting fluid – this also works on bleached oak furniture.
Mrs S McMillan, Accrington

It makes me smile

Unloading my basket at the supermarket check-out, I piled up ten tins of dog food and two bottles of whisky. The cashier said: "Let me guess – it's a Scotch terrier."
Trevor Bishop, Kilpeck

Make a difference - volunteer!

Could bedside broadcasting be for you?

Hospital radio helps to combat the boredom and isolation that afflicts many patients. The mix of music and chat provides them with comfort and entertainment. Many an aspiring DJ has started his or her career on hospital radio and most volunteers are keen to go on air but if you prefer you can just visit the wards, chat to the patients and collect requests, or help with the technical side of broadcasting.

Volunteers should be able to communicate well in English (some stations in Wales also ask for Welsh speakers). It helps if you are outgoing and enjoy meeting people. You don't need expert knowledge of music or any technical expertise – a willingness to learn is more important.

◆**To find out more, contact your local hospital or NHS Trust or call the Hospital Broadcasting Association tel: 0870 321 6002. Internet: www.hbauk.co.uk**

Here's health

Check any mole changes

Sunburn in childhood is partly responsible for the number of moles present in the skin of an adult. Moles are made up of collections of melanocytes, the cells responsible for producing the melanin pigment found in our skin which helps to give us a suntan. Fortunately, most moles are not a problem, although they can cause anxiety that they might be cancerous. Get any changes in your moles checked out by a GP, particularly if they bleed, crust over, itch or grow bigger.

My pet

Say cheese and watch the birdie! Mrs G Pead of Bexley took a photo of Lucy trying to take a photo of her.

MY PRAYER

Trust God's wisdom thee to guide;
Trust His goodness to provide;
Trust His saving love and power;
Trust Him every day and hour.

Trust Him as the only light,
Trust Him in the darkest night.
Trust in sickness – trust in health,
Trust in poverty and wealth.

Trust in joy and trust in grief,
Trust His promise for relief.
Trust Him living – dying too
Trust Him all the journey through.
        Elizabeth Mead, Maldon

Great garden idea

If you have a patch of the notorious weed horsetail in your garden, don't panic. It will gradually disappear with regular weeding, especially if the soil increases in fertility over time. In some ways it is beneficial because its penetrating root system brings up nutrients from deep in the soil. Let it grow in a damp corner, harvest it regularly and use it in your compost.

June 20-26

Every picture tells a story

My parents were never in the higher income bracket, therefore my dad took on another job to help pay for one week's holiday in Hastings. We were there in June 1949 when my mum celebrated her birthday and I remember the ice cream seller gave her a free ice cream as a present. I am the one in the middle of the photograph, aged seven.

Great garden idea

Brighten up containers by mulching around the base of the plants with decorative materials such as coloured glass, polished pebbles, slate, rustic gravel or moss taken from a shady part of the garden. You can even take old CDs – especially those that come through the post as junk mail – and smash them up to create a novel mulch that's completely free! Wear gloves because the shards can be quite sharp.

Let's get cooking!

Beef in Black Bean Sauce

(Serves 4)
- 8 oz (225 g) basmati rice
- 5 tablespoons (75 ml) black bean sauce
- 1 tablespoon (15 ml) dry sherry
- 1 tablespoon (15 ml) tomato purée
- 2 x 6 oz (175 g) packets stir-fry beef
- 2 bunches spring onions
- 1 red pepper
- 1 yellow pepper
- 1 small courgette
- 4 oz (100 g) Chinese leaf
- 2 tablespoons (30 ml) light soy sauce

1 Rinse the rice until the water runs clear. Place in a saucepan and add water to cover by one inch (2.5 cm). Stir and bring to the boil. Stir again and reduce the heat to a low simmer for 15 minutes.
2 Spoon the black bean sauce, sherry and tomato purée into a bowl. Add the beef, stir, and leave to marinate.
3 Slice the spring onions and cut the peppers into long, thin strips. Diagonally slice the courgette and roughly chop the Chinese leaf.
4 Spray a wok with a little oil. Fry the spring onions, peppers and courgettes for a few minutes, then add the beef mixture. After five minutes add the Chinese leaf and soy sauce. Stir-fry for one minute, then serve with the rice.

RECIPE COURTESY OF SLIMMING MAGAZINE

OLD-FASHIONED CLEANING REMEDY

Terracotta floor tiles (and other unglazed tiles) can be cleaned with a solution made up of half water and half white vinegar.

Wit and wisdom

The surest way to be late is to have plenty of time.
Leo Kennedy (1885-1965)

Make a difference - volunteer!

Calling volunteers aged 50 plus

The last week in June is Get Active week for the Retired and Senior Volunteer Programme (RSVP) that operates under the umbrella of Community Services Volunteers (CSV). The aim is to provide companionships for thousands of people who are housebound through age or disability. CSV also hopes to encourage many more people, aged 50 plus, to become volunteers. People like 66-year-old Peggy Trotter from Doncaster who helped to tackle the local drug problem by creating a community garden from waste land.

The first RSVP project was set up in 1989 following the discovery of an elderly man who had been left dead in his London flat for four years. Since then, volunteers have worked to combat isolation in the community. During Get Active Week, the focus is on events throughout the UK including tea dances, theatre nights and coach trips to the seaside, but RSVP says the opportunities are as diverse as the volunteers themselves.

◆ **To find out how you can be involved, contact CSV, 237 Pentonville Road, London N1 9NJ. Tel: 020 7278 6601. Internet: www.csv.org.uk**

My pet

Loopy belongs to Jean Eden of Feltham's daughter and likes to wear her sun shade to get in the holiday mood.

Senior moment

My wife Barbara and I have been on a diet. When we went out for meal with some friends, instead of chips she asked for 'scampi with a side saddle'.

Ron Bird,
Leighton Buzzard

Top tip

It is easier to remove the skins from frozen tomatoes if they are rinsed in cold water.
Mona Sharpe,
Isle of Man

MY PRAYER

I said a prayer for you today and know God must have heard,
I felt the answer in my heart, although He spoke no word.
I didn't ask for wealth or fame, I knew you wouldn't mind,
I asked Him to send treasures of a far more lasting kind.

I asked that He be near you at the start of each new day,
To grant you health and blessings, and friends to share your way.
I asked for happiness for you in all things great and small,
But it was for His loving care for you my friend
I prayed the most of all.
Mrs M M Bevan, Langley

Here's health

At risk when flying

Before you book your holiday flight, make sure you are fit to travel. If you have had recent surgery, heart or respiratory problems, you may be at higher risk of deep vein thrombosis (DVT) which occurs when a clot blocks a major vein. Some experts believe DVT is associated with air travel. When you are in the air, you should avoid dehydration by taking a non-alcoholic drink every hour. Get up and walk around to keep your circulation going. When sitting, rotate your feet, wiggle your toes and, if possible, raise your calves.

A Walk in the Wild
Darting dragonflies

Pollution and habitat destruction threaten these dazzling water dwellers

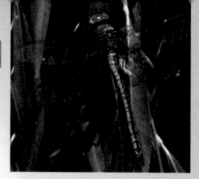

Dragonflies are amazing insects with majestic powers of flight and beautiful vivid colouring. Their ancestors flew above the carboniferous forests 300 million years ago, before the dinosaurs roamed the earth. Dragonflies are classified into two sub-orders: Damselflies (Zygoptera) and Dragonflies (Anisoptera). Both types thrive in unpolluted water that supports plenty of vegetation which provides egg-laying and emergence sites. They favour situations that are open to sunlight with some protection from strong winds.

Dragonflies have a complex life cycle consisting of a long larval phase (varying from eight weeks to five years) underwater, followed by a relatively short adult phase. In the larval stage they feed on insect larvae, water fleas, snails – even small fish and tadpoles. Adults hunt for food in woodland glades and grassy meadows and along hedgerows. Their diet consists of small flies, midges and mosquitoes. Some of the larger species, such as the Emperor, will eat butterflies and damselflies. Both the larvae and adult dragonflies are voracious predators.

Dragonflies are visual hunters. Their large compound eyes are made up of as many as 30,000 facets or lenses. The ability to see colour as well as ultraviolet light and polarised light allows them to see reflections of light on water.

Most people notice dragonflies when they are in flight as the sunlight catches their wings and the iridescence on their bodies. Thanks to powerful flight muscles and wings that move independently, they are perfectly adapted for flight and are able to hover, fly forwards, backwards and sideways as well as to change their speed and direction rapidly. Hawker dragonflies can achieve a speed of 36km an hour.

For more information, contact the British Dragonfly Society.
Tel: 01743 282021.
Website: www.dragonflysoc.org.uk

WARTIME WEDDINGS
No whisky galore

The air raid shelter served as a buffet table at Doris Carruthers of Rainham's wedding reception

Joe and I were married on 3 June 1944 – three days before D-Day. The vicar had to write to his commanding officer to get permission for Joe to come home. My friend lent me her wedding dress and the bridesmaids' dresses were lent by my sister-in-law. We scraped together enough clothing coupons to buy the material for my six-year-old niece's dress and bonnet. The flowers were real, not artificial. We were lucky to get a photographer as film was sparse.

Friends and relations pooled their dried fruit rations etc for the cake, which was iced very thinly. We held the reception at home with the buffet laid out on top of the indoor Morrison air raid shelter. My brother managed to get one bottle of whisky which was shared out between the men. We ladies made do with home-made ginger beer.

Then we had three days at a girls' boarding school at Walton-on-Thames which my firm had taken over so that employees could get away for a short break from the bombing. As we arrived before dinner was ready we were given a meat paste sandwich. We spent that night running up and down the long corridor to the toilet with upset tummies (probably the meat paste) – it was more of a nightmare than a honeymoon!

Models wanted, apply within

Every week Linda Lewis went to her local hairdresser to be practised on by trainees. She'd rather not remember the hairdryer hell, limp curls and tight curlers, thank you…

My friends spend a small fortune every month on visits to the hairdresser. I never go. In fact, I haven't been since I was seventeen.

I keep my hair long, wash it often, dye it rarely, and let it dry naturally. I don't even own a hairdryer or a can of hairspray. Should my hair need a trim, I manage, with skilful use of mirrors, to cut it myself

Sometimes I secretly want visit a hairdresser and get them to transform me, but I can't. The memories are still too painful.

It all started when I was eleven. I never minded what I looked like, clothes wise. We didn't have much money so my outfits were usually secondhand or from the market stall. For most of my childhood, my hair was left long and loose, sometimes held back by a band or a slide, but usually just left free.

Then one fateful day, my other saw an advert in a hairdresser's window – 'Models wanted'.

Of course, what the sign really should have said was 'victims' heads needed for trainee hairdressers to torment and torture', but I don't suppose that would have got the required response.

For a year afterwards, I spent most Tuesday evenings at the mercy of a band of apprentice hairdressers. My hair was curled, cut, washed, permed, blow dried, back brushed and made stiff with spray. The hands that washed my hair gently one minute had me yelping in pain the next.

It was the time spent under the driers that I hated the most. The heat and noise always made my head throb and the smells literally got right up my nose.

I used to have to go there straight from school. As I sat on the bus, I prayed for red traffic lights, a break down, anything to delay my arrival at the dreaded salon.

Time went into slow motion as soon as I got there, then, when the torture was over, I was expected to be pleased with the results.

"Not every young girl gets their hair done every week. I wish I'd been so lucky when I was a child," said my mother, sometimes insisting I sat for a photo when I got home.

From the day I was old enough to decide for myself, I vowed to avoid hairdressers at all costs. As (bad) luck would have it, I did go once more, when I was seventeen.

One of my best friends, Gill, decided to get married. She wanted her girl friends, myself, Peta and Alex, to be her bridesmaids, and she wanted us all to have lots of curls. I was at the hairdressers on the morning of the wedding for five hours. I emerged just in time for the ceremony. Almost at once my hair began to lose its curl.

So now, when I see my friends looking good after visiting the salon, I congratulate them, say how good they look, and thank my lucky stars I don't have to go, ever again.

Above right: Linda's new hairdos, aged 12, in 1967. Below: Alex, Peta, Linda, Bob and Gill

July 2005

Friday
1

Tuesday
12 Bank Holiday N Ireland (Battle of the Boyne)

Saturday
2

Wednesday
13

Sunday
3 Final day of Wimbledon Championships

Thursday
14

Monday
4

Friday
15 The BBC Proms begin

Tuesday
5

Saturday
16

Wednesday
6

Sunday
17

Thursday
7

Monday
18

Friday
8

Tuesday
19

Saturday
9

Wednesday
20

Sunday
10

Thursday
21

Monday
11

Friday
22

Saturday
23

Sunday
24

Monday
25

Tuesday
26

Wednesday
27

Thursday
28

Friday
29

August **Yours** on sale

Saturday
30

Sunday
31

IT HAPPENED THIS MONTH

5 July, 1952
The last London trams were withdrawn after 91 years of service

9 July, 1984
York Minster was devastated by a massive fire causing damage estimated at £1 million

11 July, 1934
Fashion designer Giorgio Armani was born

13 July, 1985
The Live Aid pop concert raised over £50 million

14 July, 1789
The storming of the Bastille marked the beginning of the French Revolution

17 July, 1979
Sebastian Coe set new record of 3 min 49 secs for running the mile

20 July, 1969
American astronaut Neil Armstrong was the first man to walk on the moon from lunar module Apollo II

24 July, 1965
Bob Dylan released Like A Rolling Stone

PIC: REXFEATURES

VILLAGE CRICKET

The village green and two o'the clock;
A perfect day for sport,
Where, like a country proverb,
The scoreboard says 'nought or nought';
And A G McDonnell's shade shakes hands
With Hugh de Selincourt.

The side consists of a postman, a printer,
An out-of-work jazz musician;
Two farmers, two teachers, a sales rep,
a clerk
And an overweight obstetrician
Who's forged a Surrey sweater just
To frighten the opposition.

Wives and girlfriends gossip and giggle
And clatter and clink and clup
As they chop and spread and slice and cut
And the sandwiches greyly pile up;
And they brew that deadly orange tea
That sets when it hits the cup.

It's during tea that the dog appears
From the depths of a shady thicket;
He pads across and sniffs the stumps
Then cocks his leg at the wicket,
No player and no gentleman,
But a connoisseur of cricket.

Nigel Forde

30 July, 1991
Italian tenor Pavarotti celebrated 30 years in opera with a free concert in Hyde Park

June 27–July 3

My pet

Rescue dog Meg ignores television until Neighbours comes on, says Edith Adcock of Nuneaton, then she howls!

Great garden idea

All weeds can go on your compost heap – even the vigorous perennials. Just dry them first in the sun until they're crisp, then add them to the compost. If you don't add the weeds you're wasting all the nutrients they have extracted from the soil. However, avoid adding weeds that are seeding because many seeds will survive the composting process.

MY PRAYER

Lord God, in heaven and earth there is no one like You. You keep covenant with us all and show us Your love.
Hear our prayer Lord.
In Your home in heaven hear us and forgive all the little wrongs we do and thoughts that are not nice. If any of Your people in heartfelt sorrow stretch out their hands, listen to them. You alone know the thoughts of the human heart. Deal with each of us as we give them comfort from broken homes, abuse, cruelty, neglect and starvation. They didn't ask to be born and they are our hope for years to come.
We give thanks for the lovely things in the world. The trees, the flowers, the mountains, rivers, seas and lakes. The wild life, the sun, the moon and the stars a guide for travellers of old. Lord Your blueprint of life is best, give us Your peace that the world cannot give. We ask this in the name of Jesus our Hope, our Saviour and Friend. Amen

Joan Green, Hemel Hempstead

Oh, happy day!

Sylvia and Reg Hamley celebrated 40 wonderful years together

Our ruby wedding anniversary fell on 27th July. The weather was high summer on that wonderful Sunday when we had arranged to renew our marriage vows during the morning service at our church, the Plymouth Methodist Central Hall, in front of the regular congregation and 60 of our family and friends. After the service, we took a short drive to a lovely house within a local park that caters for parties and receptions.

We had drinks on the terrace overlooking the park in the beautiful sunshine before the simple buffet meal, which was very enjoyable. The ages ranged from two to 88 years and everyone got on well together.

Before the event, my husband and I decided to ask for donations for the National Children's Home in lieu of presents and we were able to send them a cheque for £300.

The funniest comment on the big day came from our son and daughter who amazed us by revealing: "We have never seen you two kiss before!"

A nice little earner

To be a farmer's boy was not the ambition of David Sampson of Wakefield

When I was nine, my Uncle Frank, a farm manager, agreed that I could earn some extra cash after school by helping out on the farm. The first evening we herded the cows into the milking shed and my Aunt Ivy sat herself down on a small three-legged stool with an enamel bucket placed between her legs. She began deftly squeezing the cow's teats, indicating to me to take note. I wasn't relishing the thought of touching those large pink protuberances, so I shied away. I paid no heed when Uncle Frank warned me to stand between the cows and my position was at the back of the animal. The cow began to empty its bowels – I stood back, out of range, but it coughed (twice!) and I was covered from head to foot. I ran the mile home faster than Roger Bannister and took a paper round instead.

OLD-FASHIONED CLEANING REMEDY

A little chopped onion left overnight in the loo will dislodge limescale.

Charlotte Primrose, Manningtree

It makes me smile

My four-year-old granddaughter was pestering me to take her for a walk. When I asked her to say the 'magic word', she said: "Abracadabra."
Richard Hough, Ringwood

Top tip

Wet wipes are very useful household cleaners for dusting, cleaning specs, removing tea stains from cups and tarnish from silver.
Jane Thomas, London

Here's health

Pack up your pills

If you are planning a holiday, make sure you take enough of your prescription medicine with you. Pack your medicine in your hand luggage in case your suitcase goes astray and write down the correct names of any medication you take so that if you do lose it, you will know what to ask for.

Let's get cooking!

Pan-cooked Liver and Onions

(Serves 2)

- ◆ 1/2 oz (15 g) butter
- ◆ 1 onion, thinly sliced
- ◆ 3 oz (75 g) smoked bacon lardoons
- ◆ 1 clove garlic, crushed
- ◆ 2 large sprigs fresh thyme
- ◆ 8 oz (225 g) lamb's liver, sliced
- ◆ 1 tablespoon (15 ml) flour
- ◆ Salt and black pepper
- ◆ 1 teaspoon (5 ml) balsamic vinegar or red wine vinegar
- ◆ 1/2 pint (275 ml) boiling water
- ◆ 1 tablespoon (15 ml) gravy granules

1 Heat the butter in a large frying pan. Add the onion, the bacon lardoons, garlic and thyme. Cook for 2-3 minutes.
2 Coat the liver in the flour seasoned with salt and pepper.
3 Add the liver to the pan and brown for around 5 minutes. Add the vinegar and the boiling water in which the gravy granules have been dissolved. Bring back to the boil.
4 Serve with parsnip mash and seasonal vegetables.

RECIPE COURTESY OF THE ENGLISH LAMB AND BEEF EXECUTIVE

July 4-10

Remember the '60s?

'I was there!' says England football fan Peter Edis of London

On 30 July 1966 I left home with three England rosettes proudly pinned to my jacket. I was treated like a pools winner by everyone on the journey to Wembley as a ticket for the final was like gold dust. The nation was united in expectation and excitement. I was in Block D, Entrance 7, East standing enclosure, right behind the goal where Geoff Hurst scored the controversial goal which restored England's lead over West Germany in the final.

Thirty years later, I saw a television documentary called We Won the Cup and was amazed to recognise my swinging Sixties self among the crowds celebrating in Trafalgar Square. I recall being perched on the back of one of the four lions with several other fans; the one sitting on its head passed down a bottle of whisky for the rest of us!

Let's get cooking!

Fettuccine with Spinach
(Serves 2)
- 8 oz (225 g) dried fettuccine or tagliatelle
- 1 onion, chopped
- 4 oz (100 g) ricotta cheese
- 4 oz (100 g) baby spinach leaves
- 1 teaspoon (5 ml) pine nuts, to garnish

1 Bring a large pan of lightly salted water to the boil and put in the pasta. Cook for 12 minutes, or according to the instructions on the packet.
2 Meanwhile, dry fry the onion in a saucepan, adding a splash of water to moisten the pan.
3 Stir in the cheese and spinach, season and cook over a low heat for a couple of minutes.
4 Drain the pasta and add it to the pan with the cheese and spinach.
5 Divide between two plates and serve with a sprinkling of pine nuts.

RECIPE COURTESY OF SLIMMING MAGAZINE

Great garden idea

Many weeds can be eaten. Nettles are rich in vitamins and the young leaves make a tasty soup. Dandelion leaves are also a valuable source of vitamins and minerals and can be added to salads. Fat hen can be used instead of spinach and contains higher levels of vitamins, minerals and calcium. So, get out your wild flower book and identify the edible weeds in your garden.

My pet

'They say that dogs are like their owners and this is certainly true of our boxer, Jack', says Alanna Allen of Cowes. 'Saggy jowls, large ears, and looks grumpy even when he's happy – but he does come obediently to heel when called. (Don't tell my husband I said so!)'

Make a difference - volunteer

Neighbourhood newshound

If you have ever had a yen to be a journalist, why not become a freelance news correspondent for your local newspaper? Armed with a reporter's notepad or a small tape recorder, you will find yourself covering everything from fundraising events to parish council meetings. Being able to type or use a personal computer is obviously a big advantage when writing up your contributions. And if you can use a camera and provide pictures to go with the words, even better. Once you have built up a network of contacts in your community – clubs, churches, schools, charities – you will be surprised to discover how much is going on right on your doorstep. And while covering everything from church socials to golden wedding celebrations, you are bound to meet many people and make new friends.

So, if you have always dreamed of coming up with a scoop, why not start by phoning your local newspaper to see if they need a newshound in your area.

Wit and wisdom

My formula for success? Rise early, work late, strike oil.
John Paul Getty
(1892-1915)

Here's health

Keep drinking
As we grow older, we are more prone to dehydration so it's important to drink enough fluids in hot weather. In a very hot climate, drink between three and five litres of non-alcoholic liquids a day and boost your salt intake by eating crisps or taking salt tablets. Avoid intense physical exertion, stay in the shade and take frequent dips in cool water.

MY PRAYER

Deep peace of the running wave to you
Deep peace of the flowing air to you,
Deep peace of the quiet earth to you
Deep peace of the shining stars to you,
Deep peace of the gentle night to you
Moon and stars pour their healing light on you.
Deep peace of Christ, of Christ
The light of the world to you,
Deep peace of Christ.

Joan Carr,
Wakefield

Senior moment

When I visited my daughter I saw a photo of her dog Jack who had died only a few weeks previously. I asked her: "Was the photo taken before he died?"
Mrs D C Walker,
Chesterfield

OLD-FASHIONED CLEANING REMEDY

To keep your home smelling fresh, make you own pot-pourri from dried herbs or flower petals. Peppermint, sage, thyme, lemon verbena, bay leaves, rosemary and lemon-scented geranium are all good. Mix with ground cinnamon or cloves and a sprinkling of ground orris root for a preservative.

July 11-17

Let's get cooking!

Berry Brulée

(Serves 4)

- 12 oz (350 g) mixed summer berries (strawberries, raspberries, blueberries)
- 1 teaspoon (5 ml) Tate & Lyle icing sugar
- Seeds from half a vanilla pod
- 1 x 5 oz (150 g) pot of no-fat Greek yogurt
- 1.4 pt (150 ml) virtually fat-free fromage frais
- 3 oz (75 g) Tate & Lyle demerara sugar

1. Mix the berries, icing sugar and vanilla seeds together and divide between four shallow heatproof dishes
2. Mix the yoghurt and fromage frais together and spoon over the fruit in an even layer.
3. Sprinkle the sugar over the top of the yoghurt mixture, then caramelise under a hot grill for 5 minutes (or use a cook's blow-torch, if you have one).
4. Chill for 10 minutes before serving.

RECIPE COURTESY OF TATE & LYLE CANE SUGARS

My first...

Mrs N J Glander of High Littleton near Bristol loved her first swimsuit

In this picture I am in the middle, wearing my first swimsuit which was red, made from thin rubber like babies' waterproof pants. (Smelt lovely when new!) It wasn't considered proper to wear it with no clothes underneath, though. My sisters had to tuck their clothes into their knickers, as the adults did, because it was unseemly for ladies to wear a swimsuit on the beach in the 1930s. Don't they just look grotesque in their 'passion killers'?

We used to walk to the next village for the train to Weston-super-Mare and another mile walk from the station to the beach – which seemed more like six miles to little legs. Then we'd collapse on the beach to make sand pies.

Sometimes, we would get to paddle in the sea, but at Weston the tide goes out so far you seldom saw it on a day trip. They could never keep me out of the water, even if it was only a puddle.

Great garden idea

Brighten a dark patch in your shrub border where herbaceous flowering plants don't grow well by placing a few cut flowers in a watering can in the centre. You'll be amazed at the difference it makes. Cosmos is a hardy annual that grows easily from seed sown straight into the soil, so add a row in your vegetable garden then cut them to bring colour to gloomy corners.

Make a difference - volunteer!

Education, education, education

You might be surprised to learn that the largest single volunteer force in the country is school governors. In England there are 350,000 governor places and around 12 per cent of these are vacant so there is always a demand for new recruits, especially in the inner cities. No qualifications are needed to become a school governor but enthusiasm, commitment and an interest in education are important qualities to bring to the role. Management and business skills are also useful.

Governors work in partnership with the head teacher and other school staff to promote high standards of educational achievement at the school. A school's governing body has three key roles: Setting strategic direction, ensuring accountability and monitoring and evaluation.

◆ **For more information contact the DfES School Governor Recruitment Team on 01325 391290 or email gov.recruit@dfes.gsi.gov.uk**

My pet

Pat Lennon of Lawford in Essex 'framed' her cat Molly after she found her tearing a rug to pieces. Molly also stands accused of chewing most of the fabric on her owner's bed – and still has room for meals!

It makes me smile

A workman who was doing a job in my house asked if he could have some water. I said: "Do you want it in a bucket?" and he replied: "No, in a cup with sugar and milk, please." He got a cup of tea for his cheek.
Mrs S Plester, Birmingham

Top tip

When taking flowers to someone in an old people's home try to take a jug or vase with you (easily obtainable at charity shops) as it is sometimes difficult to find a suitable container to put them in.
Joan Gibbons, Liverpool

MY PRAYER

Thank You Lord for the special times,
These days I set apart.
The times of joy and happiness,
Are stored within my heart.
Thank You for the days of youth,
When the entire world was new.
When plans and schemes were only dreams,
That never would come true.

Thank You for those other times,
When things went sadly wrong.
Through love and care and answered prayer,
You helped me to be strong.
For all the happy special times,
So many I recall.
For joy and tears throughout the years,
Lord, thank You for them all.
Ruby Ainsworth, Wakefield

Here's health

Harmony at home

Your surroundings influence your wellbeing so give your home a summer makeover and the chances are your health will improve, too. The Chinese say feng shui is a way of harnessing chi energy to create calm harmony in your surroundings. Bring in fresh flowers and plants to give good yang energy and hang wind chimes to break up stagnant energy.

July 18-24

Every picture tells a story

My brothers carried this picture of my mother right through the war with them. I was living in Broadstairs with my parents. We were glued to our little box wireless for the news of Dunkirk when a call came from our local radio station asking for men's clothing as so many of our troops were throwing off their uniforms to swim out to the boats. Mum jumped up and ran upstairs, turning out dad's chest of drawers for shirts, pullovers etc. Dad was equally desperate to help but was getting worried he might not have anything left. Mum packed a bag and off she went to Margate harbour where some of the boats were coming in. She told us she found one young lad with tears pouring down his face with relief at being back on home ground so she gave him a cuddle and he told her all about his own mother. Mum came home that evening not far from tears herself.

*June R Davis,
Broadstairs*

 Let's get cooking!

Strawberry Cheesecakes
(Makes 4)
- 3 oz (75 g) reduced-fat digestive biscuits
- ½ oz (15 g) reduced-fat spread
- 5 oz (150 g) Quark
- 2 x 5 oz (150 g) pots reduced-fat strawberry yoghurt
- 1 tablespoon (15 ml) granulated sweetener
- 4 tablespoons (60 ml) gelatine, dissolved according to instructions on the packet
- 2 fresh strawberries

1 In a pan, crush the digestive biscuits and melt the spread over a low heat. Stir the melted spread into the biscuit crumbs and divide the mixture between four small foil-lined muffin cases.

2 In a bowl, beat together the Quark, yoghurt, sweetener and dissolved gelatine.

3 Spoon the mixture over the biscuit base in the muffin cases. Chill for two hours or until set. Top each cheesecake with half a strawberry.

RECIPE COURTESY OF SLIMMING MAGAZINE

My pet

Going on holiday? Not without me! Lady is determined her owner, Shirley Backhouse of Wakefield, is going nowhere without her.

Here's health

Save your skin

It's never too late to protect your skin from the sun so don't give up just because you have a few wrinkles! Stay out of the sun between 11am and 3pm and when you do go out, stay in shade and wear a hat to keep the sun off your face. Wear sunglasses to protect your eyes and make sure any exposed skin is covered in sunscreen with SPF 15 or above.

MY PRAYER

Dear Lord, let Your light shine
Over every dark corner of the land
In every region of the earth
Fashioned in beauty
Yet despoiled by men
Who pollute the air
With soot-encrusted monuments
Creating jungles of despair.

Let Your light shine in continents
Where those whose craving for power
Torture, imprison, maim and kill
Subjugating the people with constant fear
And nearer still
Where the unsuspecting bullet justifies
A fanatical hatred
And the bomb, not cross, now crucifies.
Madeleine Croll, Whitstable

Great garden idea

Bindweed can be a real problem when it's twining among your plants. Try and untangle a few stems and encourage them up a cane angled into the ground. Once the stems have become firmly attached and are moving away from your plants, apply a systemic weedkiller such as glyphosate.

Make a difference - volunteer!

You can't lick a lollipopper

Come rain or shine, school crossing patrols (affectionately known as lollipop ladies – although there are lots of lollipop men, too) have become part of the daily scene since they started in 1954. Originally aimed at protecting the safety of children crossing roads to and from school, their remit now extends to adults as well. Provided they are correctly equipped with coat, cap and stick, lollippers have legal powers to stop traffic.

If you would like to join the day-glo ranks, you need to pass a medical, sight test and Criminal Records Bureau check. The amount of training given varies from one area to another and the pay is around £5 an hour with a retainer paid during the school holidays. Most patrols operate half an hour each side of school time – morning and afternoon – but some cover may be required at lunchtime.

◆ **To find out more, contact the road safety department of your county or metropolitan borough council.**

July 25-31

My pet

Oh, I do like to be beside the seaside! Pam Mahon of Whiston with her boxer Blue who enjoys nothing better than a dip in the briney.

MY PRAYER

Lord, we look to You
To permeate the impermeable;
To abridge the unabridged;
To expiate the unexpiated;
To bridge the divide;
To bring meaning to our lives;
To include the excluded in our lives.
To make happen what is not:
To bring about the inevitable,
Once the evitable has happened.
To show us in our immediacy
That You love us;
That we are loved by You.

Anne Hadley. Slough

Great garden idea

Tear paper into strips to mix it with your compost. It contains carbon which will prevent the compost becoming too wet if there's an abundance of grass clippings. Add all your vegetable waste from the kitchen but make sure any diseased plant material is deeply buried within the compost where temperatures get high enough to kill off the pathogens.

OLD-FASHIONED CLEANING REMEDY

Apply a paste of mayonnaise and cigarette ash to scratches on polished furniture. Leave for a while before removing, then buff up with a damp cloth.

Make a difference - volunteer

Neutral meeting place for families

The National Association of Child Contact Centres (NACCC) is a national charity that supports Child Contact Centres. The Centres provide a neutral environment where children of separated families can spend time with one or both parents or other family members. The Centres are run by trained volunteers who put the needs of the children first and don't take sides with either parent. As well as listening impartially, the volunteeers' tasks include preparing the Centre before people arrive (there are toys and games for the children to play with) and tidying up after it is closed. They welcome the families, show them around, and provide refreshments.

◆ If you would like to play a part in making life better for the youngsters affected by family breakdown, contact NACCC, Minerva House, Spaniel Row, Nottingham NG1 6EP. Tel: 0845 4500 280.

Dear Diary

In 1954 Les Williams of Malvern cycled from North Wales to Blackpool to join his family on holiday

I left work at 2pm on Wednesday and at 3pm was on my way. I had quite a good ride and arrived in Blackpool at 6.40pm, just in time to get in to the hotel before it poured with rain. The family waited for me to change and then we went to the Queen's Theatre where we saw a grand variety show with Josef Locke, Harry Bailey and company. One of the best variety shows I have ever seen. The next day we spent around the shops and the Tower where we saw Reginald Dixon on the organ. At night we all went to the Opera House where we saw Harry Secombe, Eve Boswell and the John Tiller girls in Top of the Town. Again, first class.

The next day we had some fun on the beach. After dinner I got ready to return home the next day. The weather was quite windy and it took me seven and a half hours to get home.

Les (right) had a holiday to remember

Let's get cooking!

Dark Fruit Roulade
(Serves 8)
- 5 oz (150 g) caster sugar
- 2 oz (50 g) cocoa powder
- 9 egg whites at room temperature
- Pinch of cream of tartar
- 1½ teaspoons (7 ml) vanilla extract
- 1½ teaspoons (7 ml) dark rum
- 1 lb (450 g) strawberries, hulled and chopped
- 5 fl oz (150 ml) reduced fat crème fraîche

To decorate
- icing sugar ◆ strawberries ◆ mint leaves

1 Line a 13 in x 11 in (32.5 cm x 28 cm) Swiss roll tin with baking parchment. Preheat the oven to Gas mark 4, 180°C, 350°F.
2 Sift together 7 tablespoons of the caster sugar and all the cocoa powder. Set aside.
3 Whip the egg whites and cream of tartar together until foaming. Continue to whisk while adding the remaining sugar in stages until stiff peaks form.
4 Fold in the cocoa powder mix, vanilla and rum. Spoon into the lined tin and spread out evenly. Bake for 20 to 30 minutes, until the cake just springs back when touched.
5 Meanwhile, mix the strawberries and crème fraîche together in a bowl.
6 Place a clean tea towel on a work surface with a piece of greaseproof paper on top. Sift the icing sugar on to the paper.
7 Take the cooked roulade from the oven and invert it on to the greaseproof paper. Peel off the backing paper. Spread the filling over and roll up. Chill for a short while and then serve decorated with strawberries and mint leaves.

RECIPE COURTESY OF SLIMMING MAGAZINE

It makes me smile

My friend has rather large feet but when she asked the shop assistant if she had the pair of shoes she liked in her size, she was told: "Sorry, madam, we don't have the room to stock your size."
Marion Bassett, Stroud

Top tip

A drop of clear nail varnish on a spectacle screw will stop it coming out.
Mr A Barker, Northallerton

Here's health

Run away from the runs
Most cases of holiday diarrhoea and stomach cramps are due to infection by bacteria such as E coli, salmonella, campylobacter or shigella. The most common way of picking up an infection is from polluted drinking water. To be on the safe side, drink only bottled water (even to clean your teeth). Don't eat fruit or vegetables that could have been contaminated with unclean water. Avoid unpasteurised dairy products and raw or undercooked meats. Don't buy food from street vendors.

A Walk in the Wild
A rare old bird

The mating call of the capercaillie
is an unmistakable sound

The name capercaillie is derived from the gaelic 'capull collie' meaning 'horse of the forest'. It is the rarest of the grouse family in Britain and is now only found in Scotland. The capercaillie became extinct here in the middle of the 18th century and was reintroduced in the middle of the 19th century. Since then, numbers have gradually declined throughout its range.

The capercaillie is found in large coniferous woods especially at the edges and in clearings. Its enormous size (34 inches), the black plumage and rather long, fan-shaped tail makes the male unmistakable. The hen is less charismatic with pale apricot

colouring and a long rounded tail. In flight, the male can be easily recognised by his light underside. When frightened, they burst out of cover very noisily.

The diet of these large birds includes buds, shoots, berries and some insects. When the male displays or 'leks' to the female, he stands with his tail cocked and fanned and his bill held high while calling. The females choose which male they want as a mate. In spring listen for the 'clip clop' noise the huge male makes and the variety of calls that sound like anything from a popping cork to pouring liquid from a bottle. He does not join in with any domestic duties

and the female incubates the eggs alone in a mossy nest placed usually at the base of a tree.

This bird is once again threatened with extinction in Scotland, with total numbers dwindling to around one thousand. The law has recently been altered, making it an offence to disturb a capercaillie while it is lekking. Controls are also in place to limit the number of predators, particularly foxes, in forests where there are known populations.

Capercaillie can be seen at the Highland Wildlife Park, Kincraig, Kingussie, Inverness-shire.
Tel: 01540 651270.
Internet: www.highlandwildlifepark.org

WARTIME WEDDINGS

Passing out parade

**Nothing went quite right when
Cindy Hagger of Romford was wed**

Every time I see my wedding photograph I have to laugh because we don't look all that happy. Who could blame us? Everything went wrong.

I woke on 19 August 1944 to pouring rain. The wedding car broke down and we had to have another car. When that arrived the air raid siren went so we had to wait for the All Clear, which meant I was 45 minutes late at the church. When we got to the wedding reception, we learned that our parents were stranded at the bus stop.

We had booked the first night of our honeymoon in a local hotel. I requested this because it looked such a romantic place. When we arrived, I said to Jack: "Nothing can go wrong, now." How wrong I was!

Putting on my beautiful (almost

see-through) nightie with matching negligée, I went to the bathroom. I found I was locked in – the lock and bolt had jammed. The manager was sent for but he couldn't get the door open. The only thing left was to take the door right off. When it was removed and the manager saw me– a vision in pink – he passed out. Feeling awful, I stayed until he came round but as he looked up into my face, he passed out again. I thought I'd better leave and my new husband escorted me back to our room and firmly locked the door!

Logic puzzle

	Team					Mishap					Injury				
	Byklipps	Mangallgeers	Punkcherkitt	Spoakes	Zorbottam	Dog ran out	Hit spectator	Into pothole	Skid into ditch	Struck tree	Broke leg	Concussed	Cracked elbow	Dislocated kneecap	Twisted ankle
Ben Tweel															
Ian Frunt															
Jason Leader															
Noah Stamminer															
Viv Gere															
Broke leg															
Concussed															
Cracked elbow															
Dislocated kneecap															
Twisted ankle															
Dog ran out						
Hit spectator						
Into pothole						
Skid into ditch						
Struck tree						

CYCLIST	TEAM	MISHAP	INJURY

Turn to Page 157 for puzzle answers

First, read the story and at the same time use the grid to record any definite positive facts with a tick, and any definite negative facts with a cross. You should then be able to work out more as you reread the story.

This month's Tour de France is the premier cycling event of the year and is traditionally won by a European, but when will the coveted yellow vest be sported by a Briton? Last year the British teams were more determined than ever to make an impression and put out five strong contenders. But they went into the race too aggressively and… well, you've guessed it…

Noah Stamminer, who hit a spectator and went flying ending up with a cracked elbow, was neither the rider for the Zorbottam team nor for the Mangallgeers team whose cyclist, Ben Tweel, skidded into a ditch. The rider who twisted his ankle after he struck a tree, was Ian Frunt while the rider leading the way for the Punkcherkitt team was Viv Gere. The Spoakes team rider who broke his leg in a nasty accident wasn't Ben Tweel who, in turn, wasn't the unfortunate cyclist who rounded a corner only to go straight into a tree. The unlucky rider who dislocated a knee when trying to avoid a dog which ran out, didn't ride for the Zorbottam team.

Can you last the course, match each rider to his team and work out which mishap each one experienced and what the resulting injury was?

Short story

A rose without a thorn

Beastly Mr Benson is not amused when his garden is raided but Claire tries to shield her admirer from his wrath

"Happy birthday, Miss!" Oliver Knight was looking unusually angelic as he held out the bunch of creamy white roses and beamed up at her.

"That's very sweet of you, Oliver. They're my favourite colour." Claire took the flowers gingerly and wished she wasn't wondering exactly where he'd got them. It was probably best not to know, but she had the uncomfortable feeling that she'd find out sooner or later. Endearing as Oliver was, he had the knack of attracting trouble.

In the staff room, she unwrapped a Bart Simpson serviette from the stems of the roses and shook out what looked like cake crumbs into the bin. She guessed the serviette had come from Oliver's sandwich box and the roses from one of the gardens along his route to school. She hoped no one had spotted him. He'd already been in trouble twice this week and she'd overheard Richard Benson telling another teacher that Oliver was disruptive and rude. He wasn't disruptive and rude in her classes – well, okay, he might be a bit lively at times, but he wasn't a bad kid. He just always seemed to do the right things in the wrong way.

Richard Benson had joined the staff last term and already he was gaining a reputation as the sort of teacher who didn't stand any nonsense. He was tall and bearded and rather straight-faced and before the end of his first week he'd earned himself the nickname of Beastly Benson.

Claire put the roses in water, enjoying their sweet scent as she carried them back along the corridor. She was almost at the classroom when she bumped into Richard Benson striding towards her. "Lovely morning," she smiled at him, but he didn't return the greeting. He was staring, rather intently, she thought, at her roses.

"Where did you get those?" he asked, so sharply that she was taken aback.

"They were a present," Claire replied. She found herself flushing without knowing why. She looked into his angry blue eyes. "It's my birthday…" She tailed off, taking an involuntary step backwards.

Richard looked as though he would have liked to say a lot more, but was struggling to contain himself. With one more furious glare at the roses he stalked off

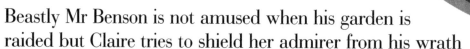

She unwrapped a Bart Simpson serviette from the stems

By Della Galton

"So, you've come back for the last one?"

PIC: ILLUSTRATION WORKS

At break time Claire approached Oliver and discreetly asked him where he'd got the roses. "From a garden down near the park, Miss," he answered, artlessly, "There was a big bush – they won't miss those few."

"That's not the point, Oliver. How would you feel if someone came into your garden and picked your flowers?"

"Wouldn't mind if they were for you. We haven't got a garden, anyway."

"Well, promise me you won't do it again?"

He looked suitably chastened, but Claire was still worried. Later, she asked Gwen, who taught music, if she knew where Richard Benson lived. Gwen said: "Park Avenue, I think. Why do you ask?"

Claire told her and Gwen choked with laughter.

"It's not funny," Claire said. "He guessed they were his roses. You should have seen his face."

"Well, it's not your fault, is it? And there's not a lot you can do about it. Unless you fancy dragging Oliver round to apologise."

"No chance!" Claire shuddered.

"Then just forget about it. If it was anyone else you'd be able to tell them and have a bit of a giggle – but not Beastly Benson!"

Claire nodded. Gwen was right. All the same, as she drove home that night, with her roses on the back seat, she couldn't resist turning down Park Avenue to see if she could spot the desecrated bush. It wasn't difficult; most of the gardens in Park Avenue had fences too high to see over, only one had a low wall, over which rose bushes tumbled. She parked her car and, feeling like a criminal, she sneaked back for a closer look.

Oliver had exaggerated when he claimed the rose bush still had plenty of other flowers. There was actually one left. One beautiful creamy white rose that bore an uncanny resemblance to the ones in her car. She sighed, and was about to turn away when a voice from behind her said softly, "So, you've come back for the last one, have you?"

She swung round in shock. Richard Benson was standing behind her, his arms folded, one eyebrow raised quizzically. He was wearing shorts and trainers, which explained why she hadn't heard his approach.

Claire knew she was blushing madly, but she couldn't think of a single thing to say. Not waiting for an answer, he went on: "Or perhaps you came round to tell me which of your pupils did the deed?"

She shook her head. He said: "Thought not," and sat on his wall in a gap between the rose bushes. He seemed in no hurry to let her escape. "Well then, I guess there's only one way to resolve this."

She stared at him. He actually didn't look at all stern without the suit he wore at school. Or was it that glint of amusement in his eyes?

"I can only apologise," Claire began. "I'm sure it won't happen again."

"Well it can't, can it?" he murmured, "I haven't got any roses left worth pinching."

"No, I suppose not." Claire lowered her eyes.

"I trust you've had a word with young Oliver," he continued and she nodded, startled.

"Then we'll say no more about it on one condition – that you let me buy you dinner tonight?"

This time she really was shocked and he must have seen the look on her face because he said quickly: "I'm sorry – you've got other plans – it's your birthday, isn't it?"

"Yes – I mean, no." He was having the most curious effect on her. "What I mean is I'd like to. I've no plans. That would be a very suitable way of resolving things."

"Great!" He smiled, and his whole face changed. Claire wondered how she could ever have thought he deserved his nickname. She smiled back. She had a feeling she was going to be seeing him in quite a different light from now on.

August 2005

Monday *1* Bank Holiday (Scotland)	**Friday** *12*
Tuesday *2*	**Saturday** *13*
Wednesday *3*	**Sunday** *14* Edinburgh International Festival starts
Thursday *4*	**Monday** *15*
Friday *5*	**Tuesday** *16*
Saturday *6*	**Wednesday** *17*
Sunday *7*	**Thursday** *18*
Monday *8*	**Friday** *19*
Tuesday *9*	**Saturday** *20*
Wednesday *10*	**Sunday** *21*
Thursday *11*	**Monday** *22*

Tuesday
23

Wednesday
24

Thursday
25

Friday
26

Saturday
27

Sunday
28

Monday
29
Bank holiday (Except Scotland)

Tuesday
30
September **Yours** on sale

Wednesday
31

CHILD BY THE SEA
About three, I suppose,
On the very edge of the pale grey sea
Jumping, flatfooted for splashes,
On each little curling wave
And laughing in ecstasy.
Starfish hands stiff with excitement,
Limp silk hair blowing across her eyes
Unnoticed. All the world lost.
Her bathing drawers (courtesy garment)
Are damp and low about her thighs,
The small brown body naked to the skies.
Complete absorption in the task at hand:
To jump on every curling wave
Just as it breaks upon the sand.

'Coo-ee, come back. It's time for tea.'
No response,
Only a new interest,
Stones for throwing at the sea.
Joyce Grenfell

15 August, 1950
Princess Anne
was born at
Clarence House

PIC: REXFEATURES

IT HAPPENED THIS MONTH

3 August, 1914
The Panama Canal
was opened

5 August, 1939
Start of British
transatlantic
airmail service

8 August, 1963
The Great Train Robbery
took place near
Cheddington in Bucks.
The gang escaped with
around 120 mailbags
containing £2,595,998
worth of bank notes.

16 August, 1819
400 people were killed
or wounded in the
Peterloo Massacre in
Manchester

18 August, 1941
First National Fire
Service set up in Britain

22 August, 1485
Richard III killed at the
Battle of Bosworth

25 August, 1609
Galileo demonstrated
the first telescope

29 August, 1944
Paris was liberated by
American troops

30 August, 1953
White bread
reappeared in bakers'
shops after 13 years,
priced at 6d for a
14 oz loaf

August 1-7

My pet

Sensible dogs Sandy and Rusty keep their hats on while soaking up the holiday rays. Their owner, Eileen Swift of St Helen's, reckons they are saying: 'This sunbathing makes you dog tired!'

Wit and wisdom

Love is like the measles; we all have to go through it.
Jerome K Jerome (1859-1927)

Great garden idea

When growing invasive herbs such as mint, plant them in their plastic containers to prevent them springing up all over the place. Make sure that the rim protrudes slightly above the surface of the soil to prevent the runners spreading. Any wandering stems are quite easy to pull up. In a sheltered garden, mint should produce leaves for most of the year and can be encouraged back into growth earlier with a cloche.

OLD-FASHIONED CLEANING REMEDY

To remove stains from your washing, add an egg-cupful of ammonia with the soap powder. For stains on carpet use ammonia neat on a wet hand mop. When using ammonia, always wear rubber gloves and make sure the room is well ventilated.
Shirley MacMillan, Accrington

Oh, happy day!

Ray Widdicombe of Barnstaple enjoyed a reunion with other ex-servicemen

We first met on 10 August 1943 at RAF Halton where 35 16-year-olds had just signed on the dotted line and become Royal Air Force apprentices. From there we went to RAF Cranwell for a three-year course to become engineers. During that time we got to know one another very well.

Over the next 60 years, few of us served at the same station, but in August 2003 11 of us 'fell in' at 1000 hours at the main guardroom at

Cranwell to start a day of memories. 'That accent hasn't changed', 'The walk would give you away in a crowd', were a few of the comments heard.

Where once we had marched, we now ambled, taking in the old familiar scene and reminiscing. The barrack blocks were much as

we remembered them but the old cinema had gone, as had the gymnasium. The large white building, known as the Taj Mahal, where some of the classes were held, remained as neat as a new pin. At lunch, knives and forks and delicate teacups replaced the mugs and eating irons of the past.

A nice little earner

Mrs P B Missenden of London earned enough to give her mum pocket money

At the back of our building was a warehouse where the food was unpacked and sent out to the David Grieg shops. We used to get round to the yard early and wait as they unpacked the wooden cheese crates. We grabbed them, and anything else made of wood, put it all in the old pram and took it home where we chopped it up into sticks. We bundled the sticks up with string and sold them for firewood at sixpence a bundle. We'd take enough to go to the Saturday pictures and buy peanuts (a penny a bag) and ice cream (tuppence) and give the rest to our mum – pocket money from us!

MY PRAYER

When I was married in 1938, I had a 'junior moment'. I couldn't cook so our first meal was boiled eggs. The book said three minutes in boiling water. I went into the sitting room and forgot about them. Ten minutes later, there was an enormous explosion – our new kitchen didn't look new any longer!

Kathleen Read, Breadsall

Here's health

Whoosh up a watermelon

Watermelon is the perfect fruit to enjoy right now – it cools you down and is packed with vitamins and minerals. The flesh is high in vitamin C and beta-carotene. Blend the flesh and the seeds in an electric blender. The husks will sink to the bottom, leaving the seeds (which are rich in protein, zinc, selenium, vitamin E and essential fats) in a juice. It's a great immune booster.

Let's get cooking!

Honey and Ginger Stir-fried Prawns

(Serves 2)

- 9 oz (250 g) large shelled prawns
- 3 tablespoons (45 ml) runny honey
- 1 in (2.5 cm) piece fresh ginger, peeled and coarsely grated
- 1 tablespoon (15 ml) oil
- 9 oz (250 g) white cabbage, shredded
- 4 spring onions cut into 1 in (2.5 cm) lengths
- 1 large carrot, peeled and cut into thin batons
- 1 small red pepper, deseeded and finely sliced
- 1 garlic clove, crushed
- Juice of half a lemon
- Noodles or rice, to serve

1 Combine the prawns, honey and ginger, stirring well to coat. Set to one side.
2 In a wok or large frying pan, heat the oil over a high heat, then add the cabbage, spring onions, carrot, red pepper and garlic. Stir fry for 2-3 minutes.
3 Add the lemon juice and stir fry for 1 minute.
4 Stir in the prawn mixture and stir fry for another 2 minutes or until the prawns are piping hot.
5 Serve with noodles or rice.

RECIPE COURTESY OF THE HONEY ASSOCIATION

August 8-14

Remember the '60s?

Irene Howe of London knows what it is like to be homeless

In 1962 I experienced a real life Cathy Come Home situation. I had just given birth to my youngest child when we were evicted from the flat that was tied to my husband's job. His employer had died and the business's new owners wanted premises for their own staff. Our local council could not help so the family was split up. My husband went back to his mother's. The children and I were taken to Newington Lodge, a Victorian-type workhouse.

I was lucky to be given a room for myself and the kids. We were allowed one small bucket of coal and breakfast each day. Every day we went out in the fresh air, whatever the weather, as various illnesses were rife in the place.

Fortunately, our stay was only eight weeks. We were rehoused in Battersea and became a reunited family again.

Let's get cooking!

Amaretto Baked Peaches
(Serves 4)
◆ 4 fresh peaches
◆ 1 oz (25 g) Tate & Lyle demerara cane sugar
◆ 4 teaspoons (20 ml) Amaretto liqueur
◆ No-fat Greek yoghurt and raspberries, to serve

1 Place the peaches in a single layer in a shallow heatproof dish and sprinkle over the sugar and Amaretto.
2 Cook under a hot grill for 6-8 minutes or until the sugar dissolves and caramelises.
3 Serve with the yoghurt and a scattering of fresh raspberries to decorate.

RECIPE COURTESY OF TATE & LYLE SUGARS

OLD-FASHIONED CLEANING REMEDY

To remove sweat stains from clothes, pour on a small amount of glycerine. Rub in gently then leave for ten minutes before laundering as usual.

Great garden idea

Recycle water in the garden. Used bath water is fine as long as there isn't a lot of bubble-bath oil in it but don't use water from washing machines or dishwashers as the detergents are too strong. Collect all water from downpipes and divert it with a RainSava device, available from garden centres. Prevent rubbish entering a waterbutt by tying old tights over the end of the downpipe to act as a filter.

My pet

Here's another pet who doesn't want to be left at home at holiday time. Dandelion belongs to Mrs I Danby of Preston's niece who took this photo after collecting her from a stay in the cattery.

Make a difference - volunteer!

Treatment for poorly pets

Thanks to PDSA (still remembered by many as the People's Dispensary for Sick Animals) thousands of ill or injured animals receive free veterinary treatment. The charity relieves pets' suffering and provides peace of mind for owners who can't afford to pay expensive vet fees. A small proportion of PDSA's 4,300 volunteers are PetAid hospital assistants but the vast majority work as shop assistants in one of its 176 shops or help with administrative work. In addition, volunteers are needed to plan and run fundraising events such as sponsored events and dog shows. Many of its volunteers are aged 50-65 and the charity's head of volunteering, Janet Compton, says: "PDSA recognises and is grateful for the commitment of the over 50s – they make a vital contribution."

◆ **To find out if there is a vacancy near you, phone 0800 854 194 or write to PDSA National Volunteering Centre, Unit 9 City Business Centre, Hyde Street, Winchester SO23 7TA. Internet: www.pdsa.org.uk**

Here's health

All hot and scratchy

Prickly heat is an itchy red rash you get when your sweat glands become blocked during hot weather. It can be prevented by keeping rooms cool and wearing loose cotton clothing so perspiration can evaporate. Ease the inflammation by applying calamine lotion or an oatmeal-based cream. An anti-histamine cream or a mild steroid cream will relieve the itching.

MY PRAYER

Fill me, loving Father, with the music of your love
With the rests of harmony in every time,
Let me never be sharp or flat
But always be natural,
To rise and fall as I share your wonderful gift with others,
May the cadenzas of life thrill me as the tie binds me
The arpeggios stretch me as they are rounded into a perfect cadence.
Show me how to turn,
To trill,
To shake the ornaments neatly.
Give me the sensitivity of interpretation
That the grace notes may be clean and exciting.

I would be as sustained as the semibreves,
As staunch as the minims,
As upright as the crotchets,
As reliable as the quavers, and pliable as the semiquavers,
And as dexterous as the demisemis.

As a musician, I love, adore and praise you
With heartfelt thanks.
        Dorothy M Roberts, Wellingborough

Top tip

When sending for goods from a newspaper or magazine, write the firm's address and phone number on the back of your cheque stub, then you will always know the contact details if anything goes wrong with your order.
                    Rita Weaver,
                    Rainham

It makes me smile

I enjoy watching How Clean is Your House? on TV but I think I went too far when my daughter fell down the stairs and I shouted at her not to chip the paint!
        Mary Lacey, Oxford

Mavis (left) with John

Let's get cooking!

Mediterranean Pork Chops

(Serves 2)
- ◆ 2 lean pork chops
- ◆ 2 cloves garlic
- ◆ Handful of fresh sage and thyme
- ◆ ½ teaspoon (2.5 ml) black peppercorns
- ◆ 1 tablespoon (15 ml) olive oil
- ◆ 10 oz (275 g) new potatoes, sliced
- ◆ 1 red pepper, deseeded and cut into large chunks
- ◆ 1 aubergine, deseeded and cut into large chunks
- ◆ 1 red onion, cut into wedges
- ◆ 2 tablespoons (30 ml) black or green olives
- ◆ 9 oz (250 g) cherry tomatoes

1 Using a pestle and mortar, pound together the garlic, sage, thyme and peppercorns. Mix with the olive oil and smear the mixture over the chops.
2 Place the chops in a non-stick roasting pan with the potato slices, red pepper, aubergine and onion. Scatter over the olives and roast in a preheated oven (Gas mark 4, 180°C, 350°F) for 30-40 minutes, depending on the thickness of the chops.
3 Halfway through the cooking time, turn the chops over and add the cherry tomatoes to the pan. Return to the oven.
4 Serve with the roasted vegetables.

RECIPE COURTESY OF THE BRITISH MEAT INFORMATION SERVICE

My first...

Every woman has fond memories of her first dance and Mavis Wild of Leicester shares hers

At 19, I had never been to a dance. "You must come, it will be all right; my brother will dance with you," said my friend Florence. We both worked in the gift department of Matthias Robinson, a large department store in Leeds. The year was 1954 and she was drumming up support for the social committee's dance. I was not the only shy teenager she was persuading with the same promise.

The day arrived and we went – complete with borrowed dresses and (on my part) great foreboding. The said brother, John, bravely shared himself out among the gauche non-dancing girls. He was a good dancer and coped well with my stumbling efforts. We were caught in a 'spot' dance. The men had to go down on one knee and the lady had to sit on the other one while both sang If You Were The Only Girl In The World. Talk about embarrassing!

I could not have been totally off-putting as at the end of the evening John asked me for a date and the rest is history. We have now been married 49 years and we still have the odd dance – and I'm still not very good!

Great garden idea

The cost of garden lighting has come down considerably as technology has advanced. A few solar-powered lights won't break the bank and will give you many more hours in the garden. Solar lights only produce low levels of light, but the amount they yield is enough to make the garden usable well into the evening. And just looking out on a garden that's lit at night is a visual delight.

Make a difference - volunteer!

In at the deep end

If you are fit and a good swimmer, The Royal Life Saving Society would be glad of your services. Members can get involved in activities ranging from Save a Baby's Life classes to training youngsters in competitive life saving as a sport. The National Pool Lifeguard Qualification is accepted by most swimming pools. If you live near the sea, becoming a beach lifeguard is an option. Many beach lifeguards are volunteers who work at weekends and on public holidays. Their duties include identifying hazards and taking preventative measures, giving water-safety advice and administering basic first aid.

◆ **To find out more contact The Royal Life Saving Society UK, River House, High Street, Broom, Warwickshire B50 4HN. Tel: 01789 773994. Internet: www.lifesavers.org.uk**

My pet

Clever Sophie alerted her owner, Margaret Box of Great Yarmouth, by barking until she went out into the garden where she found her elderly neighbour, Tilly, had trapped her hand in the chain-link fence. Tilly was freed and Sophie was rewarded with a lovely biscuit.

It makes me smile

The notice on the field gate read: 'The footpath across this field is free, but the bull is likely to charge'.
Mrs A Grimes, Bridlington

OLD-FASHIONED CLEANING REMEDY

Brown staining caused by dripping taps can be cleaned with a paste made by dissolving four tablespoons of cream of tartar in the same amount of water.

Top tip

Save yourself the expense of an electric paper shredder. Instead, put hot soapy water in a washing-up bowl and leave all the papers you wish to destroy in the bowl overnight. In the morning, just throw the congealed mass (that is impossible to read) into the bin.
Margaret Cranston, Manchester

 ## MY PRAYER

Loving Lord
Hold my hand
Guide me through
Your precious land.

Gentle Jesus
Kind and true
Help me now
To follow You.

Caring Christ
O hear my prayer
This quiet time
With Thee I share.
Marian Bythell, Tarporley

Here's health

Best foot forward

Foot odour can be an embarrassing problem but it is easy to prevent. Avoid wearing shoes or socks made from man-made fibres – these don't allow the feet to breathe so they stay wet. Instead, wear only cotton socks and leather shoes. Wash and dry your feet twice a day. Try a salt water foot bath with a few drops of tea tree oil added, or spray your feet with surgical spirit morning and evening.

August 22-28

My pet

"When Pippa wants to play football, she'll bring a ball to our feet," says Mrs P J Odell of Hampton. "As we approach, she dances with delight, her tail gently swaying, her eyes aglow. Pippa also likes to listen to music. Her favourite CD is a selection of light music with catchy tunes."

Top tip

When changing a light bulb, if the bulb comes out but leaves the metal part behind, take a cork from a wine or sherry bottle and use this with pressure to pull it out easily, avoiding those lethal wires that are left behind.

Rosalie Martin,
Dover

Great garden idea

A pile of rubble can look unsightly but, if it's too much hard work to remove it, let a climbing plant scramble over it. If you plan to clear the eyesore away in the future, use an annual climber as this will only last a year. Eccremocarpus has scorching red trumpet-shaped flowers, ipomoea has intense blue flowers and sweet peas come in a wonderful range of colours. All will grow well in a sunny position.

Here's health

Act swiftly with shingles

Shingles often strikes when the body's immunity is low. The first sign is a tingling pain and a raised red rash which later blisters. It is important to obtain medical help quickly so that anti-viral therapy can be prescribed to minimise the severity of the attack. Soothe the rash with ice cubes and apply calamine lotion to cool any burning sensation. Avoid scented bath products, wear natural fibres, and take vitamin A, B complex and E supplements that are beneficial to the skin and nerves.

Make a difference - volunteer!

Coming to terms with crime

If you have a sympathetic ear and a couple of hours a week to spare, you can give emotional support and advice to someone who has been the victim of a crime. Victim Support's 14,000 local volunteers give practical assistance to people who have suffered anything from a burglary to the murder of a relative. Volunteers visit people in their homes and help by allowing them to talk through their feelings to overcome the effect the crime has had on them. Training is given to develop listening skills and provide practical, relevant information (for example, about police and court procedures). A police check is carried out on all volunteers, although having a criminal record does not automatically exclude people from doing this type of work.

◆ **For more information, contact Victim Support National Office, Cranmer House, 39 Brixton Road, London SW9 6DZ. Tel: 020 7735 9166. Internet: www.victimsupport.org**

Every picture tells a story

When this photo was taken, the war was over and the summer fête in Greenford was coming up. I was elected Victory Queen 1945 and was dressed in a gold satin gown which had been hired from Gainsborough film studios. It had been worn by Margaret Lockwood in the film Love Story (with Stewart Grainger and Pat Roc), when she played the Cornish Rhapsody at a concert in the Albert Hall. It was very exciting to visit the film studios in Shepherd's Bush to try on the dress. It was hired for the weekend and valued at £34 – a fortune! The big day came and, with an escort of the local sea cadets, I declared the fête open, saying: "And let the revels begin." It was a wonderful day.

Beryl Langford-Dover,
Greenford

OLD-FASHIONED CLEANING REMEDY

Fresh white bread can be used to gently rub grubby marks from paper. Or use a crust of fresh bread to clean slatted blinds; hold the crust around each slat and run it along from one end to the other.

MY PRAYER

A prayer said in silence
Or a prayer said out loud
Will be heard in solitude
Or in a thronging crowd.

Because the one who listens
Knows us best of all,
In times of woe or heartache
He will answer to our call.

Whatever you may ask of him,
There's no doubt that he'll be there,
For you'll receive if you believe
In the eternal power of prayer.
Betty Elliott, Tyne & Wear

 **Let's get cooking!**

Citrus Salad with Watercress and Apple
(Serves 4)

◆ 1 orange
◆ 1 grapefruit
◆ 1 pink grapefruit
◆ 1 x 3 oz (75 g) pack of watercress
◆ 1 Cox's apple, cored and diced
◆ 2 oz (50 g) sultanas

1 Peel the citrus fruits and carefully remove all the pith. Slice thinly and divide between four plates.
2 Arrange the watercress on top of the orange and grapefruit slices.
3 Mix the apple and sultanas and scatter over the top.
Serve immediately.

RECIPE COURTESY OF THE WATERCRESS ALLIANCE

 **Senior moment**

I once heard myself saying to my sons: "Don't keep eating those biscuits. What do you think I buy them for?"

Mrs R Band, Windsor

A Walk in the Wild
The hunter on the hill

Scottish wildcats are territorial creatures

At first glance, Scottish wildcats may look similar to a pet cat, but on closer observation there are differences. The wide, flat head, ears pointing more sideways, a bushy blunt-ended tail encircled with dark rings, and a distinctly striped coat all distinguish the true wildcat from feral cats. Research has also revealed differences in their genetic make-up, blood type and skull features. Unlike the domestic cat, the wildcat is a seasonal breeder.

The ancestors of our domestic pet cat, Felis catus, may have been the African wildcat or the Indian desert cat. In Britain, the pet cat arrived with the Romans. Today, there are many domestic cats 'gone wild'. These feral cats

can interbreed with the Scottish wildcat, and produce fertile hybrid cats. Such cross-breeding may put the future survival of the Scottish wildcat at risk.

The Latin name for the elusive wildcat, Felis silvestris means 'woodland cat'. Human persecution and habitat destruction led to its extinction in England, Wales and southern Scotland by 1880. The remote Highlands provided a last refuge.

The Scottish wildcat is now fully protected by law and is recognised as a separate sub-species, Felis silvestris grampia, confined to the Central and Northern Highlands of mainland Scotland. During the day, they lie up in a den among rocky cairns

or among tree roots typically in upland forest or moorland. The wildcat preys on rabbits and rodents and other birds, reptiles, amphibians and insects.

Solitary and territorial, the wildcat is active at night, particularly around dawn and dusk. Territory is marked out by urine and droppings, and by scratches on tree trunks. The male's home range may overlap that of the female and young males may be nomadic. The young leave their mother at about five months and establish their own territories.

You can see wildcats at the Highland Wildlife Park, Kincraig, Kingussie, Inverness-shire. Tel: 01540 651270.

WARTIME WEDDINGS
Oh, what a giveaway!

Shirley Smith of Potter's Bar recalls when stray confetti caused some blushes

Eric and I got engaged on my 18th birthday in December 1941. In March Eric joined the RAF and in May I started my basic training in the ATS. Then I received a telegram requesting me to get 14 days leave to get married on 1 August 1942.

A lady who lived a few doors from my home lent me a wedding dress that fitted perfectly. I had a pretty pair of white gloves I had cherished but never worn. The bridesmaids' dresses were party dresses my sister and I had before the war – one aunt did wonderful things with them and another aunt lent me her headdress and veil. Eric had lost all his clothing twice in air raids so it was Hobson's choice for him and I was glad he looked so handsome in his uniform.

The local shops helped and we had a really wonderful spread. In the middle of the table there was a beautiful two-tiered wedding cake. I was surprised, to say the least, when

the outer covering was taken off; it was a thin type of cardboard.

We were both in uniform when we went on our honeymoon to Richmond in Surrey. We travelled on a 27 bus and when we arrived we went into a restaurant to have a meal. When Eric opened his jacket, masses of confetti flew out. We were so embarrassed we picked up our cases and rushed out of the place. I can't imagine young folk being so sensitive today!

Spaghetti what?

In the first fever of love and preparing for marriage in 1960, Sandra Stagg decided it would be a good idea to sign up for a cookery course...

My mum had always been willing to let me mess about in her kitchen but this was the love of my life I was about to marry. He deserved some special looking after, some proper recipes, something different.

My newly married cousin, Cathy, decided to enrol me for cookery lessons and we presented ourselves on the top floor of my old school. This cooking lark was new to me.

That first evening we learned how to make Spaghetti Boulannaise, (yes, that's how she spelt it). Real exciting stuff this. Hamburgers the next week (with rolled oats to pad them out) were followed by Stuffed Baked Pork Chops.

We mixed sage and onion stuffing and spread it over our chops, balancing slices of cooking apple on top and baked them. My long-suffering dad pronounced the result to be 'very good'. Cathy's husband refused to try them till she'd 'scraped all that muck off first'.

Nothing daunted, we tackled pastry next and discovered that a flan baked 'blind' had nothing to do with opticians or specs but had to be weighted down with dried peas during the first ten minutes in the oven to stop it rising in the middle.

Since tin foil was not yet with us, we raced against the clock, trying to pick burning hot peas out of the pastry with our fingers before returning our efforts to bake for another ten minutes while we prepared the filling.

An onion peeled, (this was news to one of our number who hadn't seen the need to remove the skin) and chopped, was then lightly fried with some scraps of bacon; we were learning fast just how useful these could be.

Two beaten eggs completed our filling and after another 20 minutes in the oven, we had a yet another meal for four.

We learned that egg whites whipped up for meringues responded to the 'fork on a flat plate' treatment more quickly if we stood outside in the draughty corridor.

It appeared that one person from each class would be awarded a scholarship to Athol Crescent – and she had chosen me. Being a language student, I had never heard of it and was unaware this was the Scottish equivalent of Cordon Bleu or Prue Leith.

I was mystified my teacher didn't see that marrying my beloved was more important to me and, since I was moving from Edinburgh to Southampton, commuting was not an option.

I did develop a love for cooking, though, and was very proud that in the first six weeks of marriage, I didn't duplicate a single dish. My husband, like my father, would try anything...

Several years and two children later, we moved to North Wales and made many friends. One of our favourite couples was John and Sally. Sally had been a cookery teacher, and used to lament that 'the problem with being a cookery teacher was that people expected you to be able to cook'.

One evening my husband mentioned I'd won a scholarship to Athol Crescent. I explained I didn't go because I got married instead.

Sally was incredulous. "You mean you gave it up to marry HIM?"

My husband never felt quite the same about her after that.

September 2005

Thursday *1*	**Monday** *12*
Friday *2*	**Tuesday** *13*
Saturday *3*	**Wednesday** *14*
Sunday *4*	**Thursday** *15*
Monday *5*	**Friday** *16* Southampton International Boat Show starts
Tuesday *6*	**Saturday** *17*
Wednesday *7*	**Sunday** *18*
Thursday *8*	**Monday** *19*
Friday *9*	**Tuesday** *20*
Saturday *10* Last night of the BBC Proms	**Wednesday** *21*
Sunday *11*	**Thursday** *22*

Friday
23

Saturday
24

Sunday
25

Monday
26

Tuesday
27

Wednesday
28

Thursday
29

Friday
30

October **Yours** on sale

IT HAPPENED THIS MONTH

1 September, 1976
The first of 11,500 standpipes were connected in Yorkshire as reservoir levels fell

7 September, 1952
The actress Gertrude Lawrence died in New York where she had been appearing in the musical The King and I

11 September, 1962
The Beatles recorded Love Me Do at the Abbey Road studio

16 September, 1977
T-Rex singer Marc Bolan was killed in a car crash in London

22 September, 1955
London's first independent television programmes were broadcast by the ITA

27 September, 1968
The musical Hair opened in London, one day after theatre censorship was abolished

29 September, 1758
Horatio Nelson was born at Burnham Thorpe in Norfolk

PIC: REXFEATURES

RUTH

She stood breast high amid the corn,
Clasped by the golden light of morn,
Like the sweetheart of the sun,
Who many a glowing kiss had won.

On her cheek an autumn flush,
Deeply ripened; – such a blush
In the midst of brown was born,
Like red poppies grown with corn.

And her hat, with shady brim,
Made her tressy forehead dim; –
Thus she stood amid the stooks,
Praising God with sweetest looks:

Sure, I said, heaven did not mean,
Where I reap thou shouldst but glean,
Lay thy sheaf adown and come,
Share my harvest and my home.

Thomas Hood

19 September, 1949
Leslie Hornby (later known as Twiggy) was born

Great garden idea

Christmas is still many months away but it's not too early to buy some prepared hyacinths from your garden centre to flower over the festive season. Place them in a container of bulb fibre and put them in a cool, dark place. After a few weeks, when you can see that the flower bud has emerged from the neck of the bulb, bring the container out into a cool, bright place. As the flower opens move the container to a place where you can enjoy the blooms.

A nice little earner

Margaret Gott of Ripon recalls that earning a few extra pence wasn't 'easy money'

There were three of us at the younger end of the family who were eligible for household chores for which we earned 3d a week pocket money. First, cleaning windows, which we did with vinegar and screwed up newspaper. In the bedrooms this involved sitting on the outside window ledge, holding on to the frame with one hand, legs dangling inside the room – a rather frightening experience for a child.

Then there was the washing (on hands and knees) of the front step and our bit of pavement, finishing off by 'donkey stoning' the edges in white. The third job was cleaning the brasses, taps and fenders with Brasso and blackleading the grate with Zebo. There were many other household jobs we had to do as a matter of routine but these extra ones earned us our pocket money.

Let's get cooking!

Chinese Pork with Crispy Noodles

(Serves 4)
- ◆ 1 lb (450 g) lean pork fillet
- ◆ 1 red onion, cut into wedges
- ◆ 1 red pepper, cut into strips
- ◆ 4 oz (100 g) baby sweetcorn, sliced in half
- ◆ 1 carrot, peeled and cut into thin batons
- ◆ 1 tablespoon (15 ml) oil
- ◆ 4 tablespoons (60 ml) plum sauce
- ◆ 2 tablespoons (30 ml) sweet chilli sauce
- ◆ 2 teaspoons (10 ml) soy sauce
- ◆ 2 oz (50 g) sugar snap peas
- ◆ Crispy rice noodles, to serve

1 Put the onion, pepper, sweetcorn and carrot in a roasting pan. Drizzle over the oil and mix together.
2 Place the pork fillet on top.
3 Mix together the plum sauce, chilli sauce and soy sauce and drizzle over the pork. Cook in a preheated oven (Mark 4, 180°C, 350°F) for 25-30 minutes.
4 During the last 10-15 minutes of cooking time, add the sugar snap peas. Stir into the vegetables and return to the oven.
5 Serve the pork fillet cut into slices with the roasted vegetables and crispy rice noodles

RECIPE COURTESY OF THE BRITISH MEAT INFORMATION SERVICE

Oh - happy day!

Pam Barrett of Dover felt privileged to pay tribute to 'Our Thora'

I was fortunate to get two tickets for the service of thanksgiving for the life and work of Dame Thora Hird. My friend, Barbara, accompanied me. We went by coach to London. Our first port of call was to have coffee then we took a taxi to Westminster Abbey. We had to be seated by 11.15 am. Music played before the service, during which time many famous people came in, led by Thora's daughter and grandchildren.

At precisely 11.30 am the Salvation Army band marched through the Abbey playing a rousing rendering of Onward Christian Soldiers. This set the tone for the whole service and was followed by prayers. The congregation enjoyed singing What A Friend We Have In Jesus, followed by Victoria Wood reading from the preface to Dame Thora's biography, Nothing Like a Dame. Alan Bennett's address showed he knew her very well. The last hymn was sung with great gusto by all. The whole service had a very happy atmosphere and was a tribute to a very great lady.

My pet

During the war, Rinty the terrier was the family pet of Mrs E V Cohen of London. When he heard the sirens, he would dash through the house, out into the garden and down into the Anderson Shelter – ahead of the everyone else!

My Prayer

They who are near me do not know
That you are nearer to me than they are.
They who can speak to me do not know
That my heart is full with your unspoken words.
They who crowd my path do not know
That I am walking alone with you.
They who love me do not know
That their love brings you to my heart.
Betty Cross, Wolverhampton

Top tip

If you need a quick dessert for unexpected guests just add sliced fresh fruit to tinned ones. Add a layer of macaroons or digestive biscuits and chopped nuts then top with whipped cream.
Mrs H Scott, Cumbria

It makes me smile

My young niece did a drawing of her granddad. "That's his fat belly," she pointed out, "and that's his boiled head!"
Charlotte Macauley, Co. Down

Here's health

Cuddle up, pet!
Did you know pet owners have lower stress levels, make fewer visits to their GP and cope better with traumatic events like bereavement? Walking the dog can be therapeutic because while you are out you may chat to people who are unaware that you have been bereaved or been ill and this has a 'normalising' effect. It has been shown that cat owners recovering from breast cancer, for example, benefit greatly from the comfort of cuddling their pet.

September 5-11

Let's get cooking!

Banana, Raspberry and Honey Smoothie
(Serves 1)
- 1 large banana, chopped
- 2 tablespoons (30 ml) runny honey
- 7 fl oz (200 ml) semi-skimmed milk
- 5 tablespoons (75 ml) Greek yoghurt
- Handful of raspberries, to taste

1 Place the banana, honey, milk, yoghurt and raspberries in a blender and blend until smooth.
2 To serve, pour into a tall glass and enjoy.

RECIPE COURTESY OF THE HONEY ASSOCIATION

Top tip

When my mother and grandmother patched the tough moleskin trousers my father wore in the coal mines, she used to run the needle through her hair and it then went through the tough fabric much more easily. It really does work.
Annice Collyer, Alfreton

Remember the '60s?

Now living in the Outer Hebrides, Lyn Lowe recalls the shock felt when D H Lawrence's novel Lady Chatterley's Lover was published

My father was the vicar of Denford in Northamptonshire. When he saw copies in a neighbouring village shop, he was so upset about the bad moral infuence they might have on the youth of the area that he asked the shopkeeper not to sell them. Of course, the shopkeeper could not afford to throw away his profit so, on condition that no further copies would be ordered, my father purchased the whole stock, then took them back home and burned the lot, one by one, in the church stove.

As a young person, I'd often found his moral convictions irksome, but now I am proud to remember his courageous stands.

Here's health

A drop of what you fancy
Now that the evenings are drawing in, there's no need to feel guilty about enjoying a mellow glass of sherry before supper. Researchers have found that sherry, like red wine, could actually be good for your heart. Both contain chemicals called polypehnols which help to control cholesterol levels and reduce the risk of coronary heart disease. Spanish scientists found that chemicals found in sherry boost the production of 'good' HDL cholesterol while keeping 'bad' LDL cholesterol levels under control.

OLD-FASHIONED CLEANING REMEDY
Remove difficult gardening dirt from your hands by mixing sugar with your soap.
Charlotte Primrose, Manningtree

Make a difference - volunteer!

Experience counts, every time

The Experience Corps (TEC) believes the life experience gained by people aged 50 and over, can be of enormous value to society. TEC is an independent company set up to encourage the over fifties to offer their skills and experience to benefit others in their local communities.

TEC has a team of nine Animators working in every region of England whose primary task is to match its members with voluntary opportunities from national, regional and local charities and other community-based organisations. It now has thousands of imaginative and innovative voluntary work opportunities on its database including the Pets as Therapy project shown in the picture. Many of its 190,000 members are from the Sikh, Muslim, Hindu, African Caribbean and Chinese communities.

◆ **Anyone interested in becoming a member of The Experience Corps should ring on 020 7921 0580 or go to**

www.experiencecorps.co.uk for further information. You will then be put in touch directly with an Animator who will match your individual skills with a local voluntary work opportunity.

MY PRAYER

(Said to have been written by a 19-year-old servant girl)
Lord of all pots and pans and things,
Since I've no time to be
A saint by doing lovely things, or
Watching late with Thee,
Or dreaming in the dawnlight, or
Storming heaven's gates,
Make me a saint by getting meals and
Washing up the plates.

Although I must have Martha's hands,
I have a Mary mind;
And when I black the boots and shoes
Thy sandals, Lord, I find.
I think of how they trod the earth
What time I scrub the floor;
Accept this meditation, Lord,
I haven't time for more.

Warm all the kitchen with Thy love, and
Light it with Thy peace.
Forgive me all my worrying, and make
All grumbling cease.
Thou who didst love to give men food,
In room or by the sea,
Accept this service that I do –
I do unto Thee.
         Mrs E H Payne, Burgess Hill

Senior moment

I was going shopping and my son asked me to get him some milk. I asked: "Do you want full cream or semi-skilled?"
         Mrs E J Arnold, Ramsgate

My pet

What was that about a shaggy dog story? Joshua was Jackie Norris of Halifax's 'granddog'. He belonged to her daughter Juliet, and unusually for a Briard, lived to the ripe old age of 17.

Great garden idea

Divide your lawn roughly into square metres and, taking one section a day, rake it thoroughly to remove thatch. This is hard work but not only will it get you fit, it will improve your lawn no end. Once all the debris has been removed (you can put it on the compost heap), aerate the lawn by inserting a garden fork to a depth of 3in (8cm) in rows about 6in (15cm) apart, then top-dress with a mixture of compost, grit and a general organic fertiliser.

September 12-18

It makes me smile

OLD-FASHIONED CLEANING REMEDY

Use hot vinegar on a rag to remove bird mess from windows.

Mrs V Watson, Colchester

Visiting an old lady of 92, I found she was trying to measure her curtains. She said: "I can't understand tape measures now. How long have they had these centipedes on them?"

Joyce Green, Rotherham

My first...

Brian Fisher of Northampton waxes poetic over his first set of wheels

My first car was purchased for £50 in 1958 during my two years' National Service. It faithfully carried me between Northampton and Liss in Hampshire, including once when it skidded into a deep ditch on an icy road and had to be rescued by a Land Rover. The steering and brakes were not too hot and I have grave doubts whether it would have passed an MOT test today. The hairiest moment came when I was giving the Sergeant Major's wife a lift to the railway station and one of the back wheels came off. It overtook us as we slid to a stop in a shower of sparks. When I had to consign it to the scrapheap, it was with a heavy heart.

It was a '39 Austin – FKH 107,
It had been up to Glasgow and down to Devon.
Yes – it was mine, my very first car,
I was really quite proud of my old 'jamjar',
Good old banger.

It used to stand there, battered and worn,
Looking rather bedraggled and rather forlorn,
It had seen good service and gone round the clock,
But now struggled hard to get round the block.
Did my banger.

My faithful transport had run its last mile,
And now it was just a name on a file.
Down the yard, as they winched it up high,
Did I hear a wistful parting sigh
From my old banger?

Let's get cooking!

Apricot and Nut Flapjacks

- 6 oz (175 g) butter
- 3 oz (75 g) soft brown sugar
- 3 oz (75 g) honey
- 9 oz (250 g) rolled oats
- 2 heaped tablespoons (50 g) plain flour
- 1 oz (25 g) shelled pistachio nuts
- 1 oz (25 g) pecan nuts
- 3 oz (75 g) ready-to-eat dried apricots, chopped

1 Preheat the oven to Gas Mark 4, 180°C, 350°F.
2 In a large pan, gently heat the butter, sugar and honey, stirring until melted and combined.
3 Add the oats, flour, nuts and apricots and mix well.
4 Using the back of a spoon, press the mixture into a lightly greased baking tin and bake for 25 minutes.
5 Remove from the oven and allow to cool for 5 minutes before cutting into bars.
6 Leave the flapjacks to cool completely in the tin, then store in an airtight container.

RECIPE COURTESY OF THE HONEY ASSOCIATION

My pet

Benji thinks everything in the garden's lovely. He lives with Bob and Joyce Pierson of Nettleham in Lincolnshire.

MY PRAYER

We give thanks, oh Father,
for the beauty of this earth,
For the wonder of each birth
For the joy of family and friends,
For Your love which never ends.
Keep safe, we pray, all those who ask
Your help in completing each new task.
Forgive us, please, when we just pray
For something wanted every day
And often we forget to say
Thank you, Lord!

Throughout our world, please grant peace
So that enmities henceforth shall cease;
And Your creation, happy then,
Shall sing Your praises for ever,
                    Verica Peacock, Harlow

Here's health

Confucius he say

According to traditional Chinese medicine, you should aim to adjust your exercise routine to be in harmony with the seasons. Autumn and winter are 'ying' months; a time of harvesting and storage, rest and reflection. The longer nights and colder weather of autumn call for deep breathing and stretching exercises to wind down for winter when yoga and t'ai chi are thought to be the most appropriate exercises. Less strenuous than step aerobics!

Make a difference - volunteer!

Have a say in grassroots politics

Instead of grumbling about your local parish council (we all do!) why not join them and have a voice in what happens in your own backyard? This a voluntary job that provides the perfect way to improve local amenities and make your opinion heard on local issues.

The parish council is a tier of local government and elections are held in May and when a vacancy occurs. The term of office is four years.

The parish clerk is responsible for producing the minutes, agenda and correspondence for the monthly meetings. The hours you have to put in depends on the size of the parish. In small parishes, a quarterly or monthly meeting is held to discuss planning applications, grants, conservation and financial matters.

◆ **If you are interested in getting involved, contact your parish or district council office.**

Great garden idea

If there's a walled corner of your garden that is rather dark, paint it white and cover it with a piece of trellis in a contrasting colour. With the addition of well-positioned terracotta pots the result can look almost Mediterranean. Add a mirror to reflect light (make sure you seal it around the edges to prevent the silvering becoming damaged by water) and you'll make the previously shady spot even brighter.

Top tip

To remove stubborn labels from glass jars needed for home-made jams, score the label then spray with furniture polish. Leave to soak in for a few minutes, then rub off. If there is still some of the label left, repeat the process before washing the jar.
Ruth Reeves,
Oswestry

September 19-25

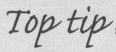

MY PRAYER

Dear Lord, I'm frequently unkind,
Help me humility to find.
In others' goodness help me see,
And let your mercy shine on me.

In thoughtless haste, just passing by,
Help me to recognise a cry
Of pain of sadness to be free,
And let your mercy shine on me.

In talk of someone else's sin,
Do I too joyfully join in,
Help me of malice to be free,
And let your mercy shine on me.

You've given me hearing, sight and voice,
So many blessings I rejoice.
To use them wisely is my plea,
So let your mercy shine on me.

Enid Gill, Tavistock

Great garden idea

Although you can sow sweet peas in autumn and spring, autumn sowings produce the best plants. Choose Rootrainers (available from all larger garden centres) and sow one seed in each, using multipurpose compost. Once they've germinated, grow them on in an unheated greenhouse or coldframe, pinching out the growing points once the seedlings are about 3in (8cm) in height to encourage branching.

My pet

'Ding dong bell – Simba's in the well'. His owner Edna Heath says he like to sit in there if he finds himself locked out in wet or windy weather. Good thinking, puss!

Make a difference - volunteer!

First Aid is just one facet

Uniformed St John Ambulance volunteers are most often seen providing First Aid at large public events but this is only one facet of its work in the community. Examples of other voluntary opportunities include working for the library service it operates in hospitals and residential homes, reading to patients or organising book stocks. Another aspect of the service is working with the homeless unit.

If your interest is in First Aid, you will be expertly trained to treat everything from headaches to heart attacks. You can build up your skills to undertake patient transfer duties or even crew an accident and emergency ambulance. Volunteers are taught the skills required to assist a doctor, nurse or paramedic in some specialist techniques.

◆ **To find out about all these facets, write to St John Ambulance, 27 St John's Lane, London EC1M 4BU. Tel: 08700 10 49 50. Internet: www.sja.org.uk**

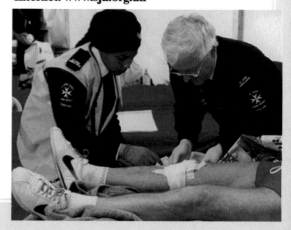

Every picture tells a story

These days owning a bicycle is the norm for most children but back in the '50s, things were different. How I craved a cycle. It didn't have to be bright and shiny, as long as it had two wheels and was rideable. Unfortunately, there was no money to spare and it seemed my dream would not come true. Then my Aunty Vi came to the rescue. She worked as a cashier at the local cinema and was a well-known sight in the area, pedalling furiously back and forth to work. The time came when she needed a replacement machine and the discarded one was passed on to me. Alas, I was only eight and it was far too big for me.

However, my father renovated it and put it away to await a growth spurt. Every night I prayed hard for that day to arrive and I can still remember the elation I felt. The world was my oyster. This photograph shows a very proud and happy Brownie trying the cycle for size.

Margaret Jesson,
Bridgnorth

 Let's get cooking!

Pork and Bramley Apple Sausage Roll
(Serves 6-8)
◆ 1 lb (450 g) sausages, skinned
◆ 8 oz (225 g) Bramley apples, peeled, cored and chopped
◆ 2 tablespoons (30 ml) snipped fresh sage or 2 teaspoons (10 ml) dried sage
◆ Black pepper, ground
◆ Flour, for dusting
◆ 1 x 13 oz (375 g) pack of ready-rolled puff pastry
◆ Beaten egg, to glaze

1 Preheat the oven to Gas Mark 7, 220°C, 425°F.
2 Mix the sausagemeat with the apples and sage, and season with ground black pepper
3 Unroll the pastry and place on a large lightly-floured baking sheet. Place the sausage mixture down the centre of the pastry, shaping it into a fat sausage shape. Use a knife to make ½ in (1.2 cm) wide and 2 in (5 cm) cuts at an angle of 45° on either side of the sausagemeat.
4 Brush the edges with beaten egg and fold the two ends of pastry over the sausagemeat. Then weave the cut edges together, overlapping each side to make a plaited pattern.
5 Brush with more egg and bake for 25 minutes or until golden and crisp. Allow to cool for 5 minutes before transferring to a serving plate.
6 Serve warm or cold, in slices.

RECIPE COURTESY OF THE BRAMLEY APPLE INFORMATION SERVICE

Senior moment

The shop assistant laughed when I went to a large store and asked for 'income support tights'.

Joan Richardson,
West Bromwich

OLD-FASHIONED CLEANING REMEDY

A small piece of chamois leather can be used to clean pearls or to polish gold jewellery.

Here's health

Oil those creaky joints

Granny's insistence on a daily dose of cod liver oil has turned out to be very wise. Scientists now know that cod liver oil not only lubricates healthy joints but helps to repair arthritic ones, too. It contains Omega 3 fatty acids which slow down enzymes that damage cartilage, reducing inflammation in the joints. People waiting for hip and knee replacements could benefit from taking a daily cod liver oil supplement.

September 26-October 2

Great garden idea

The leaves will soon come tumbling down and removing them from your pond is a chore that has to be done to prevent the water from becoming murky. Most leaves blow into a pond rather than fall straight into it so, before the first autumn winds, erect a temporary plastic mesh fence about 2ft (60cm) high around it. Netting can be purchased by the metre from your garden centre. Place all the leaves on the compost where they'll break down slowly.

OLD-FASHIONED CLEANING REMEDY

When painting window frames, keep the glass free of paint by placing dampened newspaper around the edges of each pane. If you still manage to get some on the window, freshly dried paint can be removed with a solution of three parts warm water to one part vinegar.

Dear diary

Wasps are a hazard at this time of the year as Doreen O Lane of Whitstable recorded in her diary

10 September 2001
Up early to catch the coach for holiday in Cotswolds. Received a wasp sting when near Oxford which caused an anaphylactic shock. Rushed to the cottage hospital at Bourton-on-the-Water. Excellent care after being told it was 'touch and go'. No bed available there, so taken by ambulance to Cheltenham General Hospital where again I received exellent care.

25 September 2001
On steroids and piriton. Still itching but swelling going down. Feel awful. Had chest X-ray – okay. Kept in for second night. Received phone calls from family. Doreen adds a postcript: *"Glad to say I fully recovered from this experience but sincerely hope it never happens again!"*

Let's get cooking!

Roasted Vegetable Paté
(Serves 6)

◆ 8 oz (225 g) carrots, peeled, roughly chopped, and parboiled
◆ 8 oz (225 g) parsnips, peeled, roughly chopped, and parboiled
◆ 1 red pepper, halved and deseeded
◆ A few sprays of one-calorie oil
◆ 4 oz (100 g) tinned chickpeas, drained and rinsed
◆ 2 tablespoons (30 ml) reduced-fat crème fraîche
◆ 1 tablespoon (15 ml) fresh parsley, chopped
◆ 1 tablespoon (15 ml) lemon juice
◆ 12 slices of French bread
◆ 6 lemon wedges, to garnish

1 Preheat the oven to Gas Mark 6, 200°C, 400°F. Put the carrots, parsnips and red pepper halves into a roasting pan and spray with the oil. Season well and roast, uncovered, for 25 minutes.
2 Remove the vegetables from the oven. Allow the peppers to cool before peeling off the skins.
3 Put the cooked vegetables in a food processor with the chickpeas, crème fraîche, parsley and lemon juice. Blend for a few seconds to form a chunky paste.
4 Transfer to a dish and chill for one hour before serving with slices of hot French bread, garnished with lemon wedges.

RECIPE COURTESY OF SLIMMING MAGAZINE

Make a difference - volunteer!

Helping folk down on their luck

Originally known as the Distressed Gentlefolks' Aid Association and renamed in 2000 in honour of its founder, the Elizabeth Finn Trust gives financial help to people in need whose former careers have been interrupted or ended through illness, mental problems, sudden redundancy, or family breakdown. The charity also helps pensioners who struggle to make ends meet.

The charity needs volunteers to visit current beneficiaries and new applicants in their region. At a one day training course, volunteer visitors will learn what help the charity can give, how to address sensitive issues with the new applicant or current beneficiary, and how to make the charity aware of any extra help a beneficiary could receive.

This volunteer opportunity is especially for people who would like to help in their community, but don't want to fit into the set pattern of, for instance, working in a charity shop. Visits take between one or two hours and volunteers can decide the number of beneficiary visits they would like to take on. Travel expenses are reimbursed.

◆ **For more information, please contact the Elizabeth Finn Trust on Freephone 0800 413 220.**

My pet

Olive Bussell of Holywood, County Down, took this photo of her dogs Rex (on the right) and Nel with her sister Dorothy. Rex always preferred to collect bottles to bones and did his bit for the environment by keeping the local park litter-free.

Top tip

Clean your liquidiser or food processor by filling it with hot water and a squirt of washing-up liquid, then switch on.
    K Croft, Hayling Island

Wit and wisdom

Drama is life with the dull bits cut out.
Alfred Hitchcock (1899-1980)

It makes me smile

As I was leaving the travel agent, I met a friend who congratulated me on my slimness. I told her: "My husband and I are going to aerobics." She gave me a blank stare. "But I thought you liked Majorca," she replied.
    Joy Smithson, Ferndown

Here's health

Polly, put the kettle on

Scientists have confirmed what we Brits have known for centuries – you can't beat a nice cup of tea to perk you up. American researchers in Boston (scene of a famous historical tea party) found that drinking five or six cups a day boosts your immune system. The magic ingredient is L-theanine which is broken down into antigens that fight infection. Letting the pot brew for three to five minutes gives the maximum benefit. So put your feet up and have a cuppa.

A Walk in the Wild
Frolicsome hunter of fish

The semi-aquatic otter must have clean water to survive

The otter is one of the best loved mammals in Britain, largely because of its secretive and yet playful habits. Otters belong to the Mustelid family which also includes badgers, weasels and stoats.

Otters generally live a solitary lifestyle and the female and male only come together to mate. Cubs can be born more or less at any time of the year although in the north they tend to have two main seasons – spring and autumn. The female is largely responsible for bringing up the cubs although, on occasions, you may see a family group including the male. Strangely enough,

young otters with their fluffy coat are not natural swimmers, so they are often dragged into the water by their mother. Cubs stay with their mother for over a year even though they can hunt for themselves by about six months.

Otters are semi-aquatic, which means they use both the land and water environments. Most people associate otters with rivers but by far the greatest numbers in Britain are found on the coast. In fact, if you want to see one in the wild your best chances are on the West Coast of Scotland and the Hebrides, or Shetland. Here otters are not nocturnal but can be seen

in the day hunting among the seaweed in the shallows; the International Otter Survival Fund has its offices on the Isle of Skye.

Otters are great ambassadors for a clean environment – both the land and water they use must be in pristine condition. In the past they declined throughout Europe as a result of chemical pollution, habitat loss, disturbance and hunting. Now the situation is improving and otters are slowly returning.

For further information contact: Grace Yoxon, International Otter Survival Fund, Broadford, Isle of Skye IV49 9AQ. Tel: 01471 822 487.

WARTIME WEDDINGS
Spam and salad for wedding breakfast

Margaret Finney of Ashbourne, Derby had to milk the cows before heading for the church

In the war I was working on my father's farm in the village of Loxley, near Uttoxeter, and my intended was a sergeant in the RAF. I was determined to have a white wedding so I managed to get some coupon-free lace from Darley Market Hall made up by a local dressmaker – but the biggest laugh was the lining! We were allowed clothing coupons to buy cloth for washing the cows' udders before milking and the local draper allowed me to buy some satin with those! My veil was borrowed and so were my silver shoes.

On the wedding morning I got up and hand-milked six cows and swilled down the blue-brick yard. We were married on 16 December 1944 at Uttoxeter parish church but we couldn't have any music because the organist was working making armoured cars.

The reception was at a cafeteria. I think it was Spam and salad. And there was a cardboard covered cake which lifted off to reveal a small plain cake underneath. Our honeymoon was spent in a village about eight miles away where my parents had bought a cottage for their retirement.

My husband had to return to his post on the Isle of Man two days before Christmas and I did not see him again until March. On his demob in 1946 we were very lucky to be able to buy a ten-year-old semi-detached house for £950.

Puzzles

Codebreaker

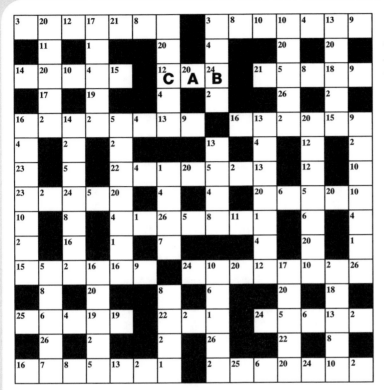

There are no clues in this crossword. Instead, each number in the grid represents a letter. We've placed one word to start you off, which shows that 12=C, 20=A and 24=B. Write these letters wherever their numbers appear in the grid and you should then be able to start working out the identity of the other letters. The completed grid will include all 26 letters of the alphabet. Use the reference boxes to keep track of the letters you've used.

A B C D E F
G H I J K L M
N O P Q R S T
U V W X Y Z

Turn to Page 157 for puzzle answers

1	2	3	4	5	6	7	8	9	10	11	12	13
											C	

14	15	16	17	18	19	20	21	22	23	24	25	26
						A				B		

Six of the Best

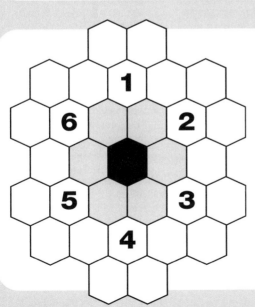

The six-letter answers to these clues should be written clockwise around the appropriate numbers in the grid so that all six solutions interlock. Once you have solved the puzzle correctly, you will find that the central shaded hexagons, reading clockwise, will spell out the name of a bird.

Clues

1 Mist or steam
2 Deep valley or gorge
3 Infertile, sterile
4 Public speaker
5 Paramour, beau
6 Choice, alternative

A different direction

Hazel will miss the meandering journey into town
– but you never know what's around the next bend

Hazel stood up as the number 38 bus came into view. She was the only person waiting in the little wooden shelter at the end of the village, making this last journey seem all the more poignant. Boarding the bus with a heavy heart, she nonetheless managed a cheery 'good morning' to the driver as she showed her bus pass before taking her usual seat by the window halfway down the aisle.

There was plenty of room. Most people preferred to travel by car, especially since the new dual carriageway had been opened, enabling them to speed directly to the town centre and avoid the winding lanes along which the number 38 meandered. These days, it seemed, people just didn't have the time to take the scenic route.

And nor did the bus company; today was the last time that Hazel would be able to enjoy the rural view on her weekly trip into town. As from Monday, the 38 bus was being re-routed along the new road.

The single-decker passed the last of the houses and swung out across the countryside. The horses were in the lower field today, Hazel noted, counting them. She frowned. Only eight. Oh no, there was the bay, standing beneath a tree in the corner. Nine. All present and correct.

The trees were beginning to lose their leaves. She would miss seeing autumn slowly weave its tapestry of gold, russet and brown before giving way to the thrilling whiteness of winter, which would in its turn submit to the fresh green of spring. These fields and hedgerows were a living calendar to Hazel.

The bus pulled in at the next village where a dark-haired woman got on with two toddlers in tow. Mrs Dalby smiled at Hazel before ushering the children into a seat near the front. Hazel had watched the Dalby family grow over the years. At first, Mrs Dalby had struggled on with a baby and a folding pushchair. By the time

the little girl could climb up the steps on her own, the pushchair was needed for her baby brother. The pattern had repeated itself when the youngest came along and now the eldest was at school.

As the children looked out of the window, their mother pointed out a blackbird sitting on a hedge. Hazel had always thought that one day she'd bring her grandchildren with her on the bus but all she'd have to show them now would be the new housing estate.

Other regulars came on board as the bus continued its journey. They acknowledged Hazel with a smile or a nod but the seat beside her remained empty until Mr Jesson lowered himself down.

"Bit blustery today," he said, removing his cap.

"It is, indeed."

There was a short silence, then Mr Jesson said: "I don't suppose I'll be seeing you next week. You'll be on the express and I'll be on the toytown minibus they're giving us."

The 38 bus was being re-routed along the new road

PIC: PHOTODISC

The bus picked up a number of passengers but none of them were familiar faces

Hazel suddenly felt quite emotional. Mr Jesson's conversation had rarely ventured beyond the weather – not even when they both worked in the bank before she was married, nor on all the occasions they had sat together on the number 38 following his retirement, but she would miss him all the same. "Perhaps we'll still bump into each other," she managed to reply.

The hedgerows were replaced by terraced houses, then rows of shops, as the bus neared the town centre, finally coming to a halt at the terminus. Mr Jesson replaced his cap and stood aside to let Hazel go first.

After bidding him good day, Hazel headed for the high street. Three hours later, she treated herself to a cup of coffee and an almond slice at the bus station café, her carrier bags tucked under the table, before making the return journey home.

This time the atmosphere was slightly different. The passengers were mainly young people, students perhaps, chatting into their mobile phones or listening to music on the headphones clamped to their ears. They didn't seem to notice the bus going over the humpback bridge as it crossed the river. There had been a time when all the passengers would exclaim as they felt their stomachs lift with the bus. Now, she supposed, it was nothing compared to the theme park rides that were so popular. Everything was so much bigger and faster.

Hazel rang the bell just before her stop and, gathering up her bags, she got off the bus, pausing only to thank the driver.

And that was that. The end of an era.

The following Friday, Hazel caught the number 38 at the usual time and sat in her usual seat but this time the bus turned right at the new roundabout, then sped off along the smooth, straight road towards the Wood Estate where all the streets were named after trees. There was Ash Avenue, Sycamore Close and so on – but precious few real trees, noticed Hazel.

The bus picked up a number of passengers but none of them were familiar faces and Hazel slipped into her own thoughts. Suddenly she felt a light tap on her shoulder.

"Hazel?"

She looked up in surprise at the woman sitting down next to her, recognition slowly dawning. "Good gracious! Lilian. How lovely to see you. It must be – how long?"

Lilian laughed. "Put it this way, probably the last time we met was when our boys left high school and I'm just off to buy David a fortieth birthday card. How's your Anthony?"

"Middle-aged."

They both chuckled and started to swap stories. They were still chatting away, when, all too soon, the bus pulled into the station.

"And I haven't heard half your news, yet," said Lilian.

"Nor I yours," agreed Hazel." She looked across at the café. "Have you got time for a coffee?"

As they sat at a table by the window, Lilian raised her cup: "Here's to the number 38 bus for bringing us together again. I vote we make this a regular event."

The new road may be straight, thought Hazel, but life was still full of twists and turns, thank goodness. "I'll drink to that," she said.

October 2005

Saturday
1

Sunday
2

Monday
3

Tuesday
4

Wednesday
5

Thursday
6

Friday
7

Saturday
8

Sunday
9

Monday
10

Tuesday
11

Wednesday
12

Thursday
13

Friday
14

Saturday
15

Sunday
16

Monday
17

Tuesday
18

Wednesday
19

Thursday
20

Friday
21

Saturday
22

Sunday **23**	Thursday **27**
Monday **24**	Friday **28** November **Yours** on sale
Tuesday **25**	Saturday **29**
Wednesday **26**	Sunday **30** British Summer Time ends, clocks go back
	Monday **31** Hallowe'en

IT HAPPENED THIS MONTH

4 October, 1957
The Soviet Union launched the Sputnik

8 October, 1959
The American tenor Mario Lanza died in Rome at the age of 38

12 October, 1915
Nurse Edith Cavell was executed by the Germans

15 October, 1928
The Graf Zeppelin airship completed its first transatlantic flight

22 October, 1811
Franz Liszt, composer and pianist, was born in Hungary

24 October, 1950
Errol Flynn married his third wife Patricia Wymore in Monaco

30 October, 1974
Muhammad Ali defeated George Foreman in seven rounds at Kinshasa in Zaïre

26 October, 1951
Clement Attlee resigned as Prime Minister after Labour was defeated in the General Election

28 October, 1965
The death penalty for murder was abolished in Britain

PIC REX FEATURES

FIREWOOD VERSE

Beechwood fires are bright and clear
If the logs are kept a year.
Chestnut's only good they say,
If for long 'tis laid away.
Make a fire of Elder tree
Death within your house shall be
But Ash new or Ash old
Is fit for a queen with crown of gold.

Birch and fir logs burn too fast
Blaze up bright and do not last.
It is by the Irish said
Hawthorn bakes the sweetest bread.
Elm wood burns like churchyard mould,
E'en the very flames are cold.
But Ash green or Ash brown
Is fit for a queen with a golden crown.

Poplar gives a bitter smoke,
Fills your eyes and makes you choke.
Apple wood will scent your room
With an incense like perfume.
Oaken logs, if dry and old
Keep away the winter's cold.
But Ash wet or Ash dry
A king shall warm his slippers by.

Anon

October 3-9

Great garden idea

Leaf mould is great for your borders and is easy to make. Gather up the leaves and place them in dustbin bags. Once the bags are full, tie them at the top then pierce them several times so that air can penetrate. Leave the bags in a corner of the garden and after a year or so you should have crumbly compost. Avoid adding large quantities of leaves to the compost as they take a long time to rot down.

Oh, happy day!

After being housebound with agoraphobia, Ann Macnaughtan of Dunbartonshire visited Niagara Falls

Did you know Niagara Falls are slap bang in the middle of a town? For many years I thought they were somewhere in an African jungle! When we were on the Canadian side, wearing our blue bin liners, I saw a long line of people in yellow bin liners snaking their way down the cliff. "I want to do that!" I said. And we did.

We went down in a lift; a group of total strangers trying to pretend we did not look completely ridiculous. We followed the guide up the walkway, through the mist of the falls, grasping the slimy wooden handrail and scrabbling to stay on our feet as we scrambled upwards.

Clinging to the rail for dear life, I raised my eyes and saw the sign 'Hurricane Deck'. The water thundered down on top of us; we laughed uproariously as we got soaked and battered. We hugged, and thrilled at the most amazing piece of serendipity ever to come our way.

There's no law that says middle-aged people can't experience the thrill of a lifetime – and that was it for me!

 ## Let's get cooking!

Bramley Apple and Sage Toad-in-the-hole
(Serves 4)
- 8 pork sausages
- 2 tablespoons (30 ml) vegetable oil
- 4 oz (100 g) plain flour
- Pinch of salt
- 1 teaspoon (5 ml) dried sage
- 3 large eggs
- 7 fl oz (200 ml) milk
- 12 oz (350 g) Bramley apples, peeled, cored and cut into wedges
- Onion gravy, to serve

1 Preheat the oven to Gas Mark 7, 220°C, 425°F. Place the sausages and oil in a large roasting pan and bake for 5 minutes.
2 Meanwhile, sift the flour and salt into a large bowl.
3 Add the sage and eggs and beat with an electric whisk until smooth. Gradually beat in the milk to make a smooth batter.
4 Remove the roasting pan from the oven, add the apples and stir well. Pour the batter into the hot pan.
5 Bake for 25-30 minutes until the batter is risen, golden and crisp.
6 Serve hot with onion gravy.

RECIPE COURTESY OF THE BRAMLEY APPLE INFORMATION SERVICE

OLD-FASHIONED CLEANING REMEDY

A few drops of baby oil on scrunched-up kitchen paper restores the shine to stainless steel hobs and ovens.
Mona Sharpe, Isle of Man

A nice little earner

Mr W J Fitzgerald of Skelmersdale gave the local chemist a helping hand

Behind our house was a row of shops and one day a posh car pulled up outside the chemist and a man started to unload the boot. I went over and asked if he wanted any help. When we finished unloading the car he gave me 6d. I offered to help other suppliers unloading goods and also went into the shops to ask for jobs, usually tidying up the yards and stacking boxes.

After a few weeks, the chemist gave me a job on odd days washing the used medicine bottles, Eventually, he allowed me to weigh the cough candy (while whistling to stop me eating it). After school I delivered medicine to houses on my bicycle. For my first week's work he offered me five shillings or a Coronation crown. I decided to take the crown and gave it to my mother.

Senior moment

When I took my elderly mother her cup of tea in bed one morning, I found that she had put her teeth on the bedside table and her watch in the glass of water!

Mrs M Hopley, Redruth

My pet

Chanel is a devoted cat. When her owner, Mrs M Quent of Farnborough, was ill and unconscious for two days, Chanel didn't leave her side – even to eat.

Here's health

Stay in touch with your pals

Keeping in touch with your friends is beneficial to your health. Researchers in California who spent seven years studying men and women in their 70s found that those who had the most demanding friendships had better mental function. Other studies have revealed – surprisingly – that people with lots of friends are less likely to catch colds and flu than those who lead more isolated lives. So get on the phone and arrange to meet for a chat very soon…

MY PRAYER

Another day draws to its end.
To the Lord my prayers I send.
I thank Him for giving me today,
For guiding me along life's way.

I pray the night be quiet and calm,
For Him to keep me free from harm.
That the day to come will bring peace.
For all worldly ills to cease.

When day breaks fresh and new
I thank Him for the morning dew.
Welcome its newness like a bird,
I thank the Lord, my prayers he heard.
                                    Josie Rawson, Selston

Top tip

If you have bought a new hot water bottle, add a few drops of glycerine when filling it for the first time. This will keep the rubber supple for longer.
Roy Maddox, Hinckley

October 10-16

Great garden idea

A small shrub will fill a large gap in a border much more quickly if you layer the outside stems into the surrounding soil. Bend down vigorous young branches of shrubs such as cornus or rhododendrons until they touch the soil and make a slanting cut in the underside. Then peg down the branches with wire loops.

My pet

If Mr Charlie has a resigned look on his face it's because he knows when Chloe gets her mitts on him there isn't much he can do about it, according to Chloe's granddad, Adrian Williams of Swansea. The dog gets a hug, like it or not!

MY PRAYER

*Whenever I am troubled
Or lost in deep despair,
I bundle all my troubles up
And go to God in prayer.*

*I tell him I am heartsick,
Lost and lonely, too,
That my mind is deeply burdened
And I don't know what to do.*

*But I know He stilled the tempest
And calmed the angry sea,
So I humbly ask if, in his love,
He'll do the same for me.*

*Then I just keep quiet
And think only thoughts of peace,
And if I abide in stillness,
My restless murmurings cease.*
   Mary Cox (no address supplied)

OLD-FASHIONED CLEANING REMEDY

Try rubbing badly scuffed leather shoes with a piece of raw potato before polishing.

Wit and wisdom

He had decided to live forever or die in the attempt.
   Joseph Heller (1923-1999)

Remember the '60s?

A return to the office worked wonders for Jean Kennett of Crediton

Towards the end of the decade, the Government was making urgent requests for married women to return to the workplace. Family finances were at an all-time low so, when the youngest was established at school I returned, in fear and trepidation, to work after an absence of 15 years.

My life was transformed as I once again became 'me' instead of someone else's wife or mother.

Little had changed during the years I had been away; manual typewriters, carbon paper and shorthand were still the order of the day. Things were becoming more casual, though, and almost everyone was addressed by their Christian names, making for a friendlier atmosphere. I was fortunate to return when I did – had I been confronted with computers, fax and e-mail all at once, I doubt I could have coped.

Make a difference - volunteer!

Just 'awalkin' the dawg'

We all know that walking is the best exercise but setting off for a solitary stroll is not an exciting prospect. What better companion than a dog that would not otherwise have the chance of a good run in the fresh air? If you don't have a pooch of your own, you can volunteer to be a dog walker for someone who does not have the time or is too infirm to take their pet out themselves. And rescue centres don't always have enough staff to ensure the dogs in their care are taken out regularly.

◆ **Place a card advertising your dog-walking service in your local shop or in the free ads column of your local newspaper. Or contact the RSPCA, the Blue Cross or Wood Green Animal Centres in your area (look under Animal Welfare Societies in the Yellow Pages). You could gain some extra pocket money as well as the health benefits!**

 Let's get cooking!

Baked Pear Tart

- ◆ 4 sheets 12 in x 7 in (30 cm x 17½ cm) filo pastry
- ◆ ½ oz (15 g) low fat spread
- ◆ 3 firm Comice pears
- ◆ 1 teaspoon (5 ml) lemon juice
- ◆ 3 tablespoons (45 ml) runny honey
- ◆ 1 tablespoon (15 ml) grated lemon rind
- ◆ 1 tablespoon (15 ml) demerara sugar

1 Preheat the oven to Gas Mark 6, 200°C, 400°F. Place a pastry sheet on a 13 in x 9 in (33 cm x 23 cm) non-stick baking sheet.
2 Melt the low fat spread in a saucepan and brush the sheet with it. Put a second sheet on top and brush again. Repeat this process twice more.
3 Halve and quarter the pears and remove the cores. Slice each quarter into 3 and toss in a bowl with the lemon juice. Arrange the slices over the pastry sheets.
4 Mix 1 tablespoon (15 ml) of the honey with grated lemon rind. Drizzle it over the pears, sprinkle with the sugar and cook for 30 minutes. Lift out on to a wire rack as soon as possible so the pastry doesn't soften.
5 To serve, drizzle with the remaining honey.

RECIPE COURTESY OF SLIMMING MAGAZINE

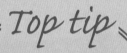 Top tip

When taking curtains down to wash, mark the position of each hook on the curtain tape with a felt tip pen. Replacing the hooks afterwards will be much easier.
Ruby Ainsworth, Wakefield

It makes me smile

I spotted this advert in our local paper: 'Beautiful lady's contemporary ring, 18 cwt white gold with 2 small diamonds. Never worn'.
Audrey Bruce, Banff

Here's health

Do you suffer from winter blues?

Seasonal Affective Disorder (SAD) usually starts between September and November and continues until March or April. Symptoms include difficulty in staying awake, fatigue and lethargy, mood swings, loss of libido, overeating, anxiety, irritability, loss of self esteem and feelings of misery. The diagnosis is only made if people have suffered the same symptoms for three consecutive years. Light therapy is an extremely effective treatment. *For more information, contact SAD Association, PO Box 989, Steyning BN44 3HG. Internet: www.sada.org.uk*

October 17-23

My first...

Ted Hay of London's first walk up the aisle was a rather uncomfortable one

I must have been six or seven when I was asked to do the honours as a page boy at a cousin's wedding. The dressmaker who was making the bridesmaids' dresses would also make a white satin suit for me to wear. Came the great day and I remember being praised after the service by numerous people for 'being such a good boy and standing so straight and still throughout the ceremony'. Little did they know that every time I moved even an inch something kept sticking in me, so I didn't have much choice but to remain motionless!

We eventually moved on to the wedding breakfast. As a member of the wedding party, I was seated at the top table but halfway through I could stand it no longer and left my seat to make my way to my mother, seated further down the hall. Having told her my tale of woe she took me into a side room and found the dressmaker had failed to remove a couple of the pins she'd used when making the suit!

I'm 84 and even after all these years I still wonder if those pins were left in by accident or design!

Let's get cooking!

Moroccan Pork Fillet

(Serves 1)
- 1 teaspoon (5 ml) cumin seeds
- ¹/₂ teaspoon (2.5 ml) all spice
- ¹/₂ teaspoon (2.5 ml) cinnamon
- ¹/₂ teaspoon (2.5 ml) dried mint
- 1 tablespoon (15 ml) oil
- 1 lean pork fillet
- Tabbouleh, cous cous or rice, to serve

1 Mix together the cumin seeds, all spice, cinnamon, dried mint and oil. Smear the mixture over the pork fillet until evenly coated.
2 Cook in a preheated oven, Gas Mark 4, 180°C, 350°F, for 25-30 minutes.
3 Serve thinly sliced on a bed of tabbouleh, cous cous or rice with a tomato and spring onion salad and a spicy tomato chutney or yoghurt dip.

RECIPE COURTESY OF THE BRITISH PORK EXECUTIVE

Top tip

When using glue for craftwork, remove it from your hands with a dusting of flour, then rub hands together and it will peel off easily.
Marjorie Hotston-Moore, Milborne Port

MY PRAYER

Do not look forward to what might happen tomorrow. The same everlasting Father who cares for you today will take care of you tomorrow, and everyday. Either He will shield you from suffering or He will give you unfailing strength to bear it. Be of peace then, and put aside all anxious thoughts and imaginings.

Florence Webb, Leigh on Sea

Make a difference - volunteer!

The children's charity

If you would like to make a difference to the lives of children like these homeless youngsters in Afghanistan, then Save the Children is the charity for you. The work the organisation does to help countless children living in poverty in the UK and around the world is made possible by the thousands of people who give their time to raise vital funds and publicise its efforts.

Whether you can spare an occasional hour or two days every week, your time could make a huge difference. There is no such thing as a 'typical' Save the Children volunteer; people from all walks of life can make a contribution. The charity has a variety of volunteering opportunities including campaigning on key issues, working in one of its high street shops, teaching school children about its work and taking part in local fundraising events.

◆ **To learn more about all these call 0845 606 4027. Internet: www.savethe children.org.uk/volunteer.**

Here's health

The all-too-common cold

By the age of 75, most of us have spent as much as two to three years of our lives suffering from the symptoms of the common cold. Keep colds at bay by:

◆ Boosting your immune system by eating a balanced diet that includes five portions of fruit and vegetables every day.
◆ Exercising every day – even a short walk boosts immunity by transporting the white cells that fight infections around the body.
◆ Taking a zinc supplement.
◆ Eating plenty of garlic which has antibacterial and antiviral properties.

Senior moment

On visiting the doctor's surgery, I asked the receptionist for an appointment for a 'ju flab'.
M Haslam, Sheffield

OLD-FASHIONED CLEANING REMEDY

Pour soda water on red wine spills before soaking in cool water then washing in the normal way.

Great garden idea

Autumn is an ideal planting time as the soil is still warm from the summer sun but moist so the roots can grow away happily. And it gives you something to look forward to enjoying next year. The climber clematis tangutica is a year-round delight with nodding yellow bells in late summer followed by silky seedheads which last all winter. It's simple to prune, just cull the stems within 6in (15cm) of the ground every spring.

My pet

Bonnie enjoys a nap after her walkies. She always stops and sits expectantly at the door of the local Post Office and has to be coaxed to carry on. Her owner Mrs D A E Armstrong of Nottingham says: "If I was allowed to draw my pension every time we pass that door, I'd be a very rich pensioner!"

October 24-30

MY PRAYER

O Lord, Thou knowest how busy I must be this day. If I forget Thee, do not Thou forget me.
Anne McCallum, Lymm

Great garden idea

Don't let gardening become a chore

◆ Instead of struggling to lift heavy bags of compost, borrow one of your grandchildren's skateboards and use this instead.

◆ When weeding use a kneeling stool, not a mat. A stool has handles on the sides which make getting up and down easier.

◆ Use ratchet secateurs when pruning large stems as these are easier to grip.

My pet

Ben is a very laid back cat, says his owner, Maggie Watson of Dunstable, who reckons he is thinking 'What's all this activity for? Chill out!"

Here's health

Seeds can stop you feeling seedy

Don't throw away the seeds from the Hallowe'en pumpkin; they are a rich source of iron which is vital for healthy red blood cells. If you don't have enough iron you could suffer from anaemia and end up feeling permanently tired and lethargic. Iron is also found in leafy green vegetables, red meat, dried apricots and cherries.

Top tip

Peel and grate a piece of fresh root ginger. Stir into a small jar of runny honey. Spread on buttered toast for breakfast, or put a spoonful on your porridge. I've not had a cold for the past five years since taking this every morning from October to March.
Pam Collins, Truro

OLD-FASHIONED CLEANING REMEDY

To clean small items of silver, dip them in a pan of simmering water that contains a piece of aluminium foil and two teaspoons of washing soda. Dry carefully before polishing with a soft cloth.

Make a difference - volunteer!

Preserving the rural scene

For 75 years the Campaign for the Preservation of Rural England (CPRE) has been working to protect the beauty, tranquillity and diversity of the country. Its 50,000 members live in towns as well as villages and the countryside. If you are concerned about issues such as the effect on the landscape of new roads and traffic growth, the quality of housing development or the future of farming, then the CPRE would be glad of your voluntary help. Other issues that the charity campaigns on are water resources, coasts, waste, tourism and energy.

◆ **The CPRE has a branch in every county and volunteers are needed for all types of work from stuffing envelopes to organising fundraising events. Write to CPRE, 128 Southwark Street, London SE1 0SW. Tel: 020 7981 2800. Internet: www.cpre.org.uk**

Every picture tells a story

This is my mother-in-law and me proudly cleaning the Austin Seven that my husband and I bought in 1947. What a difference to the cars of today! It had a starting handle on the front and indicators on the side that came out when you wanted to turn right or left. A policeman would control the traffic at busy times and if you wanted to go straight forward at a junction, the driver put his hand on the windscreen.

I never actually drove the car as I used to ride a bicycle. After my husband passed away in his fifties, my sons persuaded me to ride a moped. I learned on an RAC training scheme along with many young lads learning to ride their motorobikes!

I did eventually have driving lessons and passed my test on my fourth attempt. I currently drive a Vauxhall Corsa – a far cry from the Austin Seven!

Mrs D Willis, Southampton

It makes me smile

A former school friend bumped into me in the street and said: "I can never remember whether it was you or your brother who died."

F Bourne, Birmingham

 Let's get cooking!

Moroccan Roasted Vegetables with a Watercress Salad
(Serves 6)

For the vegetables:
- 1 teaspoon (5 ml) cumin seeds
- 1 teaspoon (5 ml) coriander seeds
- 1 teaspoon (5 ml) paprika
- 1 teaspoon (5 ml) coarsely ground pepper
- 20 g pack fresh mint, chopped
- 20 g pack fresh coriander, chopped
- 3 tablespoons (45 ml) olive oil
- Finely grated zest and juice of 2 lemons
- 12 oz (350 g) cauliflower, broken into florets.
- 3 carrots, peeled and cut into batons
- 3 small courgettes, cut into batons
- 2 leeks, cut in half lengthways, then each half into 10 pieces

For the watercress salad:
- 1 x 85 g bag watercress
- 1/2 red onion, peeled and thinly sliced
- 1 tablespoon (5 ml) salt
- 14 oz (400 g) can chickpeas, drained and rinsed
- Salt and freshly ground black pepper
- 7oz (200 g) carton Greek yoghurt, to serve

1 Preheat the oven to Gas Mark 6, 200°C, 400°F. For the spice mix, dry roast the cumin and coriander seeds in a small frying pan for 2-3 minutes, shaking the pan occasionally. Tip into a food processor with the paprika and pepper, half the mint, half the coriander, olive oil, lemon zest and half the juice, and blend.

2 Put the vegetables in a roasting pan and spoon over the spice mix. Stir to coat all the vegetables. Pour 1/2 in (1.2 cm) water into the base of the pan, cover tightly with foil and roast for 30 minutes. Remove foil and cook for a further 30-45 minutes.

3 Place the red onion in a small bowl and sprinkle with the salt and enough water to cover. Set aside for 30 minutes. Drain and rinse under cold running water. Put in a bowl with the chickpeas, the remaining herbs and lemon juice and seasoning. Mix well.

4 Serve the vegetables topped with the salad and a spoonful of yoghurt.

RECIPE COURTESY OF THE WATERCRESS ALLIANCE

A Walk in the Wild
Protecting Squirrel Nutkin

PIC: JIM WILSON PHOTOGRAPHY

Scotland is the place to see the rare red squirrel

It is believed that 160,000 red squirrels live in Great Britain and three quarters of these live in Scotland with South Scotland being one of its few remaining strongholds.

The numbers declined during the 20th century for a number of reasons that include tree clearances and outbreaks of two fatal diseases. But the major factor was the introduction of the grey squirrel towards the end of the 19th century. Aggression from the larger grey squirrel was originally blamed for the decline of the reds but research has found the competition for food to be the main factor. The grey squirrel has the advantage of being able to digest large seeds from broadleaved trees more efficiently. The poulation of grey squirrels in Britain today is estimated to be around three million.

During the breeding season, which starts in January, squirrels can be seen leaping from tree to tree and running around the trunks in mating chases.

Females can have spring and summer litters, producing three young (called kittens) on average. Their survival rate is affected by the severity of their first winter with as many as 85 per cent perishing as a result of cold weather. In autumn, they gather and store caches of nuts and cones ready for winter although they do not hibernate. However, during very cold or wet weather they remain in their homes (called dreys).

Red squirrels have fur that ranges from blonde or pale orange through reddish-brown to almost black with ear tufts and bushy tails which may bleach lighter in the warmer months of the year. They use their tails for balance, and double-jointed ankles and long claws help them to hold on when running up and down trees.

To learn more, contact Red Squirrels in South Scotland conservation officer Zoe Smolka, tel: 01387 860442. Internet: www.red-squirrels.org.uk

WARTIME WEDDINGS
Our honeymoon hotel hit by storm

The boys in blue were not too welcome when Mrs Brook of Wakefield honeymooned in Blackpool

In 1943 I was posted from a bomber station to Station X in Bletchley where I first met my husband to be, Eddie. In October 1945 he was given embarkation leave and we decided to get married before he went. Eddie went to Yorkshire to get a special licence and I stayed in London to get written permission from my father.

All the arrangements were a seven days' wonder, achieved with help from good friends. We were very, very lucky – our best man got leave for a few days and so

did my sister (who was a WAAF with me at Station X) so I had a bridesmaid. Miraculously, my brother who was in the throes of going abroad got permission to come.

Due to coupons etc at the time we only had about five presents; sheets, towels, blankets and a carving knife set I still have in use 58 years after. We had a few days honeymoon in Blackpool. We walked for hours with our wedding certificate in a pocket to find a room. Finally, we found a hotel where two

RAF officers had just gone back off leave. Then the fun started – about one-thirty in the morning the chimney fell in due to a bad storm. And a couple of hours after that the RAF boys were back for their luggage, left under the bed!

Cryptic crossword

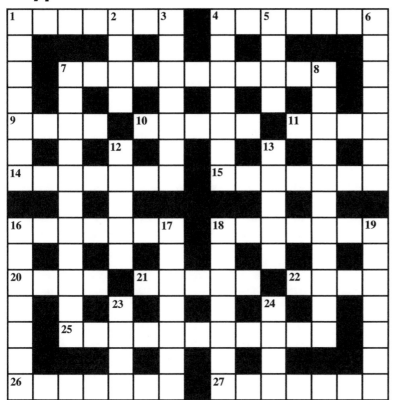

Across

1 No lunatic in charge, lacking a home? (7)
4 Brusque, stale applause (7)
7 Visit former partition in Berlin, and collapse? (2, 2, 3, 4)
9 Archbishop heard couple twice over? (4)
10 Chap compiling X-File? (5)
11 Girl embraced by man, naturally (4)
14 Film shows baseball player, we've heard (7)
15 Expression from stern expert (7)
16 Totally destroy the star, possibly (7)
18 Del Boy's runner? (7)
20 Suffer each change (4)
21 Actor's prize found in Ordnance Survey vehicle (5)

22 Two American soldiers in a movie (4)
25 Relax before speech reconstruction (11)
26 Shropshire town — left, perhaps, on ring road (7)
27 Old Reg's reformed those who pay the rent (7)

Down

1 Unspecified number on street work without a pause (7)
2 Fruit for a special day? (4)
3 Middle-of-the-road reflective sort? (7)
4 Space for the first performance (7)
5 After this panic, Jack gets a biscuit (4)
6 Turn aside from French version of Evita (7)

7 Intruder charges rate that's unacceptable (4-7)
8 Northerner destroyed rats in canal (11)
12 Leave England first? Absolutely! (5)
13 Grieving lady – wow! – is hiding identity (5)
16 Source of obscurity, in the main (3-4)
17 Ponders, possibly, how to react? (7)
18 Heavy toil, finding a path round the V&A (7)
19 Our bad form over in America is contributing towards one's downfall (7)
23 Foreign capital needed? Here's some escudos, love (4)
24 Sounds like 21 Across is reckless (4)

Reader article

Watch out, there's a postie about!

From soggy letters to cheques going up in smoke,
Francis Forrest remembers his years as a village postman

Forty-six years ago I applied for the job as a village postman in Earby, Lancashire, which boosted my income by a whole £1 a week!

I spent the first four years working in a tiny sorting office at the rear of Earby's Sub Post Office, with only four of us to cover a considerable area.

One of these was Bill, a part-timer who did the rural bit and a nearby small town. He had his arduous walk well organised, and for several years a black whippet dog – who Bill christened Blackie – used to wait for him every morning and accompany him on his round. Blackie was a great one for catching rabbits and there was many a free rabbit pie.

I can still see Bill now in his wellies, his pipe going full blast, and Blackie as ever following close to heel.

Joe, Eric and I did the rest of Earby on foot, rotating three walks and changing over each Monday. Between first and second deliveries we had to look sharp to deliver parcels, hopping on our bikes. We tied the heavy parcels round our necks with strong post office string – rather a hazardous practice, as you can imagine! At that time Earby had many thriving small shops which received lots of parcels every day. People ran catalogue clubs and I'm sure we weren't safe with all that weight on board.

Nevertheless I can't remember any of us having a serious crash or knocking anyone down, and the police always turned a blind eye to our perilous (and rather wobbly!) shenanigans, which made the job easier.

During the second delivery we did the collections from the town boxes. At one time these were sent to the main office by train but Dr Beeching put a stop to that by closing the line. From then on the mailbag was chained to the platform of a Ribble bus and collected by a postman with a duplicate key at Colne's main Post Office. We never dare miss that bus - there would have been hell to pay if we had.

Christmas was a very busy time for us, of course. No one posted their own cards by hand and the boxes used to take up to 20 minutes to empty, they were that jammed solid with Christmas cards. Each of us postmen had two students working for us. We sorted and packed their bags and they had the unenviable task of delivery but we always tried to send them out as light as possible.

There's many a memory of my years as a postman which brings a smile to my lips even now. I once asked a lady to take in a parcel for a neighbour, and she wasn't at all keen. "Oh, we don't speak," she declared, "she only ever bares her fangs."

One winter's day I pushed a

ILLUSTRATION:CARTOONLINE.CO.UK

letter through large letterbox and it bounced right back at me. Peering through the aperture I saw there was a large icicle plum centre. A very frosty reception indeed at that home, I reflected.

Whizzing a letter through a box on a glass door, my heart sank along with the mail as I watched the letter land in a bucket of water left to water the plants. I rang the door bell, confessed, and the householder retrieved the wet letter. Worse still, I'd delivered the letter to the wrong address. It was meant for next door – a double clanger, you might say.

One day I met the district nurse who appeared to be suffering with her back. "How did you come by it?" I asked. "Gardening at the weekend?" "Oh no," she said, "believe it or not I was helping an old man on with his underpants when I pulled a bit too hard."

The Catholic priest was faced one day with a hefty surcharge fee of £5, his cry of, 'Oh my God,' was very appropriate in his case but he still had to cough up.

Animals, too, could have their moments. Calling at a farm one wet and windy day in winter, I spotted the poor old sheep dog looking very miserable as he braved the elements. Sat in the old dog's kennel was a big fat cat, looking very comfy indeed.

One of our rural postmen was going up a short farm track when he saw a rabbit with its head stuck in a hole in a dry stone wall. It appeared to be having trouble getting free. On his way back, he stopped to pull the bunny out of the hole, and to his amazement, he found a weasel attached to the rabbit. It had killed the creature and was trying to pull it through the wall.

One postie told us of being invited into a rather scruffy house for a brew, the owner of which had 13 cats. She made him a slice of toast, then swiped a cat off the table with the buttered side of the toast.

Early morning starts can also bring strange happenings. A colleague was on his way to work at 5.30am when he spotted a small boy of about three walking a dog. Apparently his mum had taken some sleeping pills, had left the key in the door and young McNabs decided on an early morning stroll with his pet. A good job our man knew where he lived!

There used to be a blacksmiths in Earby and once a postie in a hurry flung in a letter, hoping for the best. Unfortunately, it went into the forge and it was months before they found it had contained a £20 cheque.

I remember one morning having a struggle to attract the attention of an old man who was hard of hearing. "You didn't ring the bell," he said. "What's the use when you can't hear?" I said. "Ah well, when you ring the bell, the dog barks and I see its jaws moving, so I know there's someone at the door." And this was long before the days of hearing dogs for the deaf.

After four idyllic years at our small Sub Post Office, we were transferred to the bigger office at nearby Barnoldswick and things were never the same. Vans replaced bikes and Land Rovers took over the rural delivery.

I've been retired now for 14 years but those 32 years and 240 days are still fresh in my memory – some bad, some good but none ever boring!

November 2005

Tuesday

1

All Saints' Day

Wednesday

2

Thursday

3

Friday

4

Saturday

5

Bonfire Night

Sunday

6

Monday

7

Tuesday

8

Wednesday

9

Thursday

10

Friday

11

Saturday

12

Sunday

13

Remembrance Sunday

Monday

14

Tuesday

15

Wednesday

16

Thursday

17

Friday

18

Saturday

19

Sunday

20

Monday

21

Tuesday

22

Wednesday
23

Thursday
24

Friday
25

December **Yours** on sale

Saturday
26

Sunday
27

Advent Sunday

Monday
28

Tuesday
29

Order **Yours** subscriptions now for Christmas

Wednesday
30

St Andrew's Day

FLANDERS FIELDS

In Flanders fields the poppies blow
Between the crosses, row on row,
That mark our place; and in the sky
The larks, still bravely singing, fly
Scarce heard amid the guns below.

We are the Dead. Short days ago
We lived, felt dawn, saw sunset glow,
Loved and were loved, and now we lie
In Flanders fields.

Take up our quarrel with the foe:
To you from failing hands we throw
The torch; be yours to hold it high.
If ye break faith with us who die
We shall not sleep, though poppies grow
In Flanders fields.

John McRae

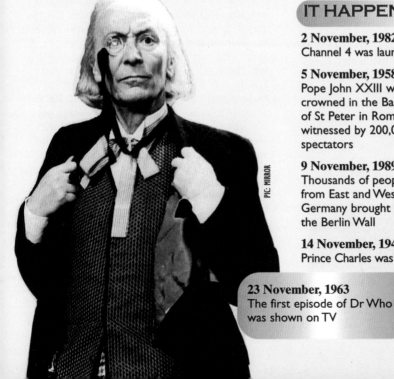

PIC: MIRROR

IT HAPPENED THIS MONTH

2 November, 1982
Channel 4 was launched

5 November, 1958
Pope John XXIII was
crowned in the Basilica
of St Peter in Rome
witnessed by 200,000
spectators

9 November, 1989
Thousands of people
from East and West
Germany brought down
the Berlin Wall

14 November, 1948
Prince Charles was born

23 November, 1963
The first episode of Dr Who
was shown on TV

16 November, 1959
The Sound of Music
opened on Broadway in
New York

22 November, 1497
Vasco da Gama rounded
the Cape of Good Hope

25 November, 1952
First performance of
Agatha Christie's The
Mousetrap at the
Ambassadors theatre

28 November, 1919
Nancy, Lady Astor,
became Britain's first
woman MP

30 November, 1936
The Crystal Palace in
Sydenham was
destroyed by fire

Great garden idea

Grow cress on your windowsill all year round. Cress is ready to harvest in little more than a week, tastes a great deal better than the cress from a supermarket and can even be grown on wet tissue paper.

Oh, happy day!

Stuart and Ann Henderson will never forget the Thanksgiving Day they spent with their grandson Thomas

As Ann had always wanted to visit the French Quarter of New Orleans our son Michael had booked us all into the Ritz Carlton hotel for the Thanksgiving holiday. The hotel was fabulous and the Thanksgiving Day buffet was fantastic. There was literally any dish you could think of; oriental and western with, of course, the roast turkey carveries taking main place. There was a running chocolate fountain into which you could dip fresh strawberries or marshmallows. In true New Orleans fashion a tuxedo-clad quartet played jazz to entertain the diners. Thomas was fascinated by the bass player and, as we stood close beside the band, the musician acknowledged his interest.

After the meal we walked round the French Quarter and got caught in a tremendous cloudburst but it didn't dampen our spirits. A marvellous day!

Let's get cooking!

Spicy Roast Lamb

◆ 3 lb (1.4 g) half leg of lamb
◆ 1 teaspoon (5 ml) ground cumin
◆ 1 teaspoon (5 ml) ground coriander
◆ 1 teaspoon (5 ml) ground turmeric
◆ ½ pint (275 ml) low fat plain yoghurt
◆ 1 cinnamon stick
◆ 5 pieces star anise
◆ 5 cardamom pods
◆ 10 oz (275 g) basmati rice
◆ pinch ground turmeric
◆ 3 ripe tomatoes, chopped
◆ 5 oz (150 g) cucumber, finely chopped

1 Trim the fat from the lamb and make deep slits into the meat. Place in a non-metal dish. Mix the cumin, coriander and turmeric in a bowl, stir in the yoghurt and season.
2 Spread the marinade over the meat, pushing it into the cuts. Cover and marinate for at least four hours.
3 Preheat the oven to Gas Mark 4, 180°C, 350°F. Transfer the meat to a roasting pan. Break the cinnamon into pieces and place on top of the lamb with the star anise. Crush the cardamom seeds and scatter over. Loosely cover with foil and cook for 1½ hours.
4 Remove the foil and baste. Return to the oven and cook for a further 20 minutes.
5 Rinse the rice and place in a saucepan. Add cold water to cover by 1 in (2.5 cm). Sprinkle in the pinch of turmeric and some salt. Bring to the boil and stir once. Reduce the heat to simmer, cover, and cook for 15 minutes.
6 Allow the lamb to stand for five minutes before carving. Serve with the rice and bowls of chopped tomato and cucumber.

RECIPE COURTESY OF SLIMMING MAGAZINE

A nice little earner

Mrs W Gelder of Great Clacton trudged many a mile for money to spend on sweeties.

In the 1920s we lived in a farm cottage away in the country; no transport in those days and winters were very bad. I earned my pocket money each day by walking a third of a mile to the farm for a pint of milk (in a can) before I went to school. I got 3d a week for that and another 3d for cleaning shoes and boots or going into the village when I left school at four o' clock for something my mother wanted. It was one and a half miles each way to school. If I cleaned the doorstep I got another 2d. We could buy two gobstoppers or two liquorice sticks for a penny.

Top tip

Keep a small piece of damp sponge handy when ironing. Rub sponge over dry creases and clothes will be evenly dampened.
Mrs V Watson, Colchester

MY PRAYER

Give me the strength to meet each day with quiet will,
Give me the faith to know Thou art my shepherd still.
Give the light to find my way when shadows fall,
Be Thou my steady guiding star, Father of all.
Mrs V Roberts, Crediton

It makes me smile

When I was watching a TV programme, the tyre on the hero's car had a blow out. As he was bemoaning the fact that it would take him half-an-hour to fix it, I thought to myself: 'Oh, good, I've got time to go and make some toast'.
Molly Climo, Hockley

My pet

When Marion Clark of Morecambe had to take Ben out for a walk in the rain she had the brainwave of making him a mac out of an old green bin bag. People laughed when they saw the words 'Refuse Only' on his raincoat but it did the trick and Ben stayed nice and dry.

Here's health

Put some ginger in you
If you feel the cold during the chilly months of the year, try eating ginger to boost your circulation to warm your hands and feet. Drink natural ginger ale made from real ginger or make ginger tea with boiling water and grated ginger root. Try eating Indian or Chinese dishes flavoured with ginger.

OLD-FASHIONED CLEANING REMEDY

To remove fresh oil or grease stains from upholstery, sprinkle with talcum powder or cornflour. Rub well, and leave until the stain is absorbed. Brush off and wipe with a damp cloth.
Roy Maddox, Hinckley

November 7-13

Great garden idea

You can create a miniature woodland area in your garden by using a multi-stemmed tree such as a silver birch. The white bark looks lovely all year round and its light canopy means you can easily grow plants beneath it. Plant bulbs in the grass beneath for spring and relax in the dappled shade on a sunny summer's day.

Wit and wisdom

Well, if I called the wrong number, why did you answer the phone?

James Thurber
(1894-1961)

My pet

What better way to clean up after a muddy walk? The star of this kitchen sink drama is Cindy, an American cocker spaniel who lives with Mrs P Corbishley of Minehead.

MY PRAYER

I am home in heaven, dear ones;
Oh, so happy and so bright!
There is perfect joy and beauty
In this everlasting light.

Did you wonder I so calmly
Trod the valley of the shade?
Oh! But Jesus' love illumined
Every dark and fearful glade.

Then you must not grieve so sorely,
For I love you dearly still:
Try to look beyond earth's shadows,
Pray to trust our Father's will.

There is work still waiting for you,
So you must not idly stand;
Do it now, while life remaineth –
You shall rest in Jesus' land.

When that work is all completed,
He will gently call you home;
Oh, the rapture of that meeting,
Oh, the joy to see you home!

Maggie Kalli, Bognor Regis

Make a difference - volunteer!

The British Legion needs you

The British Legion values its volunteers for the enthusiasm and human touch which they bring to the work they do – and this is never more evident than at this time of the year when the Poppy Appeal is in full swing. But standing on street corners in all weathers collecting money from passers by is only one aspect of working for the British Legion. Its volunteer case workers perform a range of tasks from supporting homeless ex-service people to giving advice and assistance in claiming state benefits. Fundraising volunteers give up their time to take part in the many fundraising events the British Legion organises throughout the year such as the annual Poppy Walk.

◆ **If you would like to make a contribution to any of these the contact numbers are Poppy Appeal (tel: 01622 717172), Volunteer Caseworkers (tel: 08457 725 725), Fundraising Volunteers (tel: 020 7973 7276). Internet: www.britishlegion.org.uk**

Remember the '60s?

A reader (name and address supplied) recalls a foggy night in London town

In the early Sixties, I was a motorcyclist (well, a 'scooterist'). I remember driving carefully home in a real pea-souper via Regent's Park from County Hall where I worked as a junior clerk and realising there was a whole train of cars following me. A motorcyclist, with no windscreen to obscure vision, can see marginally better in fog than a car-driver can, and they were all desperately following my tail-light. I do hope they had been intending to go the way I was going – I shudder to think what happened to them all when I turned off towards Belsize Village and left them to struggle on!

Top tip

To prevent sofas and chairs from marking a wall, fix thick strips of draught excluder to the back.

K Croft, Hayling Island

It makes me smile

I wanted a calendar with space for birthdays, appointments etc so I asked the assistant for a family planning calendar. She laughed and said: "You have left it a bit late!"

Iris Ewen, Epsom

Here's health

Eyes down, brain alert

Fancy a night out? Have a bit of a flutter and keep your brain alert by going for a game of bingo. Experts reckon bingo stimulates the little grey cells because you need to concentrate on doing several things at once. Listening and checking numbers requires rapid hand and eye co-ordination. Then there's the adrenaline rush when you win – clickety click!

 Let's get cooking!

Bramley Apple Crumble Pies
(Makes 6)

- 1 x 1 lb 2 oz (500 g) pack ready-made sweet shortcrust pastry
- 2 tablespoons (30 g) plain flour
- 2 tablespoons (30 g) ground almonds
- 1 lb (450 g) Bramley apples, peeled, cored and sliced
- 3 oz (75 g) caster sugar
- 1 teaspoon (5 ml) ground cinnamon
- 1 oz (25 g) flaked almonds
- Single cream, to serve

1 Preheat the oven to Gas Mark 6, 200°C, 400°F. Coarsely grate the pastry into a large bowl, add the flour and almonds and toss to mix.
2 Divide three quarters of the mixture between the six holes in a deep muffin tin, using your fingers to press the mixture over the base and up the sides.
3 Toss the apple slices in the sugar and cinnamon, then divide the filling between each of the pies.
4 Mix the flaked almonds with the remaining pastry mixture, then scatter on top of the apple. Bake for 20-25 minutes until the pastry is golden and crisp.
5 Serve warm with cream.

RECIPE COURTESY OF THE BRAMLEY APPLE INFORMATION SERVICE

November 14-20

My first...

Priscilla Odell says her first married home was much loved

We decided to get married on 24 May 1975, so we spent the winter months flat-hunting – our savings were insufficient for a house. We found a solidly built first floor flat in Twickenham. The owner wanted a quick sale; it became a bargain at £10,500.

All our rooms opened off a central hall. The lounge was large, furnished at first with our sideboard, table and four chairs (cost: £136.40) plus my husband Bob's radiogram. An alcove had shelving; later we added a bookcase unit. A rented TV was our entertainment. With curtains – given by parents or homemade – the flat was cheerful.

The bathroom and kitchen were old-fashioned but functional. The kitchen had a balcony where we had window boxes. A clothes line ran across the rear yard to some tall trees; it was useable 7am to 7pm daily, except Sunday. We now live in a house in Hampton, on the estate we couldn't afford in 1975.

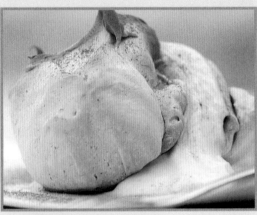

Let's get cooking!

Coffee Meringue Bites
(Makes 4)
- 2 medium egg whites
- 4 oz (100 g) caster sugar
- ½ teaspoon (2.5 ml) coffee powder
- 8 oz (225 g) reduced-fat fromage frais
- 1 teaspoon (5 ml) cocoa powder

1 Preheat the oven to Gas Mark 4, 180°C, 350°F. Whip the egg whites until stiff, then gradually whip in the sugar to form a glossy, stiff mixture. Fold in the coffee powder.
2 Drop 8 spoonfuls of the meringue mixture on to a sheet of non-stick baking paper and cook for 20 minutes.
3 Remove from the oven and cool on a wire rack. Sandwich the meringues together with the fromage frais. Dust with cocoa powder and serve.

RECIPE COURTESY OF SLIMMING MAGAZINE

My pet

When Beverley Holland of Halliwell was burgled during the night, her dog didn't even wake up but Felix the tomcat bounded upstairs and jumped on his sleeping owner, meowing to wake her up. Hearing the racket, the burglar fled!

Here's health

Don't dry out
Dry itchy skin is common in cold, windy weather. Protect your skin by moisturising daily and drinking lots of water to flush out the toxins. Eat foods such as potatoes, cashew nuts, pulses and avocado that are rich in vitamin B6. For vitamin A, eat carrots, broccoli, sweet potatoes, watercress and melon. The fatty acids found in nuts, seeds and oily fish are also of benefit.

Make a difference - volunteer!

Wide cross section at the Red Cross

Depending on your interests, you can volunteer for a whole range of activities with the British Red Cross. If you would like to be an emergency response volunteer, you will be trained to be a member of a team that provides practical and emotional support to people affected in major incidents. This includes support to the local ambulance service, in hospitals and A & E department. Less well known are activities such as the skin camouflage service which teaches individuals the simple techniques needed to apply creams effectively to cover or lessen the impact of disfiguring marks or skin conditions. An important part of this treatment is helping someone regain their confidence and self-esteem. The Red Cross also uses volunteers in its work to restore contact between close relatives who have been separated by war or natural disaster. Tracing & Message volunteers are still helping to find people who were separated by World War II.

◆ **Contact British Red Cross, 9 Grosvenor Crescent, London SW1X 7EJ. Tel: 020 7201 5454. Internet: www.redcross.org.uk**

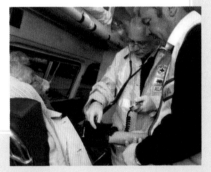

It makes me smile

Passing a cemetery in the car, my four-year-old grandson wanted to know what it was. To my husband's amusement, I replied: "It's where dead people live."
Joan Richardson, Hilton

Wit and wisdom

A critic is a man who knows the way but can't drive the car.
Kenneth Tynan (1927-1980)

OLD-FASHIONED CLEANING REMEDY

To prevent special occasion table linen from yellowing, wrap it in blue tissue paper when not in use.

Great garden idea

Improve a boring patio by lifting the odd slab and planting scented groundcover plants such as chamomile. Remove a slab adjacent to a wall and plant a climber and encourage it up a trellis (always secure a trellis on battens so the climber has room to twine its stems between it and the wall). If the wall needs to be painted, then hinge the trellis at the bottom so you can lower it down. Add texture by lifting other slabs as well and filling the space with gravel as this will soften the whole appearance.

MY PRAYER

Just trying your number, Lord,
To get the ding-aling-ling.
No answer on the line, Lord,
Just the ding-aling-ling!

First and foremost comes the answer now.
In faith, just ring the number,
He'll get the answer to you somehow.
Don't be put off by particulars not coming to review,
But give the Lord Jesus a chance to reply
And keep conversation with you.
Anne Hadley, Langley

November 21-27

 Let's get cooking!

Chicken Goulash

(Serves 4)

- ◆ A few sprays of one-calorie oil spray
- ◆ 1 medium onion, diced
- ◆ 1 red pepper, sliced into rings
- ◆ 1 yellow pepper, sliced into rings
- ◆ 2 garlic cloves, crushed
- ◆ 1 tablespoon (15 ml) ground paprika
- ◆ 4 x 5 oz (150 g) skinless chicken fillets
- ◆ ³/₄ pint (450 ml) hot chicken stock
- ◆ 2 tablespoons (30 ml) tomato purée
- ◆ 1¹/₂ lb (700 g) potatoes
- ◆ ¹/₂ oz (15 g) low-fat spread
- ◆ 2 tablespoons (30 ml) skimmed milk
- ◆ 4 oz (100 g) reduced-fat crème fraîche
- ◆ Thyme and ground paprika, to garnish

1. Spray a little oil into a non-stick pan and heat gently. Add the onion and fry, covered, for 10 minutes or until brown and soft. Add the peppers and garlic. Cook for 10 more minutes, adding a splash of water. Sprinkle in the paprika, and season.
2. Cut the chicken into large chunks. Spray another non-stick pan with oil and cook the chicken for 5 minutes. Transfer to the onion and pepper mixture. Add the stock and tomato purée and simmer for 20 minutes.
3. Meanwhile, peel the potatoes. Cook in lightly salted water for 20 minutes or until soft. Drain and mash with the low-fat spread and milk.
4. Stir the crème fraîche into the chicken goulash and season again, to taste.
5. Divide the potato between 4 plates and top with the chicken. Garnish with thyme and a pinch of paprika.

RECIPE COURTESY OF SLIMMING MAGAZINE

Every picture tells a story

As she was so beautiful and angelic we named our first baby Angela. She had a head of thick, dark brown hair and blue eyes. Her very proud nanny bought the pink floral dress she is wearing in this photo. I wish I could say she was always as quiet as her picture implies but she was a cry-baby and made us lose a lot of sleep. However, I never realised that one could feel such unconditional overwhelming love for a tiny human being. Over the years, we have had our ups and downs but I'm proud to say she has turned out to be a very courageous young woman as well as a loving, kind daughter. She was well worth all the tears, fears and heartaches.

Rosemary Medland, Letchworth

Here's health

Subduing the symptoms

There is still no cure for colds and flu but you can ease the symptoms by:

- ◆ Resting and drinking plenty of fluids (hot drinks are best).
- ◆ Sucking zinc lozenges for a sore throat
- ◆ Taking the herbal remedy Echinacea to boost white blood cell production.
- ◆ Eating citrus fruit or taking a high dose supplement to increase your intake of vitamin C.
- ◆ Use nasal decongestant for a blocked nose.

Make a difference - volunteer!

Oxfam for shopaholics

Oxfam was one of the first charity shops to be a familiar presence in the high street and in recent years it has been diversifying its presence with more than 60 specialist book shops, nine shops dedicated to music and ten specialising in home-ware and furniture. Oxfam sells many rare books and records and volunteers have become expert in spotting valuable items. These days it also has a retail presence at many of the summer music festivals like Glastonbury and WOMAD.

The charity's volunteering

manager Carolyn Myers says: "Anyone who can help us operate better as a retailing business is very welcome – from designing window displays to organising in-store events and handling the local media."

◆ **If working in a shop would not be your first choice, non-retail opportunities exist behind the scenes in areas such as marketing and public relations. Contact the Volunteering Team, Oxfam House, 274 Banbury Road, Oxford OX2 7DZ. Tel: 0845 300 0311. Internet: www.oxfam.org.uk**

Great garden idea

Winter is the time to carry out any structural work in your garden. Think about building a raised bed using railway sleepers. It saves a lot of bending and you will be able to see your flowers more easily. Raised beds are also ideal for growing vegetables, especially those with taps roots as it gives them a greater root run.

OLD-FASHIONED CLEANING REMEDY

A saucer of bath salts placed in a little-used cupboard will keep clothes fresh and prevent musty smells.

 MY PRAYER

Thank you, Lord, for being so kind. I pray to you, and I unwind. In our beautiful world there is so much stress so, to all suffering people, everywhere, please Lord, bless them with your tender care.

E Turton, Widnes

Top tip

Buy a reel of green garden wire, the flat sort that comes with a cutter, then you can cut off as much or as little as you need for sealing freezer bags.
Jean Godfrey, Coventry

Senior moment

I kept hearing a ringing noise so, thinking it might be tinnitus, I made an appointment to see my doctor. When my daughter came to see me, she said: "It's your smoke alarm - it needs a new battery!"
Mrs W Aldreg, Colchester

My pet

Flo Huck of Newcastle-upon-Tyne wrote this touching elegy for her Yorkshire terrier, Penny.
The house is so very quiet,
Quieter than I noticed before.
Everything is so very tidy,
No crumbs upon the floor.
Cushions stay in their proper place
And towels stay on the rail,
But, alas, no happy wagging tail,
No reason to walk down to the grass,
So I never see anyone pass.
Oh, what a lonely life
Without her demanding bark
And those four paws always at my side
In the daytime, or in the dark.
The pain inside is hard to stand;
Will it drift away, like quick sand?

A Walk in the Wild
Fewer bats in the belfry

You'd be lucky to catch sight of a bat flitting around at Hallowe'en

The sixteen species of UK bat range in size from the tiny pipistrelle, weighing just 4g, to the noctule, which can weigh up to 40g. Bats like to roost in habitats as varied as trees and caves to roof spaces and under soffit boards in modern houses. All UK bats are insect-eaters with large appetites – the pipistrelle can eat up to 3,000 midges in one night!

In 1991 the mouse-eared bat was declared extinct in the UK, the first mammal since the wolf 250 years earlier. Of the 16 bat species left, two are classed as endangered and nine threatened. Many of the roosting sites and feeding grounds which they need have been destroyed to make way for buildings and roads, or other changes in land use. Pesticides have not only killed many of their insect prey, but also some of the bats themselves.

Contrary to popular opinion, bats are not blind, but at night their ears are more important than their eyes. As they fly they make shouting sounds. The returning echoes give information about anything that is ahead of them, including the size and shape of an insect and which way it is going. This system of finding their prey is called echolocation. Most of these sounds are too high-pitched for humans to hear, but they can be heard with a special instrument called a bat detector.

Today there are fewer bats in the UK than ever before, so they are now protected by law. It is illegal to harm or disturb them without first seeking advice from your local Statutory Nature Conservation Organisation. The Bat Conservation Trust (BCT) is the national organisation which works to conserve bats and the places where they live. For more information call BCT's helpline on 0845 1300 228 or visit its website at www.bats.org.uk.

WARTIME WEDDINGS
Torn veil proved an omen

It was five years after her wedding day before Wyn Setters of Swindon started married life

We met in 1941 when my family moved to Brixton Hill after our house in Brixton was badly damaged in the bombing. Len lived quite near. We met and that was that. We got engaged, but at 19 years old he volunteered to join the army. After 12 weeks training, he got six days' embarkation leave and we wanted to marry.

We wanted a church wedding and all that went with it. Everything was borrowed. My sister-in-law had got married in June and offered me her dress; a few tucks were put in. Someone offered a long veil and someone offered white shoes. My mother worked in an air-raid wardens' unit, cooking for the men, so the food for the reception all came in bits and pieces. She made a one-tier cake of some sort with green icing!

The wedding was lovely; no air raids but, unfortunately, no bells. As we came down the aisle, my husband trod on the train of the veil and it split. Somebody remarked that it would be a long parting – and it was. This was on the 27th December and on the 28th he was sent to North Africa for three and a half years. The worst part came every Christmas, as the years rolled on, because when he did arrive home on leave, he had to go off again to Italy and Austria. We settled down after five years, then the family arrived!

Puzzle answers

Crossword (Page 17)

Across 1 Sect, 3 Scenic, 8 Onion, 9 Envoy, 10 Wrought iron, 11 Thomas, 12 Ache, 15 Haiti, 16 Ranch, 18 Site, 19 Pigeon, 21 Up to scratch, 23 Equal, 24 Tiara, 25 Exhume, 26 Seek.

Down 1 Stopwatch, 2 Chiropodist, 4 Create, 5 Never, 6 Cayenne, 7 Enigmatic, 13 Concentrate, 14 Arbitrate, 17 Hunchback, 18 Squeeze, 20 Asylum, 22 Touch.

Numbers (Page 17)

❤ = 9

★ = 5

☎ = 6

✏ = 7

✿ = 8

✂ = 4

I See No Ships (Page 45)

Vowel Play (Page 45)

Cryptogram (Page 59)

'We know what happens to people who stay in the middle of the road. They get run over'.

Takeaway (Page 59)

Making Tracks (Page 73)

Start at the diamond marked 2U in the fourth column and the third row.

Quizword (Page 73)

Across 7 A Touch of Frost, 8 Chalet 9 Hughes, 11 Boomerang, 14 Sheffield, 18 Taiwan, 20 Recall, 22 Spandau Ballet.

Down 1 Utah, 2 Muslims, 3 Whiter, 4 Afghan, 5 Bragg, 6 Isle, 8 Cabinet, 10 Scandal, 12 Ace, 13 Lincoln, 15 Hannah, 16 Formby, 17 Swing, 19 Alps, 21 Leek

Logic Puzzle (Page 101)

Ben Tweel, Mangallgeers, into ditch, concussed • Ian Frunt, Zorbottam, struck tree, twisted ankle • Jason Leader, Spoakes, into pothole, broke leg • Noah Stamminer, Byklipps, hit spectator, cracked elbow • Viv Gere, Punkcherkitt, dog ran out, dislocated kneecap.

Codebreaker (Page 129)

Six of the Best (Page 129)

1 Vapour, 2 Ravine, 3 Barren, 4 Orator, 5 Suitor, 6 Option. The bird is: parrot.

Cryptic crossword (Page 143)

Across 1 Nomadic, 4 Offhand, 7 Go to the wall, 9 Tutu, 10 Felix, 11 Anna, 14 Picture, 15 Grimace, 16 Shatter, 18 Trotter, 20 Ache, 21 Oscar, 22 Gigi, 25 Restoration, 26 Telford, 27 Lodgers.

Down 1 Nonstop, 2 Date, 3 Catseye, 4 Opening, 5 Flap, 6 Deviate, 7 Gate-crasher, 8 Lancastrian, 12 Quite, 13 Widow, 16 Sea-mist, 17 Respond, 18 Travail, 19 Ruinous, 23 Oslo, 24 Wild.

Short story

Lonely this Christmas

A foolish accident brings Craig home for Christmas, but does anyone in the whole world care where he is spending the festive season?

Whenever the people of Britain sat down to eat their tea, Craig Lighterman popped up on their screens. "Things must be serious if they've sent Craig out there," viewers would say, as they digested the evening news along with their meal. Famine, flood or forest fire all found Craig on the spot. Heart-strings were wrung the world over when he reported on the terrible plight of local people.

Alpine avalanches guaranteed the appearance of Craig, nattily clad in scarlet ski-jacket and bobble hat, reporting on the success or failure of the authorities' rescue. When his reports from one steamy jungle or another were shown on televisions in pubs back home, the bar staff braced themselves for a rush of orders for thirst-quenching pints. A news story from a war zone wasn't complete without Craig in the shadow of a Centurion tank (wearing a carefully chosen flack jacket – only slightly crumpled)

sombrely summing up the situation.

Craig loved writing these tense, vivid reports, then delivering them to camera. He was always conscious that the two-second delay (caused by the satellite link) between the studio asking him a question and his reply added even more weight to his words. In fact, although he would never have admitted it, these reports were the only time Craig felt he truly mattered to anyone.

He had found that in order to do his job properly – and he had won several prestigious awards for his reporting – he needed to create a defensive shell around his inner feelings. It wasn't that he didn't care about the human suffering he saw around him, but a good reporter needs to be objective. Loneliness was the price he paid for a job well done.

High points in other people's lives had become irrelevant in Craig's. Birthday cards never reached him in time because he was always on the move and nobody kept track of his

address. As his job took him to exotic locations, holidays seemed pointless – there was hardly anywhere he hadn't been. Christmas was more often than not spent in some obscure

Loneliness was the price he paid for a job well done

corner of the world, where carols from King's College, Cambridge, might be faintly heard on a crackling BBC World Service broadcast, and figgy pudding was just a figment of his imagination.

Craig had been the only child of elderly parents, who

By Yvette Verner

Lonely people were relying on him to keep them company

others about events he had not witnessed himself and felt his world had collapsed about his ears.

Christmas was approaching and, as the only newsreader without any family ties, Craig found he was almost permanently on duty. This, combined with the fact that it would be the first Christmas he'd spent in his homeland for a long time, made the festive season a singularly depressing prospect.

Just a week before Christmas, a bulging sack appeared beside his desk. After years of training in dealing with suspect parcels, Craig eyed it nervously. But the cheery wave given by the departing postman reassured him a little and he opened it, albeit with caution.

Minutes later, his desk was covered with festive parcels and cards galore. Carefully chosen ties, hand-knitted sweaters and home-baked mince pies, not to mention the odd bottle of festive spirit, all jostled for space among the discarded news bulletins.

As he sat there, bemusedly reading the letters that accompanied the gifts, Craig's spirits rose faster and more surely than the rocket launch he'd witnessed at Cape Kennedy. He realised that across the nation lonely people were relying on him to keep them company, via their television screens, over the Christmas holiday. He had more friends than he'd ever dreamed of.

For the first time in his life, Craig felt that what he did was appreciated. He was a happy man.

were proud of their son but didn't believe in showing their emotions. Although the conscientious Craig spent his childhood trying to please them, they remained aloof and never praised his efforts – except once when he had put out a garden bonfire that threatened to get out of control. And that had only been because his action had saved them from the awful embarrassment of black smoke ruining their neighbours' lines of snowy white washing.

He had been away reporting on a North Sea gas explosion, when the news came through that his parents had been asphyxiated by fumes from their central heating boiler. (Craig had warned them about it repeatedly but, true to form, they had kept the habits of a lifetime and ignored him.)

After this, Craig cut himself off even further from human contact, volunteering for assignments that took him to the ends of the earth. He would report a hole in the ozone layer in the polar regions, or provide an on-the-spot dispatch from an accident in the world's deepest diamond mine. Of course, even in places like these, he wasn't quite alone. A select crew of cameramen and sound technicians accompanied him, but it was Craig's face that the public grew to know so well.

Off-camera, he had some good times with his workmates, but made no close friends. Then one evening, when they were all relaxing at the end of a long day's filming on a South Sea island, Craig made the classic mistake of slipping on a banana-skin and sustained a very unamusing compound fracture of his leg. He could have borne the pain but what really hurt him was that his colleagues had caught the accident on film and sent it to be shown nationwide on Auntie's Bloomers.

As a result of this incident, Craig was flown home and found himself confined to the studio newsdesk. He hated reading scripts written by

December 2005

Thursday *1*	**Monday** *12*
Friday *2*	**Tuesday** *13*
Saturday *3*	**Wednesday** *14*
Sunday *4*	**Thursday** *15*
Monday *5*	**Friday** *16*
Tuesday *6*	**Saturday** *17*
Wednesday *7*	**Sunday** *18*
Thursday *8*	**Monday** *19*
Friday *9*	**Tuesday** *20*
Saturday *10*	**Wednesday** *21*
Sunday *11*	**Thursday** *22*

Friday
23

Wednesday
28

Saturday
24

Thursday
29

Sunday
25

Christmas Day

Friday
30

January **Yours** on sale

Monday
26

Boxing Day

Saturday
31

Tuesday
27

UK (Bank Holiday in lieu of Boxing Day)

IT HAPPENED THIS MONTH

7 December, 1941
The Japanese attacked ships of the US Pacific fleet anchored at Pearl Harbour

11 December, 1936
King Edward VIII abdicated the throne to marry twice-divorced American Mrs Wallis Simpson

14 December, 1911
Norwegian Roald Amundsen reached the South Pole before the British expedition led by Captain Robert Scott

17 December, 1903
Wright Brothers made their first flight at Kittyhawk, USA

20 December, 1928
Harry Ramsden opened his first fish and chip shop

22 December, 1958
General de Gaulle was elected the first President of France's Fifth Republic

25 December, 1950
The Stone of Scone (the Coronation Stone) was stolen from Westminster Abbey

5 December, 1974 The BBC broadcast the last episode of Monty Python's Flying Circus

THE UNIVERSE REJOICES

A Christmas poem from reader Valerie Jeffery of Litton Cheney in Dorset

Bells of joy at midnight sound
Vibrating wintry air
Echoing chimes around the world
In countries everywhere.

Their universal language
By all is understood,
Ringing out the message
That God is always good.

For on this night, this holy night,
His son was born and He
A true example set to us
Of what we all might be.

Heralded by angels,
Honoured with a star,
Calling hillside shepherds
And wise men from afar.

Resounding through the Heavens,
A thousand angel voices,
For with the birth of God's own son
The universe rejoices!

PIC: REX FEATURES

Top tip

To line a large cake tin for a Christmas cake, turn the tin upside down and press the cooking foil on to it. Then pop the shaped foil inside the tin – it will be a perfect fit.

Mrs J Beresford,
Middlesbrough

Great garden idea

Repair any damaged plant pots and containers while they are not in use. Shallow exterior cracks on stone or concrete pots can be repaired by applying a mixture of PVA adhesive and sand. Cracks on the inside aren't visible so simply use bitumen.

MY PRAYER

A Grandmother's Prayer
Dear child, don't let the world destroy
Your sense of childish wonder
Or dim the laughter in your eyes
Nor tear your dreams asunder.
The world can be a cruel place
That brings its share of pain
But love and laughter, friends who care
Bring happiness again.

Make time to see the lovely things
The natural world bestows,
The beauty of a butterfly,
A dewdrop on a rose.
Perhaps, one day you too will look
At eyes of palest blue
And wish for all these things for her
That I now wish for you
　　　　　　　Sheila J Leheup, Sidcup

OLD-FASHIONED CLEANING REMEDY

Rub a ballpoint pen stain on a carpet with a little methylated spirit on a clean white pad, sponge several times with warm water and blot dry.
K Croft, Hayling Island

Oh, happy day!

Nellie Heard of Guildford recalls a most unusual tableau of the nativity

My husband and I were in the Lebanon visiting our daughter Christine, son-in-law Salem and grandson Johnny. In company with Salem's mother, Badier, we drove along winding roads through mountain villages and glorious scenery to the church of the Virgin Mary at Mezziouri.

Inside the gates were life-size figures of the nativity carved in white stone. A long avenue led up to the church with statues of the 12 apostles on each side. Other biblical scenes depicted included

Christ's baptism in the River Jordan. When we entered the building, the altar was decorated entirely with white flowers, mostly roses, and their scent was unbelievable. We sat awhile in that cool, beautiful place, each alone with our thoughts.

After admiring the gardens, we saw the bridal party coming down the avenue. Two

men headed the procession, one playing a zam'mor (a type of flute) and the other a tabbel drum. We watched until they drove away with car horns hooting – a Lebanese custom. We finished the day at a restaurant with a meal of chicken pieces and sambooski (parcels of meat in pastry), kho'bizz bread and dips. Dessert was a huge basket of fruit.

A nice little earner

Fred Roberts of Lincoln reckons his days as a paper boy were the best of his life despite those early winter mornings

I remember working as a paper boy, delivering mornings and evenings, for 13 shillings a week. I was always reliable and began to collect newspaper accounts for both shops in my area, being paid an extra two shillings by each of them. This meant that I was often making over a pound a week which enabled me to indulge my interests in fishing and collecting Buddy Holly records. Although I tried my best, one of my failings was getting up early in the mornings. I really struggled to drag myself out of bed and often went on my round bleary-eyed and working on autopilot. As well as this, on cold winters, I suffered quite badly with clusters of chilblains on my toes and heels. I especially looked forward to Christmas when we called on our customers in the hope of gratuities. The average tip was two shillings – the best one a staggering five shillings!

Shopping completed, I headed for the car park, but couldn't find my key. Having searched my bag and pockets, I returned to all the shops I'd visited. Assistants and other shoppers all joined in the search. Then I remembered – I had come by bus!
Mrs A Lesley, Stoke-on-Trent

 Let's get cooking!

Vegetable Frittata
(Serves 6)

- 1 potato, chopped and cooked
- 6 oz (175 g) sweet potato, chopped and cooked
- 2 oz (50 g) baby spinach leaves
- 4 oz (100 g) sweet corn kernels
- 1 bunch asparagus, chopped
- 2 shallots, chopped
- 3 eggs
- 6 fl oz (175 ml) soya milk
- 2 tablespoons (30 g) plain flour
- 4 1/2 oz (135 g) reduced-fat Cheddar cheese, grated
- 1/2 teaspoon (2.5 ml) salt (optional)

1 Place all the vegetables in a large bowl.
2 Combine the eggs, soya milk, flour, 3 oz (75 g) of the grated cheese, and salt, if using. Stir into the vegetables.
3 Put the mixture into a lightly greased 9 in (23 cm) pie dish. Bake in a moderate oven (Gas Mark 4, 180°C, 350°F) for 40 minutes.
4. Sprinkle with the remaining cheese and place under the grill until golden.

RECIPE COURTESY OF SANITARIUM

My pet

Squirrel-proof bird feeder? You must be joking. This cheeky chappie was caught in the act by Audrey Johnson of Gant's Hill.

Here's health

Alcohol damage limitation

The party season is almost upon us. If you do over-indulge, avoid a hangover by drinking a pint of water before you go to bed to reduce dehydration. Milk thistle, available in tablet and tincture form from health food shops, limits alcohol damage by boosting the production of an amino acid that helps detoxify the liver. Take some before you go out, when you get home and again the next day for maximum effect.

December 5-11

Remember the '60s?

Mrs D E Worsley of Manchester's daughter dreaded the Daleks

We always enjoyed watching Dr Who on TV. I'll never forget the day I visited Lewis's store in Manchester with my six-year-old daughter Wendy. We were fascinated to see in one of the departments a special display of the actual Dalek figures. As we were looking at them, one suddenly started to move towards us uttering the familiar 'exterminate, exterminate'. Wendy uttered a loud shriek of terror and fled – running away down the store with me in hot pursuit! Although now grown up, she vividly remembers the occasion.

A happier Wendy with her mum

 ## Let's get cooking!

Tomato and Ricotta Tartlets
(Serves 6)
- 14 oz (400 g) shortcrust pastry
- 3 plum tomatoes, sliced into six, lengthwise
- 7 oz (200 g) reduced-fat ricotta cheese, crumbled
- 1 tablespoon (15 ml) chopped fresh basil
- 3 eggs
- 4 fl oz (100 ml) soya milk
- Large pinch of salt

1 Roll the pastry out thinly on a floured surface and use to line six 4 in (10 cm) shallow flan tins.
2 Arrange three slices of tomato, some crumbled ricotta and basil in each pastry case. Place on a baking tray.
3 Combine the eggs, soya milk and salt in a jug and whisk well. Pour into the pastry cases. Bake in a moderate oven (Gas Mark 4, 180°C, 350°F) for 20-25 minutes until the filling is set.

RECIPE COURTESY OF SANITARIUM

Top tip

For warm feet on a frosty day, I mix a few drops of tea tree essential oil with a few drops of olive oil and massage this into my feet and toes. I then slip thin plastic bags over my feet and put my tights and slacks on.
Mrs D J Flitter, Hythe

Here's health

The indigestible truth
Heartburn is more common as we get older as it's linked with the extra pounds we gain that put pressure on the abdomen. Avoid indigestion by not eating a large meal too close to bedtime and by cutting out fatty, spicy or acidic foods. Don't rush your food or wear tight clothes that restrict your abdomen. Avoid smoking, bending or lying down straight after a meal. A milky drink or a cup of peppermint tea can help to settle your stomach.

Make a difference - volunteer!

Do you dig old waterways?

Thanks to voluntary workers, hundreds of miles of our inland waterways have been saved from dereliction. In 1970, the Waterway Recovery Group (WRG) was formed to co-ordinate this work all over the country. Its largest project so far has been the rebuilding of seven locks on the Montgomery Canal on the Welsh borders. Most of the voluntary work is carried out at weekends but in the summer months WRG's Canal Camps enable longer periods of concentrated effort. Canal Camps attract people aged between 17 and 70. The restoration work is as varied as the volunteers and could be anything from bricklaying to driving a dumper. No one is asked to work beyond their capabilities and any necessary skills are taught.

◆ **If you fancy a spot of navvying in a good cause, contact The Waterway Recovery Group, PO Box 114, Rickmansworth WD3 12Y. Tel: 01923 711114. Internet: www.wrg.org.uk**

It makes me smile

My father was a captain in the Merchant Navy. One day his ship was overdue and my ten-year-old brother said: "Mammy, if anything happens to Daddy, will you marry me because I wouldn't like you to go out of the family."
Mrs J Layberry, Hawes

My pet

Mr K J Vincent of Bromsgrove calls his dog Louie the original couch potato and here he is, taking life nice and easy.

MY PRAYER

Thank You, Lord, for letting me sit down and feel content;
And Thank You, too, that I should know what solitude has meant.
Thank You for the winter snows, and for the falling rain,
To know that when they're over, summer skies will come again.

Thank You for my blissful sleep when it is getting late,
And thank You for a thousand things, too many to relate.

I've tried my best to offer help to those who needed aid;
I've tried to bring some warmth to those whose lives have been decayed;
I've tried to share with others things with which my life is blest,
Until such time as I shall face another sterner test.

Still I am happy with my lot, content with what life brings,
Sun and showers, frost and flowers, songbirds on the wing.
So thank You for the life I've led, and for the days of fun,
But forgive me, Lord, for the many things I've left undone.
Maureen Verney, Poole

Great garden idea

When planting new climbers plant them at least 1 ft (30. 5 cm) away from the wall as this will give the root ball more room to grow and avoid the rain shadow. Angle the stems towards the trellis along a cane and tie in stems as soon as you can to encourage them in the right direction. Mulch heavily as many climbers prefer a cool roots run. Protect the base of the stem with groundcover plants.

OLD-FASHIONED CLEANING REMEDY

To remove a sticky patch from the base of an iron, rub it gently backwards and forwards on a piece of paper sprinkled with salt.

 ## Let's get cooking!

Brown Sugar Meringues

(Makes 8)

- 1 medium egg white
- 1 oz (25 g) Tate & Lyle granulated cane sugar
- 1 oz (25 g) Tate & Lyle dark brown soft sugar
- 1/4 teaspoon cornflour
- 1/4 teaspoon white wine vinegar
- Few drops vanilla essence
- 1 x 5 oz (150 g) tub no-fat Greek yoghurt
- 8 fresh strawberries, sliced
- Tate & Lyle icing sugar, to dust

1 Preheat the oven to Gas Mark 2, 150°C, 300°F. Line a baking tray with a sheet of baking parchment.
2 Whisk the egg white in a clean grease-free bowl until it forms stiff peaks. Add the granulated sugar and whisk until the mixture becomes really stiff and shiny.
3 Add the dark brown soft cane sugar. Mix together the cornflour, vinegar and vanilla essence and add to the mixture. Whisk again until the mixture is glossy and firm.
4 Use a dessert spoon to heap 8 rounds of meringue on to the prepared sheet, then use a teaspoon to hollow out the centre of each on slightly.
5 Bake for 1- 1 1/4 hours or until the meringues are hard and sound hollow when the base is lightly tapped. Leave to cool.
6 To serve, top each meringue with a spoonful of yoghurt and top with a sliced strawberry. Dust with icing sugar and serve immediately.

RECIPE COURTESY OF TATE & LYLE CANE SUGARS

My first...

Teresa Rubnikowicz (below right) of London's first cooking attempt was Christmas dinner

The first time I cooked was in wartime. We were three evacuee children on our own in Berkshire, with Christmas approaching. Our parents were in London where my mother was having a serious operation.

A kind farmer gave us a duck. I didn't know how I would manage cooking Christmas lunch but, full of confidence I followed a recipe from my grandmother's Mrs Beeton book. I plucked as many feathers as I could from the duck and put it in the range, and a homemade pudding on the hob. Then we went off to church. When we got back the duck was as raw as when I started so we decided to have some of grandfather's port. The vegetables were cooked by now so we ate them – but not the duck! Later we ate the pudding and later still, the Christmas cake. But still the duck was not ready. After more port I finally put the duck on the table. We ate the odd feather, but nothing tasted better than that duck. We'd had a traditional Christmas, and it didn't matter that it wasn't in the right order.

Years later when we meet, we agree it was the best Christmas, ever. Of course, the port probably helped!

Top tip

To open a screw-top glass jar with a metal lid, stand it in a bowl of cold water and carefully pour a little very hot water over the top. Hold with a cloth and unscrew the lid, which will have expanded.
Mrs M Campion, Harwich

Make a difference - volunteer!

A lifeline for children

ChildLine is the 24-hour helpline for children who desperately need to talk to someone who is not a relative or friend of the family. Volunteers are the bedrock of this free service. ChildLine depends on them to train as counsellors and take children's calls as well as helping with administration and fundraising.

Volunteers must care about children and young people and be able to listen to distressing problems with sympathy.

No previous experience is necessary as ChildLine gives its recruits a ten-week training course.

◆ **If you wish to become a counsellor you must be prepared to commit yourself to a regular weekly three to four hour shift for one year and to continue with ongoing training. Alternatively, you can help by being an administrative volunteer or getting involved in fundraising activities. For details of all of these call 020 7650 3267 or visit the website www.childline.org.uk**

Here's health

Relief from arthritis
If you suffer from osteo-arthritis, try taking one teaspoon (5 ml) of honey dissolved in a cup of warm water with one dessertspoon (12 ml) of cider vinegar three times a day. Within 14 days, you will experience relief from pain.
Joan French, Great Clacton

OLD-FASHIONED CLEANING REMEDY
Hair lacquer stains on a mirror can be removed with methylated spirit.

MY PRAYER

Dear Lord bless all things small and weak or ugly, gross, bizarre, unique. Young and tender shoots that spring from soil and womb and egg, and bring the sweet green sap of Hope like Holy Grail to all those tired and old and frail. All things cast out, ignored, rejected, all creatures lost in pain, neglected. Wipe my eyes that I may see all of Your humility.

Sylvie Farquhar, Coventry

It makes me smile

A large board near us advertised 'Holly Missiltoe Reeves' for sale!
Mrs J M Lister, Bournemouth

My pet

Pippa has always liked sleeping in the laundry basket – her owner, Mrs C Johnson of Portsmouth, thinks the vibration from the washing mashine rocks her to sleep.

Great garden idea

Instead of throwing away an old shelf unit, paint it with one of Cuprinol's Garden Shades range (you may have to remove the varnish first) then put it against a wall on your patio and use it to display some of your favourite plants. Add a few ornaments such as gnarled driftwood or unusual pebbles.

Every picture tells a story

This photo, taken in 1954, brings back memories of the happy years my sister Betty and I spent at Shaftesbury Modern School in Dorset. It shows the boys and girls of Class 2.

At Christmas every year, our wonderful domestic science teacher, Miss Woodward, taught us to bake and decorate Christmas cakes – and we were always so proud of them. We took in our own ingredients and brought our cakes home to be eaten by the family.

Betty and I moved away in 1956 when our father's job took him to Cheltenham and I am no longer in touch with anyone in this picture but I wonder if any of our schoolfriends will recognise themselves?

Sheila Rowe (née Pearce), Penzance

Great garden idea

Don't try and keep your Christmas poinsettia from one year to the next. These are termed 'short-day' plants which means they need to be given extended periods of darkness for the characteristic red bracts to be produced. This is possible at a nursery but not in your home.

OLD-FASHIONED CLEANING REMEDY

To remove wine stains from table linen, cover with wet salt, leave for about an hour and then wash out.

F Chatburn, Heywood

Let's get cooking!

Eccles Cakes
(Makes 10)
- 6 oz (175 g) puff pastry
- 1 oz (125 g) caster sugar

For the filling:
- 4 oz (100 g) currants
- 4 oz (100 g) demerara sugar
- 1 oz (25 g) butter, melted

1 On a floured surface, roll out the pastry quite thinly and cut out as many 4 in (10 cm) rounds as possible.
2 Mix the filling ingredients together and place a heaped teaspoon of the mixture in the middle of the pastry rounds.
3 Fold the edges in towards the centre, pinch them together and flatten a little. Fit each round in a 2½ in (6 cm) pastry cutter and flatten to the size of the cutter, forming a neat round. Make 3 small cuts in the top of each round.
4 Brush the tops lightly with water and sprinkle with the caster sugar.
5 Place on a baking sheet and bake in a preheated oven (Gas Mark 7, 220°C, 425°F) for 15-20 minutes or until golden brown. Cool on a wire rack.

Top tip

Instead of expensive bath oils, fill a bottle with cooking oil – cheapest will do – then add a few drops of lavender oil or your favourite perfume.
Mrs D Hawkins, Ipswich

Make a difference - volunteer!

Bring comfort to the bereaved

Anybody who has lost someone dear to them knows that Christmas can be an especially painful time, evoking bittersweet memories. Many people bottle up their feelings of grief and even anger simply because they have no one to share them with. Cruse Bereavement Care offers free information and advice to people of all ages who have been affected by the death of a relative or close friend.

The charity needs volunteers to help people who are struggling to face the future by counselling individuals or running bereavement groups. Alternatively, you could help run a branch; this might involve fundraising, organising publicity, administration or being part of a management committee.

◆ **To find our more contact Cruse Bereavement Care, Cruse House, 126 Sheen Road, Richmond, Surrey TW9 1UR. Tel: 020 8939 9530. Internet: www.crusebereave-mentcare.org.uk**

My pet

'Who are you calling Rudolf?' Mrs J Shaw of Stoke-on-Trent sent this photo of her daughter's dog Jake waiting patiently for his portion of Christmas pud.

MY PRAYER

To all our family and our friends
We are sending you this prayer,
That God will always bless you
With His love and with His care.

The very special friendships
We have shared with all of you,
Have made our lives so complete
It's been special, warm and true.

So may God always smile on you,
And send you from above
The things that bring you happiness,
For you and those you love.

We thank the Lord we've known you all
And think you are 'just great',
So tonight we have many reasons
For us all to celebrate.

Janet York, Daventry

Wit and wisdom

If I sent a Christmas card to Gilbert Harding, he would add the words 'and Gilbert Harding' to the words 'from Hubert Gregg' and send it to someone else.

Hubert Gregg (1914-2004)

Senior moment

At my usual produce stall in the market I blithely asked for 'a pound of eggs and a dozen bananas, please'.

Patricia Soar, Doncaster

Here's health

Talking turkey

A traditional roast turkey dinner is packed full of vitamins and minerals. Brussels sprouts are little powerhouses of vitamins contining B3, B6, C and E, folic acid, calcium, magnesium, potassium and betacarotene. And they have strong anti-cancer, antibacterial and anti-viral properties. Cranberries help prevent urinary tract infection and contain flavanoids which act as antioxidants and may reduce the risk of heart disease. Finally, turkey is a good source of low-fat protein. So enjoy!

December 26-31

My pet

Jack and his sister Jill snuggle up for a snooze. They live with June van Dam of Billericay who says Jack is the one that usually gets up to mischief!

MY PRAYER

Faith came singing into my room
And other guests took flight.
Grief and anxiety; fear and gloom
Sped out into the night.
I wondered that such peace could be,
But faith said gently, 'Don't you see
That they can never live with me?'

Beryl Mole, Lee-on-Solent

Wit and wisdom

Kissing don't last: cookery do!
George Meredith (1828-1909)

Great garden idea

If you are planning a holiday and enjoy gardens, where better to stay than at a B & B which has a beautiful garden attached? Special Places to Stay – Garden Bed and Breakfast by Alistair Sawday lists hundreds of B & Bs with gardens that have featured in magazines or on television. You can order a copy by phoning 01275 464891 or by visiting the website www.sawdays.co.uk.

OLD-FASHIONED CLEANING REMEDY

If your bronze candlesticks have green marks on them, try rubbing them with turpentine. Leave to dry before brushing off with an old toothbrush. Finish off by polishing with a little oil.

Make a difference - volunteer!

Practical aid for the disabled

Two organisations that specialise in helping people with disabilities are Dial UK and Independent Living Alternatives (ILA). ILA needs full-time volunteers, with four months to spare, to work as personal assistants providing physical support for a disabled person. The work involves tasks such as helping them to get out of bed, get dressed and washed and do practical things like cooking, shopping and housework. No experience is necessary as all training is provided. **Contact ILA, Trafalgar** House, Grenville Place, London NW7 3SA. Tel: 020 8906 9265. Internet: www.i-l-a.fsnet.co.uk

The DIAL network also helps disabled people to lead independent lives and encourages volunteers who have personal experience of disability themselves. The work, which can be anything from administration to answering telephones, might include giving practical advice on matters like applying for grants.
◆ **To find out more, call 01302 310 123 or look on DIAL's website www.dialuk.info**

Dear diary

Hazel Wheeler of Canterbury wrote of a day in the life of a lollipop lady

16 December 1966
On the crossing. Milder and fine. The Hungarian lady came hurrying down the lane in a panic. Diane had arrived home with one shoe on and minus the other. And she was going to her daddy's works party tomorrow. She rushed down to school. When she came panting back, the caretaker had found it in the boys' toilets.

Another lady told me she been busy all morning varnishing the dining-room table as a surprise for her husband at Christmas. When she got home, the postman had been and the dog had jumped up in excitement on to the table, leaving pawmarks on it.

Evening: Took Caroline and Elizabeth for piano lesson. Miss Taylor said I needn't pay for the lesson, it could be a Christmas present, so I gave her a box of Turkish Delight after going to the supermarket.

Top tip

Cut old nylon tights into strips to use for tying plants to supports in the garden.
Dorothy Roberts, Bozeat

Here's health

Nourishing nuts

If you still have some bowls of nuts left over from Christmas, don't worry about dipping in. Nuts do contain high levels of fat but it is the monounsaturated type of fat that protects against heart disease. Almonds, walnuts and cashews are rich in vitamin E and a study in Finland found that people with higher levels of this vitamin in their diet were less likely to develop type 2 diabetes. Other sources of vitamin E include brown rice and wheatgerm.

It makes me smile

When my children were small Amy's friend Lisa came round to play. I heard Lisa say: "I had chicken-pox at Christmas." Amy replied: "Oh. We had turkey."
Joan Lee, Great Waltham

 Let's get cooking!

Individual Quiches

(Makes 12)
- 6 oz (175 g) shortcrust pastry
- 1 egg and 3 egg yolks
- Salt and pepper
- Grated nutmeg
- ½ pint (275 ml) double cream
- 4 oz (100 g) leaf spinach, cooked, drained and chopped
- 5 oz (150 g) leeks, thinly sliced and softened in butter
- 4 oz (100 g) red onion, finely diced and softened in butter

1 Roll out the pastry and use to line 12 2½ in (6 cm) flan tins. Prick with a fork and chill for one hour. Bake blind in a preheated oven, Gas Mark 6, 200°C, 400°F, for 15 minutes.
2 Whisk the egg yolks and the egg together. Season with salt and pepper and add nutmeg, to taste. Whisk in the cream and check the seasoning.
3 Divide the mixture into three equal quantities. Mix one with the spinach, one with the leeks and one with the red onion.
4 Spoon into the baked cases and return to the oven for 15-20 minutes or until the filling is just firm to the touch. Serve warm or cold.

A Walk in the Wild
Dappled denizens of the woodland

PIC: BRITISH DEER SOCIETY (P. MITCHELL)

Fallow deer prefer to venture out under cover of darkness

Introduced to this country by the Normans in the tenth century, fallow deer (Dama dama) were protected for sport in the Royal hunting forests. These, and escapees from the deer parks, were the forerunners of today's free-living herds.

Smaller in size than the roe, Britain's biggest deer, fallow deer, are the only British species to have palmate antlers. The antlers increase in size with age, reaching over two feet in length. In summer, the fawn coat sports distinct white spots that virtually disappear in winter. A black dorsal stripe extends to the end of the tail. Many minor variations of colouration exist, including a long-haired version found in Mortimer forest, Shropshire.

Although fallow deer are not territorial, the buck defends his rutting stand for the does that he has herded together. The doe gives birth to a single fawn in June. Despite a heavy mortality rate after birth and during the first winter, the population is increasing, although the distribution is sparse in Scotland and patchy in parts of England and Wales.

Commonly, groups of adult males and females remain apart for most of the year. Living in mature woodland, fallow deer graze on grass and broadleaf tree shoots during the summer and in the winter months they eat brambles, holly, heather and coniferous tree shoots. As farmers are well aware, they will also browse on agricultural crops. Unlike most of the other larger species of deer, fallow deer remain silent for most of the year. Does with a fawn will give a short bark when alarmed and bucks groan during the rut. Herds are active throughout the day but make more use of open spaces during the hours of darkness. Dawn and dusk are the peak activity times.

For more information about all six species of British deer, contact The British Deer Society, Burgate Manor, Fordingbridge, Hants SP6 1EF. Tel:01425 655434.

WARTIME WEDDINGS
An invitation declined

Joan Blake of Hook in Hampshire had a Christmas wedding, complete with traditional turkey

Ken and I were married in a lovely village church in East Anglia on Christmas Day in 1943 (a special concession during wartime). Ken was on a 72-hour pass from the Navy (he was a signalman doing East Coast convoy work and nearly didn't make it) and I had a week's leave from the ATS. My dress was made from curtain lace and my bridesmaid's dress was a renovated dance frock of my mother's.

My father was the local baker and we had a Christmas dinner in the village hall. The turkey was cooked in the bread oven.

After the reception we travelled by train to Bishop's Stortford for a two-night honeymoon. The hotel was used mainly to billet American officers from nearby bases. After we had shyly got ourselves into bed, there was a banging at the door and an American voice said: "Come on down, Jack. We have just heard on the wireless that the Scharnhorst has been sunk!" (The Scharnhorst was a German battleship.) Needless to say, he declined the invitation!

Competition

What was <u>your</u> best day of 2004?

Your entries flooded in for our best day of 2003 competition in last year's Year Book – and what wonderful letters and photographs you sent. Stories of family celebrations, overcoming illness and great reunions – and they were all so good, we've decided to run the competition again this year!

We'd love to hear from you if you had a memorable event in 2004, be it a wonderful day out, old friends meeting up after years or an unexpected (pleasant) surprise.

Tell us about your special day in 2004, in not more than 350 words and please try to send a photograph or two to accompany it – both of your special event and you as the author. We'll take good care of them and return them in due course (but it will take a while).

Send your entries to the address given on this page, by Friday February 25, 2005.

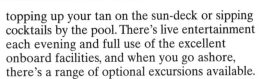

And there's a wonderful prize for the best entry!

You can win a nine-day Summer Sunshine Cruise to the Mediterranean for you and a partner, worth £1,200. Departing September 18, 2005, you'll visit Oporto, famed for its delicious port wine and see the charming Spanish city of Cadiz, where you can enjoy a traditional flamenco show. Then there's Gibraltar, with all the advantages of a foreign country, yet all the familiarity of home. You'll also visit the exotic and colourful North African city of Tangiers, as well as the attractive Spanish seaport of Vigo.

The prize includes return coach travel from selected pick-up points, or free secure parking at Falmouth, all port taxes and eight nights' full-board accommodation onboard the mv Van Gogh in a cabin with full private facilities, including air conditioning.

On board there's plenty to do, whether it's topping up your tan on the sun-deck or sipping cocktails by the pool. There's live entertainment each evening and full use of the excellent onboard facilities, and when you go ashore, there's a range of optional excursions available.

We hope to publish the winning entry, along with a selection of the best entries, in a future publication.

Please send your entries to **Yours**, Bretton Court, Bretton, Peterborough PE3 8DZ, marking your envelope BEST DAY OF 2004. Usual **Yours** competition rules apply. Good luck to you all, and we hope the coming year is equally special.

This holiday is operated by Travelscope Promotions Ltd (ABTA V5060). If you would like more information about other cruise holidays on offer please call 0870 7705010 for a free brochure quoting reference YRS/OCC. Or write to Travelscope Promotions Ltd, Elgin House, high Street, Stonehouse, Glos GL10 2NA.